Touring
MONTANA
AND WYOMING
HOT SPRINGS

Jeff Birkby

FALCON®

HELENA, MONTANA

A **FALCON** GUIDE ®

Falcon® Publishing is continually expanding its list of recreational guidebooks. All books include detailed descriptions, accurate maps, and all information necessary for enjoyable trips. You can order extra copies of this book and get information and prices for other Falcon® books by writing to Falcon, P.O. Box 1718, Helena, MT 59624, or calling 1-800-582-2665. Also, please ask for a free copy of our current catalog listing all Falcon books. Visit our website at www.Falcon.com or contact us by e-mail at falcon@falcon.com.

©1999 Falcon® Publishing, Inc., Helena, Montana.
Printed in the United States of America.

2 3 4 5 6 7 8 9 0 MG 04 03 02 01 00

Falcon and Falconguide are registered trademarks of Falcon® Publishing, Inc.

All black-and-white photos by the author unless otherwise noted.

Library of Congress Cataloging-in-Publication Data:
Birkby, Jeff
    Touring Montana and Wyoming hot springs / Jeff Birkby.
        p. cm.
    Includes bibliographical references (p.)
    ISBN 1-56044-679-X (pbk.)
    1. Hot springs—Montana—Guidebooks. 2. Hot springs—Wyoming—Guidebooks. 3. Montana—Guidebooks. 4. Wyoming—Guidebooks.
    I. Title.
    GB1198.3.M9B57 1999
    551.2'3'09786—dc21   99-17813
                                                                    CIP

CAUTION

Outdoor recreational activities are by their very nature potentially hazardous. All participants in such activities must assume the responsibility for their own actions and safety. The information contained in this guidebook cannot replace sound judgment and good decision-making skills, which help reduce risk exposure, nor does the scope of this book allow for disclosure of all the potential hazards and risks involved in such activities.

Learn as much as possible about the outdoor recreational activities in which you participate, prepare for the unexpected, and be cautious. The reward will be a safer and more enjoyable experience.

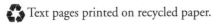 Text pages printed on recycled paper.

CONTENTS

ACKNOWLEDGMENTS

During a road trip to visit the ruins of a Montana hot springs resort, my brother Bob commented that "it's not easy to make a thriving business out of a puddle of hot water." I've learned that it's also not easy to write a book about those "puddles of hot water," and it certainly would have been impossible without the support and expert assistance of many individuals.

My thanks to Rick Newby and Randall Green, both formerly with Falcon Publishing, for asking me to write this book. Without their invitation this project would never have gotten off the ground. Thanks also to Peggy O'Neill-McLeod, my editor at Falcon Publishing, for her encouragement and sharp eye for detail.

The fascinating histories that enrich the text were generously shared by hot springs owners throughout Montana and Wyoming, to whom I am grateful. Thanks also to the many museum archivists who spent countless hours helping me bring to light the buried stories of Montana and Wyoming hot springs. These selfless individuals include Dave Walter and Lory Morrow of the Montana Historical Society, Lee Whittlesley, archivist for Yellowstone National Park, and the museum staffs of the Wyoming Historical Society, the Park County (Wyoming) Museum, the Gallatin County Historical Society, the Hot Springs Museum in Thermopolis, and the Fremont County Historical Society. Also thanks to Jessie O'Conner of the Jackson Hole Chamber of Commerce for sharing his knowledge of hot springs in the Jackson Hole area.

A note of appreciation to the late Roger Phillips of Helena, one of Montana's foremost hot springs connoisseurs. Also thanks to Marty Lord of Helena, who loaned me some of the early issues of *The Hot Springs Gazette,* edited by Phillips in the 1980s.

Thanks also to my colleagues at the National Center for Appropriate Technology in Butte, Montana, for tolerating my long absences from my "real job" for suspicious "research trips."

I'm also eternally grateful to my father, Robert Birkby Sr., and my mother, Evelyn Birkby, who taught me the joy of adventure and the pleasure of writing.

A special thanks and a free night at the Symes Hot Springs Hotel to my always supportive brother Bob Birkby. His constant encouragement and his marathon editing sessions were key to pulling this book out of the thermal mudpots of literary gibberish.

Finally, thanks to my many friends and colleagues with whom I've enjoyed soaking in the warm water of the Rocky Mountains over the last 20 years. The memories of all of those soaks are woven into the text of this guide.

MONTANA OVERVIEW MAP

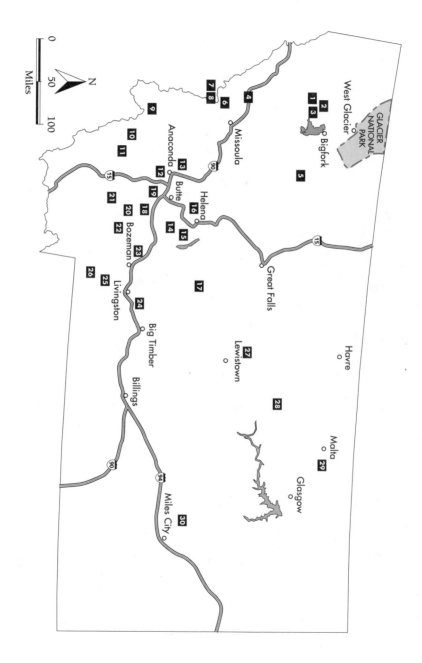

WYOMING OVERVIEW MAP

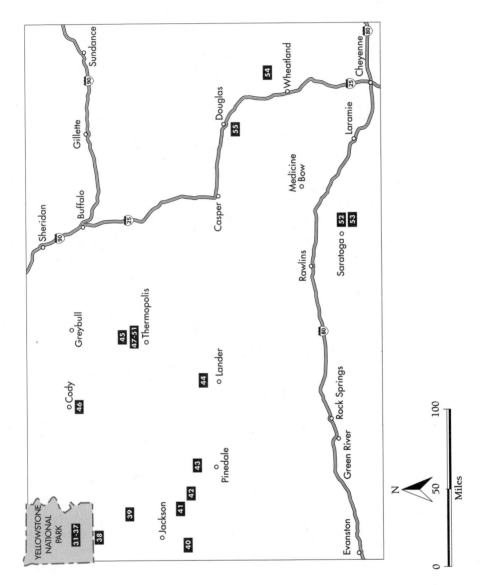

YELLOWSTONE NATIONAL PARK
OVERVIEW MAP

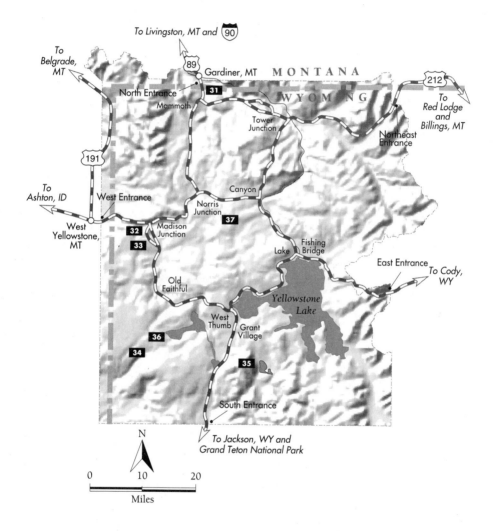

Map Legend

Interstate	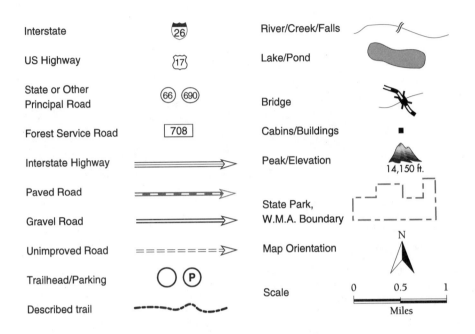	River/Creek/Falls	
US Highway		Lake/Pond	
State or Other Principal Road		Bridge	
Forest Service Road		Cabins/Buildings	
Interstate Highway		Peak/Elevation	
Paved Road		State Park, W.M.A. Boundary	
Gravel Road			
Unimproved Road		Map Orientation	
Trailhead/Parking		Scale	
Described trail			

14,150 ft.

N

0   0.5   1
Miles

INTRODUCTION

Of all the natural features of Montana and Wyoming, perhaps none has inspired as many legends or been the object of as much wonder as the region's primeval hot springs. The number and variety of thermal springs found in these two states are unsurpassed anywhere in the world. There's something for everyone here, from the beautiful mineral terraces in Hot Springs State Park near Thermopolis and the magnificent geysers in Yellowstone to Montana's secluded mountain soaks and the sleepy resorts on the eastern prairie.

Native Americans bathed in the region's hot springs for perhaps thousands of years before the arrival of European settlers. Tribes considered many springs to be sacred ground, gathering places where warring factions would call truces to soak in the pools. Members of the Crow, Arapaho, Shoshone, Sioux, and Flathead tribes frequented the region's hot springs, and fur trappers heard ancient legends of the great healing power of the water. When Dr. A. J. Hunter visited a hot springs near Livingston, Montana, in 1864, he reported seeing more than 1,000 tepees of the Crow Tribe clustered around the springs and many tribal members bathing in the mineral water.

The first explorers to discover hot springs in the region were Lewis and Clark, who visited Lolo Hot Springs near the current Montana-Idaho border in 1805. Captain Clark's diary contains the first recorded description of a hot springs in the Rocky Mountains: "[We] passed several springs which I observed the deer, elk, etc. had made roads to, and below one of the Indians had made a hole to bathe. I tasted this water and found it hot and not bad tasted. In further examination I found this water nearly boiling hot at the places it spouted from the rocks. I put my finger in the water, at first could not bear it in a second." Captain Clark's journals also contain entries indicating that he visited what is now Jackson Hot Springs, in Montana's Big Hole Valley, on his return from the Pacific Ocean in 1806.

John Colter, a member of the Lewis and Clark Expedition, also figured prominently in the early exploration of hot springs in the Northern Rockies. Colter was the first to describe the geothermal wonders of Yellowstone, as well as the geothermal area near present-day Cody, Wyoming. Colter's description of the Cody area was recounted by Washington Irving in *The Adventures of Captain Bonneville:* "A volcanic tract of similar character is found on Stinking River, one of the tributaries of the Bighorn, which takes its unhappy name from the odor derived from sulphurous springs and streams. This last mentioned place was first discovered by Colter, a hunter belonging to Lewis and Clarke's [sic] exploring party, who came upon it in the course of his lonely wanderings, and gave such an account of its gloomy terrors, its hidden fires, smoking pits, noxious streams, and an all-pervading 'smell of brimstone,' that it received, and has ever since retained among trappers, the name of 'Colter's Hell!'"

In 1832, Captain Benjamin Bonneville discovered the large hot springs near Thermopolis in what is now Hot Springs State Park. Ten years later the explorer John C. Fremont described a "gurgling springs," later named Emigrants' Laundry Tub, that served as a major landmark along the Oregon Trail in southeastern Wyoming.

The discovery of gold in the 1860s prompted a major period of discovery and development for the region's hot springs, especially in Montana. From 1864 to 1870, bathhouses and hotels were built at hot springs near gold camps in Chico, Virginia City, Boulder, Clancy, and Helena. Gold miners would soak their aching bones in the hot water, and local physicians prescribed daily soaks as the cure for a variety of diseases.

The decades from 1890 to 1920 were the heyday of the region's elegant hot springs resorts. Luxurious hotels were built at Hunter's, Chico, Corwin, and Broadwater hot springs, and the newly constructed Northern Pacific Railroad brought a constant stream of vacationers eager to enjoy these resorts.

The era of sumptuous resort hotels lasted only about 30 years. Several of the resorts were destroyed in spectacular fires, and one was severely damaged by an earthquake. The enactment of Prohibition laws forbidding the consumption of alcoholic beverages proved to be the fatal blow to several other popular hot springs resorts.

After World War II, many of the commercial facilities at hot springs in Montana and Wyoming struggled to survive. Although they often had a loyal local clientele, few of these resorts could attract sufficient tourists to really thrive. One resort had more than ten different owners in a 50-year period.

The last 20 years have seen a rebirth in the popularity of hot springs in the region. Several new resorts have been built, including the Inn at Saratoga, Fairmont Hot Springs Resort, and The Lodge at Potosi Hot Springs. Older resorts have been renovated, including the Symes Hot Springs Hotel, Boulder Hot Springs, and the Spa Hot Springs Motel in White Sulphur Springs. Not only are these resorts popular with locals, but an increasing number of national and international visitors are discovering the pleasure of soaking at these scenic escapes from civilization.

In addition to the many outstanding hot springs resorts, Montana and Wyoming are also home to undeveloped thermal pools, including Granite Falls Hot Springs, Upper Potosi Hot Springs, and the wonderful soaking areas in Yellowstone. These pristine bathing spots have remained relatively unchanged over the years, delighting generations of soakers seeking the physical and mental bliss that can only be found in the soothing water of natural hot springs.

Hot Springs Geology

Montana and Wyoming are home to the largest concentration of hot springs in the world. Not surprisingly, the majority of these hot springs lie in Yellowstone National Park, but a significant number of hot springs in Montana and Wyoming lie far outside of Yellowstone's boundaries.

Why are these hot springs found here and not everywhere throughout the United States? And what makes hot springs hot? The answers lie in the presence of a unique combination of ingredients necessary to form hot springs. These ingredients are only found in a few places in the world.

The first thing necessary to form a hot spring is, of course, heat. The earth's core is made up of molten rock, called magma, that can be as hot as 7,000 degrees F. The hottest temperatures occur at the center of the earth, more than 4,000 miles from the surface. The temperature of the earth decreases as you move away from the center. By the time you get within 50 miles of the earth's surface, the temperature is around 2,000 degrees F. Fortunately for us, the immense heat of the earth continues to cool as it approaches the surface. The top mile or so of the earth's crust has a fairly constant temperature gradient of about 1 degree F for every 100 feet of depth. This means that the temperature 1,000 feet below the surface is usually about 10 degrees hotter than the ground just beneath our feet. Temperatures at a depth of 10,000 feet would be 100 degrees warmer than the surface. This natural heat gradient in the earth is the primary ingredient needed for the formation of hot springs.

Not all of this region's hot springs rely on the earth's natural heat gradient for their temperature. Yellowstone National Park sits atop an unusually thin section of the earth's crust. The molten magma is only a few miles deep beneath Yellowstone, much closer to the surface than it is anywhere else in the region. This means the earth's temperature is much higher just below the surface of Yellowstone than in other areas, and the temperature gradient is much steeper than normal. This "hot spot" provides a perfect environment for the formation of Yellowstone's thousands of unique geothermal features.

The second element needed for forming a hot spring is a way for rainwater to penetrate the earth the thousands of feet necessary for it to get hot. Most of the hot springs described in this book occur at the edges of mountain ranges, and with good reason. Rainwater in the mountains percolates down faults, or cracks in the earth, which are commonly found in the mountains and valleys of Montana and Wyoming. These faults may extend thousands of feet into the earth, providing an easily traveled highway for surface water to follow. As the water descends into the earth, it is warmed by the natural heat gradient. Eventually this heated water enters other faults that lead back to the earth's surface. The heated water rises to the surface through a combination of natural convection and the pressure of the water column pushing from behind. The water eventually emerges at the surface of the earth as a hot spring. The entire cycle, from the time the rainwater enters the earth until it emerges as a hot spring, may take thousands of years.

Although all geothermal features are often called hot springs, there are actually five different types of thermal water phenomena in Montana and Wyoming:

Hot springs: These are by far the most common types of hot water features. A hot spring is simply a pool or spring of natural hot water that emerges from the earth at a temperature higher than normal groundwater. Hot springs usually occur in areas that have natural cracks in the earth that serve as conduits to bring the artesian water to the surface. This guidebook describes hot springs that range in temperature from 68 degrees F to some in Yellowstone that are hotter than boiling.

Mudpots: A mudpot is a type of hot spring that contains a much higher quantity of dissolved rock material than a normal hot spring. Mudpots often are very colorful, depending on the type of dissolved rock that is present in the hot water. Mudpots are rare outside of Yellowstone National Park.

Geysers: A geyser is a very rare type of hot spring, where hot water builds up tremendous pressure just beneath the earth's surface. This hot water eventually boils, and the resulting steam erupts, sending a column of steam and hot water into the air. In the Montana-Wyoming region, active geysers occur only in Yellowstone, although remnants of old geyser cones are visible near the Wyoming towns of Cody and Auburn.

Fumaroles: Sometimes superheated water emerges from the earth only in the gas phase, forming a constant steam vent called a fumarole. These geothermal phenomena occur primarily in Yellowstone on high ground well above the water table.

Hot water wells: Found mainly in eastern Montana and Wyoming, hot water wells penetrate deep aquifers of thermally heated water that have no natural outlets to the earth's surface. These wells usually were intended to be oil wells or to provide cold water, but instead they punctured an underground aquifer of hot water. Examples of hot water wells described in this guidebook include the 185-degree-F Angela Well north of Miles City, Montana, and the Sleeping Buffalo Resort near Malta, Montana.

BOOK ORGANIZATION

Montana and Wyoming offer an amazing variety of hot springs to enjoy. Some hot springs are to be visited simply to savor their historical past and offer little opportunity for bathing. Others are quiet primitive pools where you can soak in solitude in a forested mountain valley or on an endless grassland prairie. Still others have rustic mineral pools that have been cared for by the same family for generations. Some hot springs in the region are family-style resorts, while others are posh spas with gourmet restaurants and other top-flight amenities including golf courses, timeshare condominiums, and guided fly-fishing trips.

Hot springs pools have been described with a variety of names. During the 1890s, smaller enclosed hot springs pools were called "plunges." The largest, most elegant pools, such as those at Broadwater Hot Springs near Helena, were referred to as "natatoriums." Over time, these words lost their original specific meaning and thermal pools today are known as plunges, natatoriums, mineral baths, hot springs, spas, bathhouses, and resorts, and you will find all of these terms in this book. But no matter what they're called, all of these facilities provide soothing hot water soaks. Your best bet is to enjoy the experience yourself, and then come up with your own words to describe this form of heaven.

This guide covers most of the publicly accessible hot springs in Montana and Wyoming, but it doesn't list every known thermal area in these two states. Many once popular bathing resorts that are now off-limits to the public aren't included, such as Sleeping Child Hot Springs in Montana's Bitterroot Valley and Puller's Hot Springs near Virginia City. Other more primitive hot springs, such as Ringling Flowing Well in Montana's Shields River Valley, are conspicuously posted with "no trespassing" signs. These types of hot springs have also been excluded from this book.

This guide does include a few descriptions of closed hot springs when they have a compelling history and vantage points that are accessible to the public. If you visit these hot springs, please respect the private property boundaries and observe the hot springs from the public roads. If you want to enter private land to observe or soak in a hot spring, always find out who owns the land and ask permission first.

This book is divided into seven geographical sections: Northwest Montana, Southwest Montana, Northeast Montana, Southeast Montana, Yellowstone National Park, Northwest Wyoming (outside of Yellowstone), and Southeast Wyoming. Curiously, there are no known hot springs in either Southwest Wyoming or Northeast Wyoming. Each geographical section of the book presents detailed information on the hot springs in that area, with the springs arranged to facilitate travel from one hot springs to the next for those who want to plan tours to several hot springs.

The information in this book is current at the time of publication, but hot springs resorts in Montana and Wyoming have a reputation for changing ownership and accessibility. Some resorts may go out of business overnight, while formerly closed resorts may change ownership and reopen to the public. "No trespassing" signs may suddenly appear on locked gates on roads that formerly allowed access to primitive pools on private land.

If you have updated information on any hot springs in Montana or Wyoming, please send your comments to Jeff Birkby c/o Falcon Publishing, or send an e-mail to the author at jbirkby@hotmail.com. We will work your insights into the next edition of this book to keep the guide as current as possible.

USING DIRECTIONS AND MAPS IN THIS BOOK

The majority of hot springs in Montana and Wyoming are near paved roads or highways and require little navigational skill to locate. Each chapter of this book contains detailed directions on finding the hot springs, accompanied by a clear map. Although most of the springs should be easy to find with the maps and directions in this book, you may want to obtain a topographical map before visiting some of the more isolated springs (topo maps can be obtained directly from the USGS, from map supply stores, or at many outdoor recreational stores). The name of the topo map most useful in finding each spring is included in the descriptions.

Although most hot springs in Montana and Wyoming are not hard to find, the hot springs in the backcountry of Yellowstone National Park are an exception. Before heading to thermal areas away from the main roads of Yellowstone, refer to Bill Schneider's *Hiking Yellowstone National Park* (Falcon Publishing) for detailed directions, camping regulations, and map information.

PRECAUTIONS

Soaking in natural hot springs is one of life's true pleasures. Following a few safety tips helps ensure you have only pleasant memories of your experience.

Swimming in most commercial hot springs resorts in Montana and Wyoming requires no more preparation than you would make before visiting a commercial swimming pool. However, bathing in the more rustic or primitive pools requires a few precautions. Here's a quick checklist of things to remember before you head out on your next hot springs adventure:

1. Always test the water temperature before you get into a thermal pool. Hot springs can be scalding, and unfortunately there have been tragic deaths in Montana and Wyoming when people jumped or dove into thermal pools that they thought were safe to soak in. Even hot springs that you've visited before can experience drastic changes in temperature. Some hot springs are much cooler early in the spring and summer when melting snows mix with thermal water. Other thermal spots, such as the hot springs that mix with river water in Yellowstone, can be much too hot for soaking during a dry year when insufficient river water is available to cool the hot springs. Even commercial facilities can have some pools that are too hot for comfort. Play it safe before you soak, and always test the water with your fingertip, then cautiously ease into the pool. The bottom of some thermal pools can be much hotter than the surface, so be cautious even after you've settled in for your soak.

2. Keep your head above water in natural hot water pools. While commercial swimming pools are chlorinated, most mineral pools in Wyoming and Montana are not. Drinking or inhaling this water can expose you to a variety of nasty amoebae and bacteria, including Giardia and Naegleria. Try to avoid water droplets or spray, especially in primitive thermal pools.

3. Don't soak by yourself. Soaking with friends is not only more enjoyable, it's also safer.

4. Drink plenty of (nonalcoholic) fluids. Hot water soaks can increase your body temperature and can put abnormal stress on your heart. Drink plenty of water during your hot springs bath, and avoid alcoholic beverages, especially if you've been soaking for a long time. Lengthy thermal soaks and a high alcohol level in your bloodstream are a dangerous combination—stick to nonalcoholic beverages.

5. Don't soak in a hot pool for long periods of time if you're pregnant. Raising your body temperature can put undue stress on the fetus.

6. Remove your jewelry before you get into thermal pools. The sulfur found in some hot springs in Montana and Wyoming may quickly tarnish your favorite ring or bracelet.

7. Watch your children. If you're soaking with your kids, make sure they are close by at all times, especially when soaking in thermal areas with strong river currents such as Yellowstone's Boiling River.

8. Take special precautions when visiting Yellowstone's backcountry hot springs. The wild country of Yellowstone National Park requires that you familiarize yourself with techniques for hiking and camping in bear country, traveling through unmarked thermal areas, and Park Service regulations on soaking in Yellowstone's thermal areas. See the Yellowstone section of this guide book for specific information on visiting Yellowstone's backcountry hot springs.

EQUIPMENT CHECKLIST

Preparing to visit the more luxurious hot springs resorts in Montana and Wyoming requires packing little more than a swimsuit and some good books to read in the lounge chairs. However, if you're planning on soaking in one of the more rustic or primitive thermal pools in the region, the following items may come in handy:

❒ Swimsuit (optional at some springs, but take one along just in case)
❒ Towel
❒ Daypack or plastic sacks (to keep your clothes dry while you're soaking)
❒ Rubber thongs or old sneakers (to protect your feet from sharp rocks in pools)
❒ Drinking water (it's easy to get dehydrated if you soak for a long time)
❒ Snack food
❒ Sunglasses
❒ A hat that provides good shade protection
❒ Sunscreen (for your nose, ears, and other areas not submerged)
❒ Skin moisturizer (for use after soaking)
❒ Flashlight (if you think you may have to return to your car after dusk)

RESPONSIBLE BEHAVIOR

The vast majority of people who visit Montana and Wyoming hot springs know that these thermal areas are rare natural wonders, and they treat both the hot springs and other visitors with courtesy and respect. Unfortunately, a few individuals haven't been as respectful of some of the more primitive pools, and their inconsiderate actions have forced restrictions to be placed on some popular hot springs areas. Granite Hot Springs in Wyoming, Boiling River in Yellowstone National Park, and Jerry Johnson Hot Springs in Idaho used to be open at night. But after years of alcohol-related incidents, Park Service and Forest Service officials have had to close these springs to all after-dark bathing.

You can do your part both to protect the fragile nature of hot springs areas and enhance the quality of the soaking experience for both yourself and other visitors by keeping in mind a few rules of etiquette during your visit:

• Don't bring glass containers. Nothing ruins a hot soak faster than cutting your feet on a shard of broken glass.

• Pack out all your trash. And pack out as much trash as you can that's been left by others.

• Respect private property rights. Don't enter a hot spring on private land without being sure the owner allows public access.

• Keep noise to a minimum. Soaking in hot springs is an almost mystical experience to some bathers. Loud parties or blaring radios ruin the mood for everyone.

• Watch where you walk. Many hot springs have deposited beautiful ledges of fragile minerals, which may have taken decades to build up. Walking on these delicate areas can destroy these deposits.

• Follow local conventions on nudity. Several primitive hot springs in this book are clothing-optional, but use your own judgment before you strip. If you come to a primitive hot pool that's already occupied by clothed bathers, then either ask if it's OK to soak nude or follow the majority lead and wear your swimsuit.

AUTHOR'S FAVORITES

Most Historic—Emigrants' Laundry Tub

You won't find an attractive soak at this location, but for true history buffs these warm springs near Guernsey in southeastern Wyoming are at the top of the list. Emigrants' Laundry Tub was described by John C. Fremont during his first trek westward, and later the warm springs were an important landmark for thousands of pioneers traveling on the Oregon Trail. It's easy to imagine the pioneer wagons in the 1830s arriving at the warm springs a day after leaving the last outpost of civilization at Fort Laramie. Combine a morning visiting Emigrants' Laundry Tub with an afternoon exploring the nearby Oregon Trail Ruts National Historic Site, the hundreds of pioneer signatures carved into the sandstone at Register Cliff National Historic Site, and a visit to Fort Laramie.

Most Romantic—Chico Hot Springs Lodge

Located an hour north of Yellowstone National Park in the Paradise Valley, Chico Hot Springs Lodge offers all the ingredients needed for a romantic weekend. Request a room in the original lodge building (the ones with private baths and antique furnishings are best). Spend the afternoon with your partner relaxing in the outdoor pools, and then linger over a gourmet meal in the intimate atmosphere of Chico's renowned restaurant. After dinner take a stroll outside under the brilliant stars and moonlit mountain peaks, then slip back into the hot pools for a pre-bedtime soak.

Most Luxurious—Saratoga Inn Resort and Hot Springs Spa

If you're looking to be pampered, the Saratoga Inn is the place for you. The resort has invested several million dollars over the last few years to completely renovate the facilities, and the attention to detail and guest comfort is unmatched. Located about an hour north of the Colorado border in southeastern Wyoming, the Saratoga Inn is furnished in the style of a luxurious Western dude ranch, with oversized leather chairs and couches in front of massive stone fireplaces and feather quilts and Pendleton wool blankets in the bedrooms. Food and beverage offerings include an on-site microbrewery, a gourmet restaurant, and warm chocolate chip cookies delivered to your room every evening. Don't miss luxuriating in one of the five thermal soaking pools in the enclosed courtyard, followed by a professional massage or an aromatherapy session.

Best for Families—Hot Springs State Park

Great family vacation spots have attractions for harried parents and enthusiastic children. Hot Springs State Park, located in northwest Wyoming near the town of Thermopolis, fills all the requirements for a perfect family adventure. The third most visited park in Wyoming after Yellowstone and Grand Teton national parks, Hot Springs State Park is home to one of the largest hot springs in the world. Take the kids on a walking tour of the colorful terraces formed by the hot water, then drive on the loop road past the buffalo pasture, where you may see two dozen bison grazing in the distance. When you're ready to swim, there are five separate public and commercial facilities with hot mineral soaking pools, saunas, water slides, and wading pools. Both the Holiday Inn of the Waters and the Quality Inn Plaza Hotel offer mineral water pools and great family accommodations. Not far from the state park are other great places to visit with kids, including the Wyoming Dinosaur Center and Petroglyphs State Park.

Wild and Natural—Boiling River

There's no better way to experience firsthand the raw power of the earth's geological forces than by soaking in Yellowstone National Park's Boiling River. Located 2 miles from the north entrance of the park, Boiling River pours more than 1,200 gallons of hot water every minute over travertine ledges into the cold Gardner River. Adventurous soakers slip into the warm pools formed where the hot water and the Gardner River mix. Wildlife is abundant in the area, and you may have to wait for a buffalo to cross the trail to the springs before continuing on to the soaking area. Bathers sometimes spot elk and bighorn sheep on the opposite banks of the river. After your soak, continue 2 miles farther south to see Mammoth Hot Springs, the largest hot springs terrace in the world.

Most Isolated—Angela Well

Located 28 miles north of Miles City in extreme eastern Montana, Angela Well is a hot springs you've got to really want to visit. Once you reach the isolated town of Angela, you'll still have another 6 miles of gravel road and then 4 miles of dirt ruts to travel before you arrive at the hot water well. But the long trip is worth it—every minute, over 1,200 gallons of 185-degree-F water pour out of the well onto the prairie to form a brilliant white terrace that looks like a small version of the terraces at Mammoth Hot Springs in Yellowstone. Prairie grassland and wheat fields stretch to the horizon in all directions, with only a few cows sharing the view.

Northwest Montana

From the Kootenai River to the rugged peaks of Glacier National Park, northwest Montana is a geographically diverse area known for its wild mountain country and wide prairie basins. The region is home to the Flathead Indian Reservation, the city of Kalispell, the National Bison Range, and Flathead Lake, the largest natural body of water in Montana.

The hot springs of northwest Montana include a cluster of resorts near the aptly named town of Hot Springs. Quinn's Hot Springs is east of the town of St. Regis, and Sun River Hot Springs flows from the foothills of the eastern edge of the Bob Marshall Wilderness.

1

Camas Hot Springs

General description: Two hot outdoor soaking pools in the shadow of an abandoned bathhouse in the sleepy town of Hot Springs.

Location: Northwest Montana, about 80 miles north of Missoula and 65 miles south of Kalispell on the Flathead Indian Reservation.

Primitive/developed: Developed.

Best time of year: Open year-round. One local says that he prefers soaks in the steamy water in the early mornings or in the fall or winter, but bathers visit the pools every day of the year.

Restrictions: Use of the two outdoor pools is free. The nearby Camas Bathhouse has been closed for many years.

Access: Any vehicle can make the trip.

Water temperature: 120 degrees F at the springs; about 104 degrees F in the two pools.

Nearby attractions: Flathead Lake, National Bison Range, Lake Mary Ronan State Park.

Services: Gas, food, and lodging are all available in the town of Hot Springs. The nearby Symes Hotel and Mineral Baths is an excellent choice for overnight lodging (see page 17, "Symes Hot Springs Hotel and Mineral Baths," for a full description). The Hot Springs Spa, located adjacent to the old Camas Bathhouse, has 13 apartments with claw-foot bathtubs or Jacuzzi tubs filled with 96-degree-F mineral water.

Camping: Tent camping is available on the grounds of the Symes Hotel and Mineral Baths, about four blocks to the south of the springs. Big Arm public campground is located just south of Elmo on Flathead Lake, and camping is also available at Lake Mary Ronan State Park north of Dayton near Flathead Lake.

Map: Montana State Highways map.

Finding the springs: From Missoula, go north on Interstate 90 to the U.S. Highway 93 exit. Take US 93 north for 27 miles to Ravalli, then turn onto Montana Highway 200 west for 20 miles to the junction with County Road 382. Drive north on CR 382 for 16 miles to the junction with Montana Highway 28. Drive north on MT 28 for 4 miles to the turnoff to the town of Hot Springs. The town is about 1.5 miles west of MT 28. From Kalispell, head south on US 93 about 40 miles to Elmo on the west side of Flathead Lake. Head west from Elmo on MT 28 for about 20 miles to the town of Hot Springs.

Camas Hot Springs is located on a hillside on the northern edge of town. From Broadway Street in downtown Hot Springs, turn right (north) onto Spring Street. Go four blocks north to the large abandoned Camas Bathhouse. Drive through the gate that says "Camas Hot Springs" and park in the car lot. The springs are located about 20 yards northwest of the parking lot. No recreational vehicle (RV) or overnight parking is allowed. Vehicles must leave the parking lot by 10:00 P.M., although bathers can continue to soak until midnight.

The hot springs: Soaking activity at Camas Hot Springs takes place mostly in two outdoor cement pools about 25 yards northwest of the old resort building. The pools are actually the old holding tanks for the now-abandoned Camas Bathhouse resort. The Flathead Indian tribe owns the hot springs and bathhouse buildings. A local individual currently leases the land from the Flathead tribe and maintains the soaking pools.

The two cement pools make for marvelous soaks that draw an eclectic mix of long-time residents of Hot Springs, newcomers to the area, and national and foreign visitors. The larger pool, a 10-foot by 15-foot concrete rectangle about 4 feet deep, attracts the most bathers. The 8-foot-diameter second pool is located about 10 yards north of the first pool. Locals fill their water jugs at a nearby tap with the sulfurous water to drink for therapeutic purposes.

The two pools aren't the only thermal areas near the old Camas Bathhouse. Approximately 175 yards northeast of the parking lot is the Corn Hole, a soaking area famous for treating corns, bunions, and other foot and lower-extremity circulation problems. Wooden planks were laid over a mud pool, and 2-foot by 2-foot squares were cut into the planks to allow patrons to dangle

Camas Hot Springs and
Symes Hot Springs Hotel and Mineral Baths

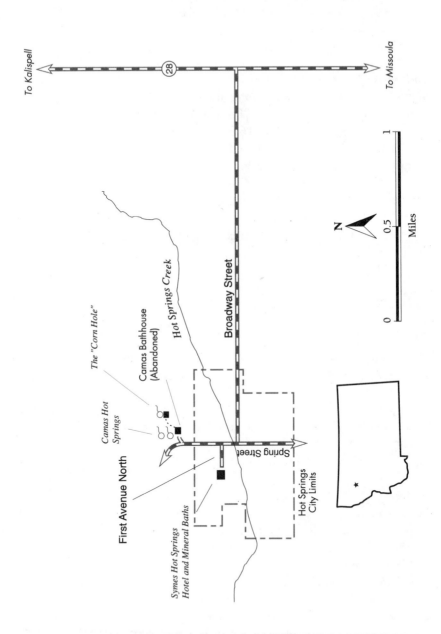

their feet into the hot, sulfurous mud that bubbled beneath them. Old-timers would sit for hours at the Corn Hole, playing checkers or chess with friends and new acquaintances as they soaked away their troubles. The remains of a small wooden bathhouse are located about 20 yards east of the old Corn Hole.

It's worth the short walk from the parking area to see the remnants of the Corn Hole and old bathhouse. Be aware, however, that this area is no longer maintained, and the loose, rotting boards and stagnant water may make for an uninviting, if not dangerous, place for your feet. It may be best to limit your soaking to the two well-maintained plunges near the parking lot.

Poem from the 1949 edition of *The Camas Hot Springs Exchange*, extolling the virtue of the hot mud at Camas:

THE PIG, HE LOVES MUD TOO

The Pig, he knows the value
of mud, to make a cure,
Of all his aches and pains
and muscles, which are sore.

Just give him mud and water,
and with health he grows and thrives.
How much more wise the Piggy
than doctored human lives.

History: The thermal waters and land around Camas Hot Springs were probably known to Native Americans for thousands of years. Early settlers in the area often observed them harvesting wild foods. A local newspaper in 1885 reported that Native Americans would visit the area to catch "wagonloads of fish in the Little Bitterroot River" and dig the sweet-tasting roots of camas plants that grew profusely on the rolling hills around the hot springs.

Everyone shared the hot springs. An 1896 article in *The Plainsman* from the nearby town of Plains described a visit to Camas, where "the Indians and others can bathe without heating rocks." The reporter wrote, "I did not need a bath as I had one some six or seven months before, but in order to be in touch with the balance of the Indians I took one."

Ed Lemoreux built the first bathing facility at Camas in the early 1900s. Lemoreux dug an 8-foot-square pool at one of the springs and constructed two mud baths, one enclosed in a log cabin and one in a frame building. A June 1911 article in the *Sanders County Signal* noted that "the accommodations for the winter were not the best, but in the summer it is the sick man's paradise. He can pitch his tent, bathe when he wants to, and eat when he wants to, and rest with nothing to worry him."

When the town of Hot Springs was incorporated in 1910, the popularity of Camas Hot Springs increased, and by the end of 1911, a new bathhouse had been built containing seven rooms and eight tubs. Baths were free to the public. In 1912 the *Sanders County Signal* reported that the water could be used to treat a condition it called the "grumps," a disease that "makes one find fault with his surroundings." Fortunately a few sips of hot water and a long soak in one of the tubs "relieves the sufferer and he comes out all smiles."

Over the following three decades, several other bathhouses were built on the site by federal agencies overseeing the Indian reservation. In 1941, the Flathead tribe assumed ownership of the springs. The tribe embarked on a major expansion of bathing facilities and in 1949 opened the $400,000 Camas Bathhouse. Featuring stark, utilitarian postwar construction, the structure had one floor for women and one for men. Mud and mineral baths could be taken in the resort's sky-blue bathtubs, and an outdoor swimming pool was in use during the summer months. Massage therapy and steam baths were also available. A three-week course of 21 baths was recommended for most ailments, and while bathing, guests were encouraged to drink glasses of mineral water.

Postcard from Hot Springs, Montana, circa 1950.

Noting that its waters provided relief from arthritis, rheumatism, skin disease, ulcers, and high blood pressure, an advertising brochure for the Camas Bathhouse boasted that it was "One of America's Finest Hot Springs and Mud Baths." A postcard from the era pictured a frail, elderly man hobbling into the bathhouse but clicking his heels with joy after treatment. "Limp In and Leap Out" became the motto of the town.

Tourism in Hot Springs boomed in the 1940s and 1950s, and the town became one of Montana's top vacation destinations. At its peak, more than 30 motels and 3 hotels stayed busy, with tourists coming to "take the waters" at Camas and the other hot springs of the area. Cures of all sorts of ailments were ascribed to the hot springs. The July 1949 *Camas Hot Springs Exchange* reported that "a gentleman came here who had no hair on the top of his head. He daily bathed and massaged his scalp with the hot springs water and left here with a new growth covering the once sensitive spot. This is encouraging."

The boom in tourism didn't last. When gasoline rationing ended at the conclusion of World War II, people began taking longer trips, often going out of state for vacations. In addition, some of the lumber mills in·the vicinity of Hot Springs shut down, causing additional economic hardships for the town. Many of the hastily built motels closed, and their empty shells can still be seen. Camas Bathhouse itself closed in the late 1970s and now stands quietly decaying in the mists of the soaking pools.

2

Symes Hot Springs Hotel and Mineral Baths

(See map on page 14)

General description: A flamingo-pink hotel with outdoor soaking pools and indoor mineral water tubs located in the quiet town of Hot Springs. The hotel décor and slow pace of the surrounding town transport guests back to the 1940s.
Location: Northwest Montana, about 80 miles north of Missoula and 65 miles south of Kalispell on the Flathead Indian Reservation.
Primitive/developed: Developed.
Best time of year: Open year-round.
Restrictions: The hotel and hot springs are privately owned. An admission fee is charged to use the pools (hotel guests soak for free).
Access: Any vehicle can make the trip.

Water temperature: The water in the smaller (upper) outdoor soaking pool is 102 to 104 degrees F. The hot water from this pool overflows into a larger, slightly cooler pool where temperatures range from 98 to 100 degrees F. Water temperature in the indoor soaking tubs is adjustable.

Nearby attractions: Flathead Lake, National Bison Range, Lake Mary Ronan State Park.

Services: The hotel features 26 hotel rooms, a suite with a private Jacuzzi, efficiency cabins, and apartments. Some kitchen facilities are available for guests. The Corn Chowder Restaurant in the hotel serves mostly organic meals (it is only open on weekends). Massage and Reiki therapists are available. Bicycles can be rented for afternoon tours of the surrounding area.

Camping: Tent camping spaces are available behind the hotel. A tepee can be rented overnight. Big Arm public campground is located just south of Elmo on Flathead Lake, and camping is also available at Lake Mary Ronan State Park north of Dayton near Flathead Lake.

Map: Montana State Highways map.

Finding the springs: From Missoula, go west on Interstate 90 to the U.S. Highway 93 exit. Take US 93 north for 27 miles to Ravalli, then turn onto Montana Highway 200 west for 20 miles to the junction with County Road 382. Drive north on CR 382 for 16 miles to the junction with Montana Highway 28. Drive north on MT 28 for 4 miles to the turnoff to the town of Hot Springs. The town is about 1.5 miles west of MT 28. From Kalispell, head south on US 93 about 40 miles to Elmo on the west side of Flathead Lake. Head west from Elmo on MT 28 for about 20 miles to the town of Hot Springs.

Symes Hotel and Mineral Baths is located in the northwest part of town. From Broadway Street in downtown Hot Springs, turn right (north) onto Spring Street. Go one block north on Spring Street, then turn left (west) onto First Avenue North. Drive two blocks on First Avenue North to the Symes Hotel. It's the only large pink hotel in town. Come to think of it, it may be the only large pink hotel within a thousand miles.

The hot springs: The mission-style Symes Hotel, with its pink-hued walls and plush red carpeting, appears as if it has been plucked out of the desert Southwest and dropped into the northern Rockies. You may be reminded of the Hotel California from the old Eagles' song, where "you can check out any time you like, but you can never leave." However, after a day or two at the Symes Hotel, you actually may never *want* to leave.

Everything about the Symes Hotel whispers to you to relax, from its tranquil setting in the slumbering town of Hot Springs to the resident cat sunning himself in the lobby window. There are no telephones or televisions in the guest rooms. Even the air conditioning system, a "swamp cooler," is a throwback to earlier times. The cooler consists of a large fan aimed at a sheet of wet fabric in such a way that it blows cool, moist air down the second-floor hallway. On hot summer days, it's a good idea to request a room near the swamp cooler.

The spacious lobby with its fireplace and piano is a comfortable gathering place in the evenings. The lobby also turns into a musical stage on the weekends for the local Hot Springs Artists' Society. Started in 1996, the Hot Springs Artists' Society is succeeding in its mission to bring a bit of culture to this isolated town. A wide variety of talent is featured during "pass the hat" performances, which include contemporary folk and blues, jazz, Celtic, and classical music. Various lectures are also presented, and a puppeteer has been known to stop by occasionally.

Off the lobby are the indoor mineral baths, where claw-foot tubs separated by wooden partitions line a hallway. Guests can adjust the temperature of the mineral water.

The second floor of the hotel includes guest rooms filled with period furniture, an open-air sunporch, and an enclosed sunroom. Brochures from the past extol the health-giving properties of the sunroom's special "vita glass" that admitted only "healthful" solar rays.

Outdoor soaking pools at Symes Hotel.

Located a few yards south of the main entrance to the hotel, the Symes' outdoor pools are especially popular on cloudless nights when stars fill the sky. Hot water from a 250-foot-deep artesian well keeps the upper pool between 102 and 104 degrees F. The water cools down a few degrees as it cascades into the larger lower pool.

Since the hotel was refurbished and the outdoor pools were built a couple of years ago, the Symes has seen a resurgence in popularity. Small groups can rent the entire hotel for a weekend, and the Symes is becoming a desirable gathering place for weddings and reunions.

History: Mr. and Mrs. Fred Symes built the Symes Hotel in 1928. Like many of the 30-plus hotels and motels built in Hot Springs at the time, the Symes Hotel prospered from the large number of tourists who came to sample the hot waters. A brochure credited the Symes' mineral baths with providing "cures for arthritis, high blood pressure, skin diseases, stomach ulcers, kidney ailments, rheumatism, asthma and many other diseases."

Another brochure printed in the 1960s boasted that "there are no better hotel facilities than at the Symes Hotel. You need not leave the hotel for baths, sweats, and massages. In its spacious lobby you meet people from everywhere and they all want to talk. In this calm and restful atmosphere people joke of their ailments and look forward to uncanny cures." The same brochure told the story of an elderly man who visited the Symes Hotel every year to bathe in the hot water. "Maybe it's a sign of old age," he commented, "but if it is, all the more reason I should grow old as young as possible."

The Symes family owned the hotel until the mid-1990s, when it was sold to current proprietors Leslee and Dan Smith.

3

Wild Horse Hot Springs

General description: An isolated bathhouse with private soaking rooms located on the arid east side of the Little Bitterroot Valley.
Location: Northwest Montana, about 85 miles north of Missoula and 60 miles south of Kalispell on the Flathead Indian Reservation.
Primitive/developed: Developed.
Best time of year: Open year-round.
Restrictions: Privately owned resort. Admission fee charged to use the private hot pools. Swimsuits optional within the private pool rooms.

Access: Any vehicle can make the trip. The highway from the town of Hot Springs and the gravel road to Wild Horse Hot Springs are plowed in the winter to keep them open.

Water temperature: 122 degrees F at the source, 104 degrees F in the private plunges (but may be adjusted by bathers).

Nearby attractions: Flathead Lake, National Bison Range, Lake Mary Ronan State Park.

Services: Two overnight guest rooms are available, complete with beds, small kitchens, and private hot plunges. Other accommodations, gas, and food are available in the town of Hot Springs, 6 miles to the southwest.

Camping: Twelve RV spots and a number of overnight tent camping spots are available for a small fee.

Map: Montana State Highways map.

Finding the springs: From Missoula, go west on Interstate 90 to the U.S. Highway 93 exit. Take US 93 north for 27 miles to Ravalli, then turn onto Montana Highway 200 west for 20 miles to the junction with County Road 382. Drive north on CR 382 for 16 miles to the junction with Montana Highway 28. Drive north on MT 28 for 4 miles to the turnoff to the town of Hot Springs. Continue north on MT 28 for 0.5 mile past the Hot Springs turnoff. Turn east on a blacktop road and follow the signs for about 6 miles to Wild Horse Hot Springs.

Private indoor plunge at Wild Horse Hot Springs.

Wild Horse Hot Springs

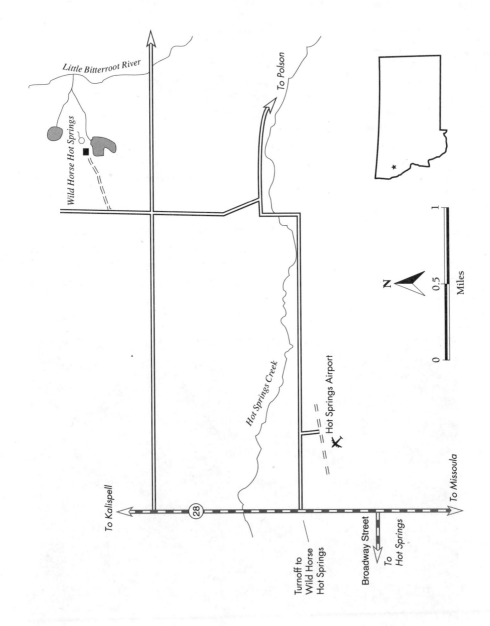

From Kalispell, head south on US 93 about 40 miles to Elmo on the west side of Flathead Lake. Head west and south from Elmo on MT 28 for about 20 miles. About 0.5 mile north of Hot Springs, turn east onto a blacktop road and follow the signs about 6 miles to Wild Horse Hot Springs.

The hot springs: The bathhouse at Wild Horse Hot Springs is contained in a blue-and-white one-story steel-sided building. Six private soaking rooms are available for hourly rental. Each room contains a 7-foot by 8-foot plunge about 3 feet deep. A shower, sink, toilet, and sauna are also contained in each room. Bathers have complete privacy in their own rooms, and swimsuits are optional. The hot water well provides 120-degree-F water to the bathhouse, but the pools are initially adjusted to 104 degrees F. Individual users can then increase or decrease the pool temperature according to their own desires.

History: The land that now surrounds Wild Horse Hot Springs was homesteaded by Mollie Bartlett, the only daughter of Montana's second governor, Robert B. Smith. Water was scarce at the homestead, and Bartlett had to haul water from the Little Bitterroot River for washing, drinking, and irrigating of crops. In 1912, she decided to drill a water well on her property to ease her burden of carrying water to the house every day. The drilling proceeded slowly. After eight days of boring through hard clay, a "huge column of hot water burst forth from the earth," according to a July 1941 article in the *Camas Hot Springs Exchange.* Close to 250 gallons per minute of 120-degree-F water shot out of the well with so much force that it created a large hole around the well. The hole grew at such an alarming rate that "drenched men and frightened teams struggled to move the little homestead house from the rapid flood." Eventually the hot water flow was controlled, and Mollie Bartlett was assured of a good supply of water for her garden.

Over the next 30 years visitors came from far distances to bathe in and drink the hot water from the Bartlett well. Because there was no readily available cold water to temper the thermal flow, soaking in comfort required ingenuity. A wooden barrel was placed near the well, and after each bath, guests poured hot well water into the barrel where, over time, it cooled. Subsequent bathers could then adjust the soaking temperature by mixing cool barrel water with hot water in a wooden tub.

In 1941 Mrs. Bartlett campaigned to raise funds to build a treatment center for children suffering from polio. The hot water well and surrounding area were renamed "Camp Aqua," and the project to use the water to relieve the suffering of afflicted youngsters was called the "Montana Warm Water Project for Crippled Children."

A public resort built later on the property retained the Camp Aqua name into the 1980s. In 1982, a new hot water well was drilled on the property with funds provided by a state renewable energy grant, and the springs owners began planning a $20 million project to use the hot water to heat an ethanol plant. The *Sanders County Ledger* reported that the ethanol plant would employ more than 70 people and would use locally grown wheat and barley to make the ethanol.

The plans for the ethanol plant fell through, however, and the hot springs returned to their historic use of providing hot soaks. In the early 1990s, Denny and Jamie Larson acquired the property and changed the name to Wild Horse Hot Springs.

4

Quinn's Hot Springs Resort

General description: A quiet family resort set in a grove of ponderosa pine trees on the banks of the Clark Fork River.

Location: Northwest Montana, 20 miles east of St. Regis.

Primitive/developed: Developed.

Best time of year: Open year-round.

Restrictions: Admission fee charged for use of the pool and Jacuzzi.

Access: Any vehicle can make the trip.

Water temperature: 120 degrees F at the springs; 75 to 105 degrees F in the pools, depending on the season.

Nearby attractions: National Bison Range, Cascade Falls Nature Trail, Clark Fork River.

Services: 16 cabins and trailer units are available, as well as a convenience store, gas, and a laundromat. A restaurant located next to the pool serves breakfast, lunch, and dinner. All other services are available at St. Regis, 20 miles west.

Camping: A dozen spots are available for tent camping at the resort, as well as 33 RV spaces with partial or full hookups. With 12 campsites, Cascade Campground is 3 miles west of Quinn's on Montana Highway 135.

Map: Montana State Highways map.

Finding the springs: From Missoula, take Montana Highway 200 north for about 68 miles to the junction with Montana Highway 135. Turn west on MT 135 and follow the Clark Fork River for 3 miles to Quinn's. An alternate route

Quinn's Hot Springs Resort

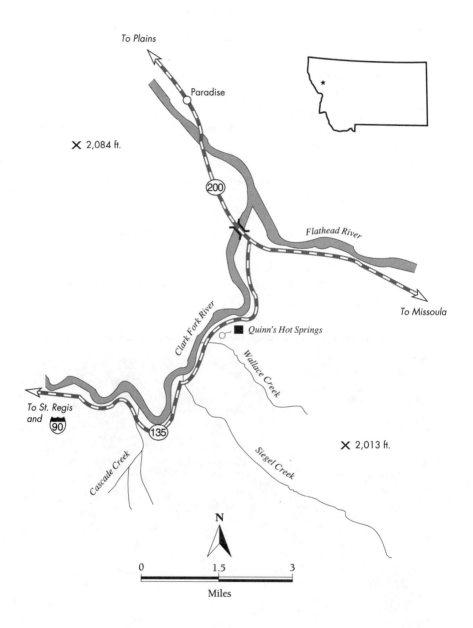

To Plains

Paradise

✕ 2,084 ft.

200

Flathead River

To Missoula

Clark Fork River

Quinn's Hot Springs

Wallace Creek

To St. Regis
and

90

135

✕ 2,013 ft.

Cascade Creek

Siegel Creek

N

0   1.5   3

Miles

is to take Interstate 90 from Missoula west for 70 miles to St. Regis. Turn east on MT 135 for 20 miles to Quinn's. The resort is about 50 yards off the highway. Look for a large sign advertising the resort.

The hot springs: Located about 200 yards above the Clark Fork River, the hot springs are 120 degrees F at their source. A large outdoor pool is maintained at 70 to 75 degrees F in the summertime but is heated to 100 to 105 degrees F in the winter. Water depth ranges from 3 to 10 feet in the outdoor pool. The 12-foot-diameter Jacuzzi is kept at 95 degrees F in the summer, but it warms to 100 to 105 degrees F in the winter. A private indoor Jacuzzi is also available. The water is slightly sulfurous.

History: In the late 1880s, an Irishman named M. E. Quinn was foreman for the Pardee Mountain Mine, located on a ridge 5 miles from the hot springs. Ore from the mine was hauled down a steep road to the Clark Fork River, where it was placed on a barge and floated 8 miles downstream to a railhead near Plains. During these river trips Quinn noticed a hot springs flowing into the river and many Native Americans camped nearby. Quinn filed a homestead on the site and a few years later built a commercial bathhouse there. During its first years, guests could reach the establishment only by climbing down a steep trail from the mountains above the hot springs or by floating down the Clark Fork River to the resort. Despite the arduous journey required to reach them,

Quinn's Hot Springs Resort.

the springs soon gained local attention. In 1896 *The Plainsman* reported that "not far from town are some remarkably efficacious hot springs owned by M. E. Quinn, which have effected surprising cures in rheumatic and kidney diseases, and are fast becoming a popular summer and winter resort."

By 1905 Quinn had constructed a hotel at the site, and in 1909 a railroad was completed through the valley. Quinn built a swinging bridge across the river to connect with the railroad, which stopped at the bridge to disembark guests. He managed the resort until his death in 1932. His family continued to operate the resort for many years, and his grandsons built the current bar and restaurant in 1948. Additions to this building were made in the 1970s, and a dance hall was added during the 1980s.

The present owner of Quinn's Hot Springs Resort is Dutch-born Andre Meleif, who acquired the property in the summer of 1998.

5

Sun River Hot Springs

General description: A warm water pool on a private guest ranch on the eastern edge of the Bob Marshall Wilderness. In the 1920s, sulfur deposits on a ledge in a nearby cave were sold for medicinal purposes.

Location: Northwest Montana, 58 miles west of Choteau.

Primitive/developed: Developed.

Best time of year: Summer and early fall.

Restrictions: The warm water pool is on the privately owned K Bar L Ranch and is only for the use of ranch guests.

Access: Most vehicles can make the trip to Mortimer Gulch Campground at the east end of Gibson Reservoir. From the campground, ranch guests are transported by jet boat to the head of the Gibson Reservoir, and then by horseback to the K Bar L Ranch, where the warm water pool is located. Hikers who want to see the springs must take the rugged 7-mile trail along the north shore of Gibson Reservoir to the springs.

Water temperature: 84 to 86 degrees F in the warm water pool.

Nearby attractions: Bob Marshall Wilderness, Rocky Mountain Hi Ski Area, Pine Butte Swamp Preserve, Freezeout Lake Wildlife Management Area, Lewis and Clark National Forest, Sun River Wildlife Management Area.

Services: Food and lodging are available to guests of the K Bar L Ranch. All other services are available in Augusta, 25 miles east of Mortimer Gulch Campground, and Choteau, 51 miles east of the campground.

Sun River Hot Springs

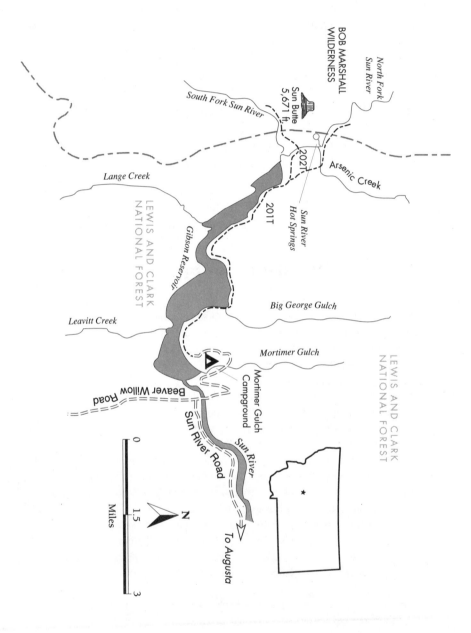

Camping: The USDA Forest Service operates Mortimer Gulch Campground at the east end of the Gibson Reservoir. Camping is allowed anywhere in the Lewis and Clark National Forest.

Maps: Montana State Highways map, Bob Marshall Wilderness Forest Service map.

Finding the springs: From Choteau, take U.S. Highway 287 southwest for 26 miles to the town of Augusta. Head west from Augusta on Sun River Road for about 25 miles to the Mortimer Gulch Campground at the east end of the Gibson Reservoir. The road ends just past the campground at the trailhead to Forest Service Trail 201. If you're a guest of the K Bar L Ranch, you'll be met at the campground by jet boat or pack horses for the trip to the ranch. If you're hiking on your own, take Forest Service Trail 201 along the north side of the Gibson Reservoir for about 5 miles until the Sun River Canyon narrows. Take Forest Service Trail 202 north until you reach the end of the reservoir. Cross the pack bridge over the Sun River, and continue north along the North Fork of the Sun River. You'll see the pool and the adjacent Sun River Hot Springs on the property of the K Bar L Ranch.

The hot springs: Sun River Hot Springs is located between the north and south forks of the Sun River at the foot of Sun Butte. The hot springs have been known by several names, including Alta Mineral Springs, Lockey's Mineral Springs, and Warm Springs. Today the springs are commonly called both Medicine Springs and Sun River Hot Springs.

Soaking pool at Sun River Hot Springs, circa 1920. PHOTO COURTESY OF MONTANA HISTORICAL SOCIETY.

The springs are on the property of the K Bar L Ranch. The ranch accepts guests from June 1 to mid-September, and during the fall hunting season. Facilities at the resort include a large lodge containing a well-stocked library from which guests can choose books to read in front of the stone fireplace. The rustic log guest cabins, heated with wood stoves, fit well with the Western theme of the ranch. Hearty Western fare fills the dining table. Up to 30 guests at a time can enjoy the facilities of the K Bar L, which offers many outdoor activities, including pack trips into the adjacent Bob Marshall Wilderness.

The hot springs supply a swimming pool with 83- to 87-degree-F water. About 50 yards from the pool are the springs themselves, near the mouth of a partially collapsed cave. A separate spring is used to run a hydroelectric generator to provide power to the guest ranch. The K Bar L is also known as the guest ranch that is "beyond all roads," a phrase that aptly fits this self-contained resort.

History: The only hot springs located in the eastern foothills of what is now the Bob Marshall Wilderness, Sun River Hot Springs was often visited in the late 1800s by nearby settlers. The March 19, 1886, *Choteau Calumet* reported that "a good bath house has been constructed over this spring, or more properly near it, and a fireplace has been constructed to modify the temperature in winter."

The warm water wasn't the only natural feature attracting visitors to the springs. Michael Leeson's 1885 *History of Montana* contained this information: "A cave inlaid and festooned with sulphur of varying thickness was discovered near the Alta Mineral Springs, on the North Fork of the Sun River, in March, 1885. The supply is unlimited, the earth surrounding the cave being impregnated for miles. There is intense excitement in Augusta, caused by the huge specimens of pure sulphur exhibited by the locators of the claim."

As word spread of the springs and the mineral deposits, more and more visitors came seeking relief for a variety of ailments. One of the visitors was Western artist Charlie Russell, who traveled by horseback from his home in Great Falls to the hot springs in 1898. A report produced in 1900 by the Montana Bureau of Agriculture, Labor, and Industry noted that "hundreds testify to the wonderful curative powers of the waters and to the sedimentary deposit of a ledge matter that contains sulphur, iron, magnesia, potash, aluminum, soda and other minerals in sulphate form and similar in ingredient to the noted Carlsbad Sprudel salts. The matter of this ledge is solvent in water and in recent years has been experimentally and successfully administered in the curing of many skin and blood diseases. When transportation reaches the vicinity and accommodations are provided for the entertainment of guests, these springs will become an American Carlsbad."

Indeed, the mineral salts oozing from the ledge in the cave did gain a national reputation. A 1921 advertising pamphlet produced by the Sun River Chemical Company of New York City promoted the salts under the name "Sun River Ointment" and claimed it would cure all skin diseases.

The area around the springs was developed into a guest ranch in 1927 and was acquired by the Klick family in 1947. Dick and Nancy Klick, the third generation of their family to own the resort, are the current proprietors.

SOUTHWEST MONTANA

Row after row of mountain ranges rise across southwest Montana, including the Absaroka-Beartooths, the Madisons, the Tobacco Roots, the Pioneers, the Pintlers, and the Bitterroots. Separating these ranges are broad valleys bisected by blue-ribbon trout streams and crystal-clear rivers, including the Missouri, Yellowstone, Bitterroot, Madison, and Gallatin. The region is rich with mining history, from prospectors panning for gold in Virginia City and Helena to the giant open-pit copper mines of Butte.

Southwest Montana is home to more than 20 hot springs, including some that once hosted the most elegant resorts ever built west of the Mississippi. Much of the early history of these thermal springs is linked to nearby gold mining in the high mountain valleys and streams.

6

Lolo Hot Springs

General description: A developed resort with an outdoor swimming pool and indoor hot plunge located on the historic Lolo Trail.
Location: Southwest Montana, about 35 miles southwest of Missoula, near the Idaho-Montana border.
Primitive/developed: Developed.
Best time of year: Open year-round.
Restrictions: Private resort. Admission fee charged for use of pools.
Access: Any vehicle can make the trip. The springs are located adjacent to U.S. Highway 12.
Water temperature: The seven springs located on the hillside just north of the pools vary from 105 to 117 degrees F. The indoor hot pool is kept around 102 to 104 degrees F. The outdoor swimming pool averages 94 degrees F.
Nearby attractions: Lolo Pass, Bitterroot Mountains.
Services: Gas, food, lodging, and camping facilities are available at the resort. Additional lodging is available at the adjacent Fort at Lolo Hot Springs (406-273-2201), which is owned and operated independently of the main resort. Other available services include cross-country skiing, snowmobile rentals, a picnic area, a saloon, and a full-service restaurant. More than 500

Lolo Hot Springs

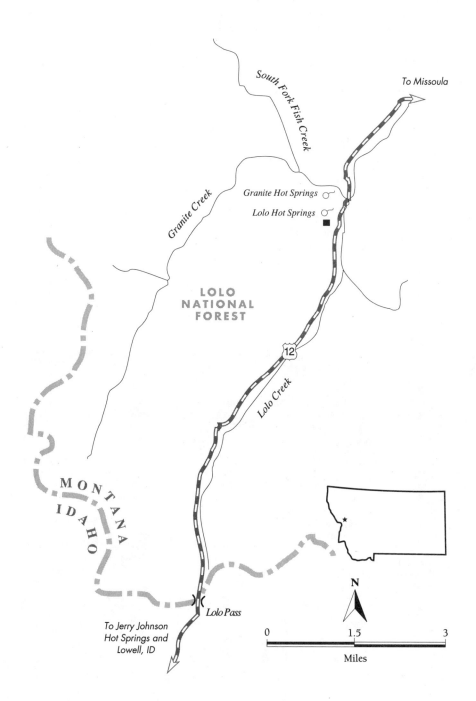

miles of snowmobile trails and extensive cross-country ski trails are available at nearby Lolo Pass. Excellent backcountry hiking is also nearby.

Camping: Tent and RV camping is available at the resort. Tepees with lanterns and wood-chip floors can also be rented for overnight accommodation. Two Forest Service campgrounds are located near Lolo Springs along US 12: Lee Creek Campground is 1 mile west of the resort, and Lewis and Clark Campground is 17 miles east.

Map: Montana State Highways map.

Finding the springs: From Missoula, drive 8 miles south on U.S. Highway 93 to the junction with US 12 at the town of Lolo. Turn west on US 12 and drive 25 miles to Lolo Hot Springs. The springs are located about 7 miles from the Montana-Idaho border.

The hot springs: The mineral pools at Lolo Hot Springs are located about 50 yards north of US 12, at the base of a striking formation of granite rock spires. Seven separate hot springs issue from cracks in the granite rock face. Water from the springs is collected into a holding tank and is then piped into the swimming and soaking pools. Every 24 hours about 75,000 gallons of water flow from the springs through the pools.

Bathers at Lolo Hot Springs in 1890. PHOTO COURTESY OF MONTANA HISTORICAL SOCIETY.

A broad sundeck surrounds the large outdoor swimming pool, which is kept at around 94 degrees F. Changing rooms and showers are connected to the pool. The indoor soaking pool, located on the west side of the changing rooms, is lit by sunlight diffused through the translucent plastic roof. The temperature of the soaking pool is maintained at a soothing 104 degrees F.

A full-service restaurant and bar are located about 100 yards west of the pools. A camping area is located south of the pools on the opposite side of US 12.

About 200 yards east of the main resort lies another thermal area, sometimes called Old Lolo or Granite Creek Hot Springs. The old Mineral Springs Hotel, a two-story structure built in 1932, is located on this property. The hotel featured a 105-degree-F soaking pool right off the lobby, which was very popular in the 1980s with cross-country skiers. The skiers would soak their sore muscles in the hotel pool after a day of skiing near Lolo Pass. Unfortunately the old hotel and the surrounding area are now closed to the public and are currently operated as a private retreat.

History: Meriwether Lewis and William Clark were the first visitors to Lolo Hot Springs to leave a written record. On September 13, 1805, the 33 men of the Corps of Discovery and their Shoshone guide, Sacajawea, reached the springs. The trail from the Bitterroot Valley had been long and hard, with dense stands of lodgepole pine impeding progress. The explorers were trying desperately to get across the Continental Divide before the winter snows covered the trail over Lolo Pass.

In his journals, Captain Clark described his first impressions: "Passed several springs which I observed the deer, elk, etc. had made roads to, and below one of the Indians had made a hole to bathe. I tasted this water and found it hot and not bad tasted. In further examination I found this water nearly boiling hot at the places it spouted from the rocks. I put my finger in the water, at first could not bear it in a second."

On their return from the Pacific Ocean in late June of the following year, Lewis and Clark had more time to enjoy the hot springs. In his journals, Clark noted the soaks enjoyed by his comrades:

These warm or hot springs are situated at the base of a hill of no considerable height. . . . The principal spring is about the temperature of the warmest baths used at the Hot Springs in Virginia. In this bath which had been prepared by the Indians by stopping the river with stone and mud, I bathed and remained in ten minutes. It was with difficulty I could remain this long and it caused a profuse sweat. Two other bold springs adjacent to this are much warmer, their heat being so great as to make the hand of a person smart extremely when immersed. We think the temperature of those springs about the same as that of the hottest of the hot springs of Virginia. Both the men and the Indians amused themselves with the use of the bath this evening. I observe after the Indians remaining in the hot bath as long as they could bear it run and plunge themselves into the creek, the water of which is now as cold as ice can make it. After remaining here a few minutes they return again to the warm bath, repeating the transition several times, but always ending with the warm bath.

Trappers followed in Lewis and Clark's footsteps, harvesting fur-bearing animals from the streams and meadows near the springs. In 1810 a Frenchman named Lolo trapped beaver in the nearby streams and became the namesake for both the old pack trail and the hot springs.

Many travelers visited the hot springs on the Lolo Trail in the 1800s. In 1885 Fred Lembke purchased the springs and surrounding land and constructed a small resort. In addition to a hot water plunge, the early resort featured a hotel, dining room, cabins, saloon, and a store. William Boyle purchased the resort around 1888. Boyle provided stagecoach transportation for guests from Missoula, charging them five dollars for the long, bumpy journey to and from the springs. The resort expanded under Boyle's ownership, and "Billy Boyle's Springs" became a favorite summer resort.

Summer supplies were brought to the springs by a four- or six-horse freight wagon, but winter provisions had to be transported through the deep snows by sleigh. The number of visitors dropped significantly in the winter because of the difficulty of travel, although some guests enjoyed the snowy isolation. An article on the springs in *Lolo Creek Reflections,* a history of the area compiled in the 1970s by the Lolo History Committe, commented on the winter guests: "Preferring the solitude, a regular clientele of bachelors would take residence for the winter."

Paul Gerber purchased the Lolo property in 1903 after a disastrous fire destroyed the hotel. He doubled the size of the resort to almost 400 acres, and business increased as road access to Missoula improved. Labor Day and the Fourth of July were especially busy. During one of these weekends, more than 500 tents surrounded the hot springs.

Lolo Hot Springs remained in the Gerber family until 1964. It then went into a period of decline and was closed until 1988, when Don Stoen, who currently owns the property, purchased the resort.

7

Jerry Johnson Hot Springs (Idaho)

General description: A series of primitive hot springs pools scattered along the banks of a rushing creek in a valley of statuesque cedar trees. Like neighboring Weir Creek Hot Springs, Jerry Johnson is not technically a "Montana" hot spring, but many Montanans claim it as their own because Missoula is the closest sizable city to this Idaho soak.

Location: Northeast Idaho, 22 miles from the Montana-Idaho border, 70 miles southwest of Missoula.

Primitive/developed: Primitive.

Best time of year: Accessible (and very popular) year-round. The hot springs pools closest to Warm Springs Creek are often washed out during the spring runoff.

Restrictions: No camping is allowed at the springs. The hot springs area is closed at night, and all bathers must leave the area by 8:00 P.M. The Forest Service is quite strict with enforcement and will issue citations to anyone staying in the springs past the curfew. Swimsuits are optional.

Access: Any vehicle can make the drive to the trailhead.

Water temperature: The temperature varies in the soaking pools, depending both on the amount of cold river water mixed in and on the time of year. The hot waterfalls that nourish the lower pools run about 115 degrees F. The soaking pools near the rock-strewn hillside farther up the creek average 102 to 106 degrees F, depending on how much river water is mixed in. The isolated large upper pool overlooking the cedar-lined meadow holds at a constant 106 degrees F.

Nearby attractions: Lolo Pass and Lolo Hot Springs, Lochsa River, Weir Creek Hot Springs, Selway-Bitterroot Wilderness.

Services: There are no services available at the springs. Gas, food, and lodging are available at Lochsa Lodge, 11 miles northeast on U.S. Highway 12, or at Lolo Hot Springs on the Montana side of the border, 22 miles northeast of Jerry Johnson Hot Springs on US 12.

Camping: Camping was allowed near the springs until the mid-1990s but is now prohibited. The closest legal camping area, Jerry Johnson Forest Service Campground, is 0.5 mile southeast of the pack bridge on US 12. Wendover and Whitehall Forest Service campgrounds are located 7 and 8 miles northwest of the pack bridge on US 12.

Maps: Idaho State Highways map, USGS Tom Beal Peak ID, Clearwater National Forest map.

Jerry Johnson Hot Springs (Idaho)

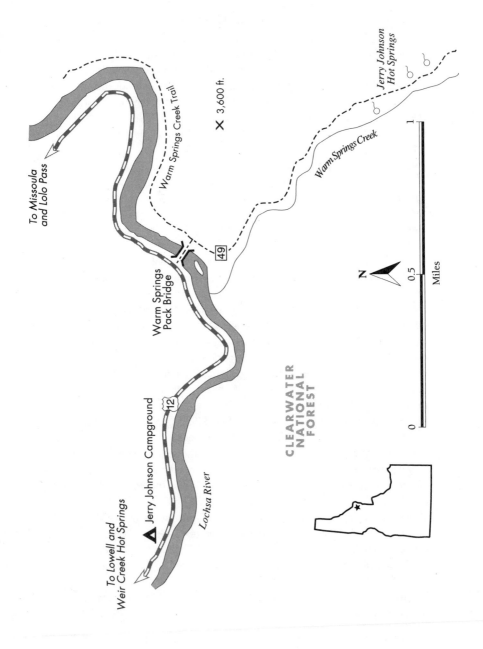

Finding the springs: If you're coming from Montana, travel west on US 12 over Lolo Pass. From Lolo Pass continue west into Idaho on US 12 for 22 miles to mile marker 151. About 0.25 mile east of mile marker 151, look for a parking lot on the north side of the highway and a well-built suspension bridge (called the Warm Springs Pack Bridge) over the Lochsa River. The 1-mile trail to Jerry Johnson Hot Springs (Forest Service Trail 49) starts at the pack bridge. Cross the bridge. The trail is well maintained, and it's an easy, almost level walk to the hot springs.

CAUTION: There have been a number of break-ins to cars parked in the Jerry Johnson parking lot. Place valuables in your trunk or take them with you.

The hot springs: Jerry Johnson consists of three separate groups of hot springs, each with a different personality. Named for a prospector who built a cabin near the springs in 1893, Jerry Johnson Hot Springs offers a variety of soothing soaking options in a pastoral forest setting.

One mile up the trail from the pack bridge, a steep side trail veers toward the creek, leading to a half dozen soaking pools fed by hot waterfalls. The short, rocky trail down to the creekbed and shallow pools can be slippery. This area is often washed out by spring runoff, but later in the year it provides a great isolated soak out of view from the trail above. Some of the pools directly under the waterfalls may be too hot for soaking, but nearby you're likely to find a cooler

Soaking pool beneath the hot waterfalls at Jerry Johnson Hot Springs.

pool just to your liking. As with all soaking locations at Jerry Johnson, nudity tends to be the rule rather than the exception.

A hundred yards farther up the main trail from the hot waterfalls, another hot spring emerges from a boulder-strewn hillside. This spring flows into a series of shallow, makeshift soaking pools. The hottest pools are located near the hillside, while the pools near the banks of Warm Springs Creek are cooler. Bathers often take breaks from a siege of hot water soaking by plunging into the icy waters of the creek, then basking on the sun-warmed rocks surrounding the pools.

Another 50 yards farther up the main trail is the final hot spring. Its large pool overlooks a cedar-lined meadow and easily holds a party of 10 or more. Maintaining a fairly constant 106 degree F temperature, the pool is about 100 yards from the creek. The pool is about 10 feet across and 3 feet deep and gets fairly muddy when disturbed. As with the other soaking pools at Jerry Johnson, this pool can get crowded, but the beautiful views and relaxed atmosphere tend to overcome any discomfort caused by the occasional lack of solitude.

In the 1970s and 1980s, the increasing popularity of Jerry Johnson Hot Springs led to occasional conflicts. A few individuals would camp for weeks near the pools, discouraging other bathers from soaking. Lack of toilets near the pools also raised concerns about water quality. The Forest Service responded by enacting an 8:00 P.M. curfew to discourage camping and monopolizing of the pools and to reduce the environmental impacts of long-term visits.

8

Weir Creek Hot Springs (Idaho)

General description: A series of secluded hot pools in a quiet grove of cedars next to a mountain stream. The short but rocky hike to the springs usually means fewer soakers than at nearby Jerry Johnson Hot Springs. Although Weir Creek Hot Springs is in Idaho, many Montanans claim it as their own because Missoula is the closest large city to the springs.
Location: Northeast Idaho, 79 miles southwest of Missoula.
Primitive/developed: Primitive.
Best time of year: Summer and early fall. Winter snows can make the 0.5-mile hike to the springs difficult, but it's worth it if you take your time and are prepared to deal with the snow.
Restrictions: None. The springs are located on Forest Service land. Swimsuits are optional.
Access: Any vehicle can make the drive to the trailhead.

Water temperature: 117 degrees F at the springs, cooling to 100 to 105 degrees F in the large upper pool. The lower pool just above the creek measures 95 degrees F.

Nearby attractions: Jerry Johnson Hot Springs, Lolo Pass, Lolo Hot Springs, Lochsa River, Selway-Bitterroot Wilderness.

Services: There are no services at Weir Creek. Gas, food, and lodging are available at Lochsa Lodge, 19 miles northeast of the springs on U.S. Highway 12, and in Lowell, Idaho, 45 miles southwest of the hot springs on US 12.

Camping: Jerry Johnson Forest Service Campground is located 8.5 miles west of the Weir Creek Hot Springs parking area. Wendover and Whitehall Forest Service campgrounds are located 16 and 17 miles northeast of Weir Creek Hot Springs on US 12.

Maps: Idaho State Highways map, USGS Greystone Butte ID, Clearwater National Forest map.

Finding the springs: From Lolo Pass on the Montana-Idaho border, drive southwest on US 12 into Idaho to mile marker 143. Continue driving southwest for 0.9 mile on US 12. Look for a small parking area and trailhead on the northwest side of the road. Park and lock your car (take valuables with you or lock them in the trunk).

It's only about 0.5 mile from the parking lot to Weir Creek Hot Springs, less than a half-hour walk on a dry summer day. However, the hike can be tricky. The Weir Creek trail isn't maintained by the Forest Service, unlike the well-manicured path at nearby Jerry Johnson Hot Springs.

Don't be seduced into taking the apparently well-used trail that heads up the mountainside. Stick to the lower trail that stays near (and sometimes in) Weir Creek. The trail is littered with tree roots, boulders, and blowdowns, so watch your step. About 0.5 mile up the trail you'll see the steam rising from Weir Creek Hot Springs on the hillside on the left-hand side of Weir Creek. You'll need to scramble about 30 feet up the hill to reach the best pools.

The hot springs: Surrounded by a cathedral of large cedars, the four hot soaking pools of Weir Creek Hot Springs are perfect for an afternoon of secluded soaking. The hot springs emerge from a granite rock face 100 feet above the canyon floor and flow through stair-stepped hot pools down to Weir Creek. The shallow and somewhat stagnant uppermost pool is large enough for a couple of bathers, but most soakers opt for the 8-foot by 10-foot main pool on the ledge looking over the creek. The main pool has a solid granite bottom and is surrounded by weathered wooden plank benches worn smooth by decades of soakers' bottoms. The pool temperature hovers around 105 degrees F, and a steady flow of hot water through the pool ensures a fresh soak.

A long wooden gutter carries the water from the main pool over a ledge,

Weir Creek Hot Springs (Idaho)

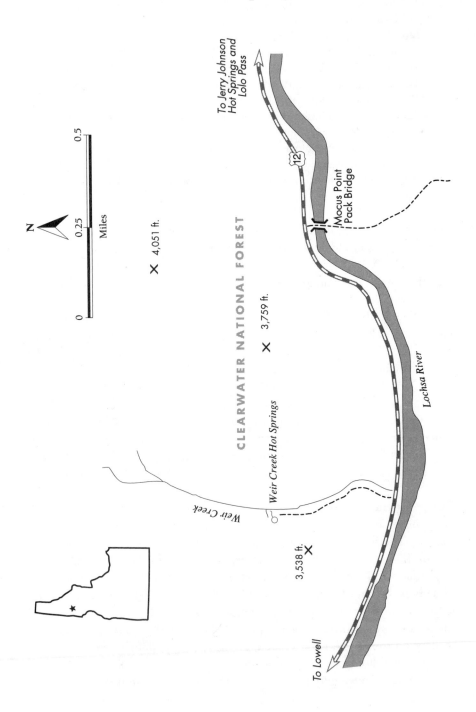

To Jerry Johnson Hot Springs and Lolo Pass

12

Mocus Point Pack Bridge

CLEARWATER NATIONAL FOREST

4,051 ft.

3,759 ft.

Lochsa River

Weir Creek Hot Springs

Weir Creek

3,538 ft.

To Lowell

N

0   0.25   0.5
Miles

creating a hot water shower into a small soaking pool below. The hot water finally flows into some volunteer pools adjacent to Weir Creek. There's no detectable sulfur smell in the hot water, just the fresh scent of cedars overhead.

Jerry Johnson Hot Springs, 10 miles northwest of Weir Creek, is closed at dusk by the Forest Service. Some hot springs enthusiasts move from Jerry Johnson to Weir Creek in the evening because there are no restrictions at Weir Creek regarding nighttime soaks. You are therefore most likely to have Weir Creek to yourself in the morning and early afternoon.

9

Lost Trail Hot Springs Resort

General description: A rustic hot springs resort in a narrow, pine-covered mountain valley along the Lewis and Clark Trail.

Location: Southwest Montana, about 90 miles south of Missoula just below Lost Trail Pass in the Bitterroot Valley.

Primitive/developed: Developed.

Best time of year: Open seven days a week from June 15 until Labor Day. The pool and restaurant are usually open after Labor Day only Thursday through Sunday, and Wednesday by reservation only. Pool and restaurant hours depend on the number of guests staying at the resort, so it's best to call ahead to be sure the pool facilities are open in the winter. Lodging is available seven days a week year-round. The resort is especially popular in the winter with snowmobilers and cross-country skiers, who enjoy the many miles of groomed backcountry trails near Lost Trail Pass.

Restrictions: Private resort. A fee is charged for the use of the pools.

Access: Any vehicle can make the trip, because the resort is just off U.S. Highway 93.

Water temperature: 110 degrees F at the source; 105 degrees F in the hot tub; 95 degrees F in the swimming pool. According to a brochure from the 1940s, the water is "not too hot and not too cool."

Nearby attractions: Lost Trail Ski Area, Anaconda-Pintler Wilderness, Selway-Bitterroot Wilderness, Big Hole National Battlefield.

Services: Breakfast, lunch, and dinner are served at the Alpine Restaurant and Lounge at the resort. Several lodging options are available, including two group lodges that sleep more than 30 people each, nine private cabins, and eight individual nonsmoking rooms. Also available are 18 full-service RV hookups.

Camping: Indian Trees Forest Service Campground is located about 1 mile south of Lost Trail Hot Springs Resort on US 93 and has 16 camping spots available. The campground acquired its name from the numerous ponderosa pine trees in the area, which were scarred by Indians who scraped off the outer bark to reach the inner bark for food.

Maps: Montana State Highways map, USGS Lost Trail MT.

Finding the springs: From Missoula, drive 88 miles south on US 93 through the Bitterroot Valley, past Hamilton and Sula, until you see a sign for Lost Trail Hot Springs on the west side of the highway (about 6.5 miles south of Sula). Turn west and drive about 0.25 mile through the pine trees past the cabins and lodges to the restaurant and pool building. From Butte, drive south about 17 miles on Interstate 15 to Montana Highway 43 (the Divide turnoff), then 70 miles west on MT 43 to Lost Trail Pass. The resort is about 6 miles north of Lost Trail Pass on US 93.

The hot springs: The 110-degree F hot springs are located on a hillside approximately 0.75 mile above the resort and are piped directly into a 25-foot by 75-foot outdoor swimming pool and an adjoining indoor hot tub. A sauna is also available. The outdoor pool varies in depth from a 10-inch wading area at one end to 9 feet at the other end. Unlike many hot springs in Montana, the

Outdoor pool at Lost Trail Hot Springs Resort.

Lost Trail Hot Springs Resort

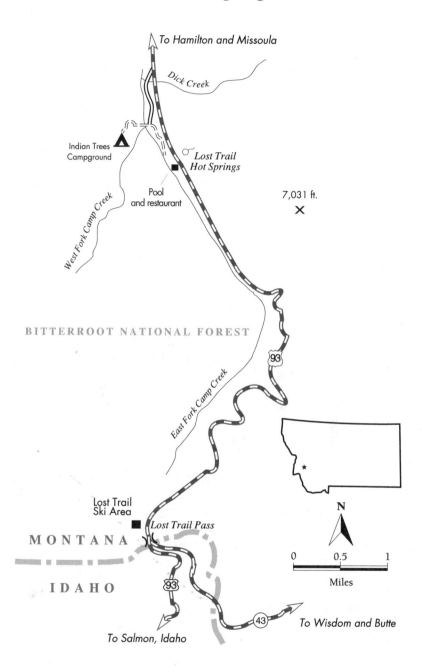

To Hamilton and Missoula

Dick Creek

Indian Trees
Campground

Lost Trail
Hot Springs

Pool
and restaurant

West Fork Camp Creek

7,031 ft.
✕

BITTERROOT NATIONAL FOREST

East Fork Camp Creek

93

N

Lost Trail
Ski Area

MONTANA

Lost Trail Pass

IDAHO

93

0   0.5   1
Miles

To Salmon, Idaho

43

To Wisdom and Butte

water at Lost Trail is odorless, with no sulfur smell. Pool temperature averages 95 degrees F year-round, and the temperature averages 105 degrees F in the hot tub. Diners near the window in the upstairs restaurant and lounge have a great view of the pool area below.

History: Lost Trail Pass gained its descriptive name due to a navigational error by the Lewis and Clark Expedition. In September 1805, as they traveled north toward the Bitterroot Valley, the explorers missed a critical trail at Moose Creek and instead headed up Fish Creek. Their miscalculation added an extra day and night to their travel over the pass. The explorers eventually descended a ridge west of Camp Creek, which flows through the present-day Lost Trail Hot Springs Resort area, and finally reached Ross's Hole, where they rested for two days to recover from their arduous trip on the "Lost Trail."

Lewis and Clark apparently didn't discover Lost Trail Hot Springs during their trek (although they did find two other Montana hot springs, Lolo and Jackson). The first recorded inhabitant of the springs was a woman who built a cabin near the springs in 1892 so she could give her ailing son therapeutic soaks in the water. A 14-room hotel was built near the springs in 1895 by Frank Allen, who sold the property to James Gallogly in 1897. The Gallogly family owned the property until the 1970s (the springs are still called Gallogly Springs on many maps). The current bathhouse and restaurant were built in 1941. In 1954 the resort became a private camp for boys and remained so until the 1970s, when the resort was reopened to the public.

10

Jackson Hot Springs Lodge

General description: A cavernous, rustic lodge and outdoor warm-water pool in the heart of the Big Hole Valley.
Location: Southwest Montana, 48 miles west of Dillon.
Primitive/developed: Developed.
Best time of year: Open year-round. Every season in the Big Hole is spectacular.
Restrictions: Privately owned; an admission fee is charged.
Access: Any vehicle can make the trip on Montana Highway 278 to Jackson.
Water temperature: 138 degrees F at the source; 96 degrees F to 98 degrees F by the time it reaches the outdoor pool.

Nearby attractions: Bannack State Park, West Pioneer Mountains, Bitterroot Mountains, Big Hole National Battlefield, Lost Trail Ski Area, Maverick Mountain Ski Area.

Services: Food and lodging are available at Jackson Hot Springs Lodge. Two other stores with gas, supplies, and food are also located in the town of Jackson.

Camping: Tent camping is allowed behind the lodge for a small fee. Several public campgrounds are within a half-hour's drive. Miner Lake public campground is the closest. From downtown Jackson, head west on County Road 95 for 7 miles, then west on Forest Service Road 182 for 3 miles. Two other public campgrounds, North and South Van Houten, are located 10 miles west of Jackson on Skinner Meadows Road (County Road 6). Go south of town 1 mile on MT 278 to find Skinner Meadows Road.

Maps: Montana State Highways map, USGS Jackson MT.

Finding the springs: From Butte, head south on Interstate 15 for 19 miles to Montana Highway 43. Follow MT 43 west for 51 miles to the town of Wisdom. Turn south on MT 278 for 19 miles to Jackson. From Dillon, take MT 278 west for 48 miles to Jackson. Jackson Hot Springs Lodge is on the east side of Main Street, which is also MT 278. The lodge building dominates this small town of only 50 residents, so you're not likely to miss it.

The hot springs: The 137-degree-F hot springs are located 1,300 feet east of the lodge and are piped underground to the town of Jackson. The water is almost odorless, with no trace of sulfur smell.

The entire town of Jackson depends on the hot springs for its water source, which makes life a little difficult if you want a really cold glass of water. Until fairly recently, residents and guests in Jackson had only hot water available from the tap. Cold water for drinking was produced by placing a jug of hot springs water in the refrigerator and waiting for it to cool. Showers were even more exciting. Guests at the lodge were each given a bag of ice to hang under the showerhead so that the hot water from the springs had a brief chance to cool before it hit their skin.

Presently the lodge has developed a system of underground pipes that allows the hot springs water to cool sufficiently for drinking and washing, and guests no longer have to endure ice bags and scalding water in the shower.

The hot springs heat the entire resort and the 30-foot by 75-foot outdoor pool. Once covered but now open to the elements, the pool is maintained at around 96 to 98 degrees F. It is connected to the cavernous 9,000-square-foot lodge. The two-story building houses a giant oak dance floor, surrounded by more than 50 wild game trophies looking down from the walls. The rustic

Jackson Hot Springs Lodge and Elkhorn Hot Springs Resort

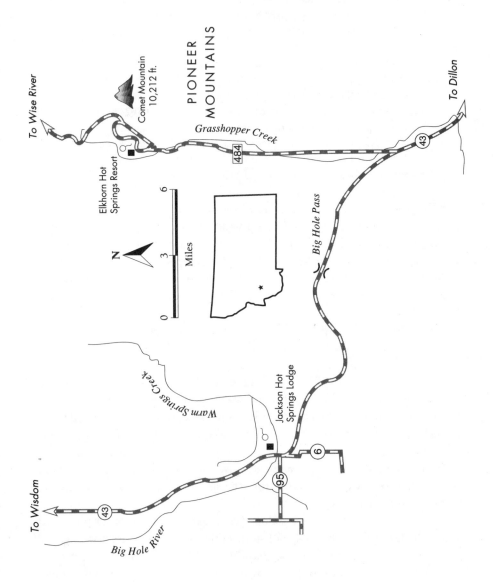

ranch theme extends to the south end of the dance floor, where dozens of sweat-stained cowboy hats hang from the rafters over the bar. A restaurant with seating for up to 45 is on the west side of the dance floor. It serves a variety of "cowboy gourmet" dinner items, including prime rib and steak, as well as breakfast and lunch.

Guest rooms aren't available in the main lodge, but cozy cabins (many featuring their own fireplaces) surround the lodge, as do a four-plex apartment, RV spaces, and tent sites.

Recreational activities abound in the area, and the lodge is popular with hunters, downhill and cross-country skiers, and snowmobilers. At 6,475 feet in elevation, cross-country skiers can literally ski out the front door of the lodge in the winter. Two downhill ski areas (Lost Trail and Maverick Mountain) are within an hour's drive.

Despite its isolation (or perhaps because of it), Jackson Hot Springs Lodge has hosted several celebrities, including Bing Crosby, Bob Hope, and Supreme Court Justice Earl Warren.

History: The town of Jackson and the hot springs were named for the town's first postmaster, Antone Jackson. However, persons other than Native Americans first saw the thermal waters in 1806, when a portion of the Lewis and Clark Expedition passed close by on their return from the Pacific Ocean.

Lewis and Clark had separated in the Bitterroot Valley. Captain Lewis headed northeast toward the Great Falls of the Missouri, while Clark went southeast to explore the Yellowstone River. Clark's journey took him through the Big Hole Valley. He noted in his journals that the valley (which he called "Hot Springs Valley") was one of the most beautiful he had ever seen, and he was impressed with the plentiful fur-bearing animals and lush grasses. Around noon on July 7, 1806, Clark and his party, including the Shoshone Indian guide Sacajawea, reached the hot springs. Clark said that the water "blubbers with heat for twenty paces below where it rises." The party settled around the hot springs for lunch, and Clark cooked a piece of meat "the width of two fingers" in the steaming water, noting that in five minutes the meat was cooked enough to eat.

A few fur trappers reported visiting the springs in the 1820s, but not much use of the springs was noted until Benoit O. Fournier took claim to the springs in 1884. Fournier built his house and a small plunge next to the springs. In 1898 the local paper reported that "a bath in the hot water is one of the luxuries which people usually take advantage of when in town."

In 1911 the springs were sold to M. D. Jardine, who built a plunge and hotel on Main Street in Jackson and piped the hot water 1,300 feet from its source to the new pool. The resort changed little until 1950, when John Dooling,

Outdoor pool at Jackson Hot Springs Lodge.

a wealthy rancher from Jackson Hole, Wyoming, purchased it. Dooling bought a number of ranches in the Big Hole, as well as many of the buildings along the main street of Jackson. But Dooling's enduring legacy was the construction of a new log inn and hot springs pool. Originally named the Diamond Bar Inn, the new lodge cost Dooling about $400,000 to build. Dooling turned the new lodge into a center of activity for outdoor enthusiasts in the Big Hole, culminating with the attraction of the International Ski Plane Races, held near Jackson in the 1950s.

The lodge has had several owners since the 1960s and has been owned by Monte and Inge Peterson since 1990.

11

Elkhorn Hot Springs Resort

(See map on page 48)

General description: A rustic mountain resort and hot springs located in the heart of the Pioneer Mountains.
Location: Southwest Montana, 43 miles northwest of Dillon.
Primitive/developed: Developed.
Best time of year: Open year-round.
Restrictions: Privately owned. Admission fee charged to use the pools.
Access: Any vehicle can make the trip.
Water temperature: 118 degrees F at the springs source. The larger outdoor hot pool is around 95 degrees F; the smaller, hotter pool is approximately 98 degrees F; the indoor wet sauna is 104 to 106 degrees F.
Nearby attractions: Pioneer Mountain Scenic Byway, Bannack State Park, Crystal Park, Coolidge Ghost Town.
Services: Food and lodging are available at the resort. All other services are available in Dillon, 40 miles to the southeast, or Wise River, 31 miles to the north.
Camping: There are four tent sites and five RV sites available at the resort. Several Forest Service campgrounds are available on the National Scenic Byway north of the springs. Grasshopper Campground, about 1 mile south of the springs, is the closest public camping option. Camping sites are also available at Bannack State Park, about 20 miles south.
Maps: Montana State Highways map, USGS Polaris MT.

Finding the springs: From Dillon, take the Jackson/Wisdom exit off Interstate 15, 2 miles southwest of Dillon on Montana Highway 278. Drive west for 25 miles on MT 278 to Forest Service Road 484 (also called the Pioneer Mountains Scenic Byway). Drive north on FS 484 for 13 miles to the springs. You can also reach the springs by traveling south from Wise River on FS 484 for 31 miles to the springs, but this road is impassable in the winter.

The hot springs: The two outdoor pools at Elkhorn are just right for a soak after a day of skiing in the nearby Pioneer Mountains. The larger, 95-degree-F pool is slightly cooler than the smaller, 98-degree-F pool. If you need even more heat, step inside the bathhouse next to the pool and enter the "Grecian wet sauna." This 12-foot by 12-foot, dark and steamy retreat averages 104 to 106 degrees F.

Outdoor pools at Elkhorn Hot Springs Resort.

The resort has 11 log cabins with wood stoves or fireplaces (wood is provided), as well as ten rooms on the second floor of the lodge. The cabins have no running water—each guest is provided with a jug of water at the lodge. Showers are available at the bathhouse, and outhouses are the rule.

The first floor of the lodge contains an informal restaurant, with dozens of moose, elk, and other trophy mounts watching the diners from the walls. A crackling fire in a large stone fireplace warms guests after dinner.

At an elevation of 7,385 feet, Elkhorn Hot Springs Resort offers access to superb winter activities. Over 20 miles of groomed cross-country ski trails are available from the resort, as well as 200 miles of groomed snowmobile trails. The resort rents cross-country skis, snowshoes, and snowmobiles. Maverick Mountain ski area, 3 miles south of the resort, offers excellent downhill skiing.

Summertime activities at Elkhorn include horse trail rides, mountain biking (bikes are available for rent), hiking, and exploring the nearby ghost town of Coolidge. Digging for quartz crystals in the 30-acre Crystal Park Mineral Recreational Area, 4 miles north of the resort, is also a popular activity.

History: Elkhorn Hot Springs was originally owned by the federal government as part of Beaverhead National Forest. A newspaper article from the 1890s declared that Elkhorn was "one of the two hot springs in the entire country which remain as government property and directly under government control."

Traveling to Elkhorn in the early days required a major commitment, according to a reporter with the initials W. E. C., in an undated newspaper article from the 1890s. The springs had "fallen into disuse and accommodations were of such nature and roads were so impassable that it necessitated a pioneering instinct to spend a few days at the healing waters."

Little development occurred at the springs before area businessmen formed a committee to solicit contributions for improving the springs. With money from both local citizens and federal sources, the committee built a 20-foot by 40-foot plunge, followed immediately by a second plunge three times larger than the first. Dressing rooms, more than a dozen summer cottages, and "one of the best camping grounds in the state" followed the construction of the plunges. A Forest Service ranger was stationed at Elkhorn to supervise the use of the springs and to ensure that the "strict rules of the national forest are rigidly enforced."

Locals were so excited about the new bathing facilities and surrounding natural beauty that they planned to petition the U.S. Congress to designate the area a national park. W. E. C. reported in the 1890s newspaper article that "Elkhorn National Park, still only a hot springs with no more than local repute, will be in time a national playground." Area residents were certain that the proposed Elkhorn National Park would soon be as well-known as Yellowstone.

Elkhorn National Park never became a reality. The federal government relinquished ownership of the land, and Samuel Engelsjard filed water rights on the springs in 1905. Engelsjard built cabins and a horse stable near the site a year later.

The resort had more than ten owners from the 1920s until 1980. The current lodge was built as a private hunting retreat in 1924 by a group of local ranchers, but little other development took place. The original poolhouse was rebuilt in the 1940s after it was damaged by a lightning strike. When acquired by Bernal Kahrs in 1980, the lodge and many of the cabins had been condemned. Fortunately, Kahrs and subsequent owners in the 1980s and 1990s rescued Elkhorn Hot Springs from disrepair. A redwood deck around the pool was added in 1992, and all of the cabins and the main lodge have been completely renovated, while still retaining their rustic charm.

12

Fairmont Hot Springs Resort

General description: A popular destination resort located between Anaconda and Butte, featuring two large recreational pools and two soaking pools.

Location: Southwest Montana, 15 miles west of Butte.

Primitive/developed: Developed.

Best time of year: Open year-round.

Restrictions: The resort is privately owned. An admission fee is charged to use the pools. Overnight guests can swim for free and can use the pools 24 hours a day. The pools and waterslide are open to the general public from 8:00 A.M. to 9:30 P.M.

Access: Any vehicle can make the trip.

Water temperature: 143 degrees F at the natural hot springs; 160 degrees F at the hot water well. The large indoor and outdoor recreational pools are kept between 89 and 92 degrees F, while the smaller indoor and outdoor soaking pools are kept between 100 and 105 degrees F.

Nearby attractions: Discovery Basin Ski Area, Montana Museum of Mining, Anaconda-Pintler Wilderness, Humbug Spires Primitive Area, Lost Creek State Park, Warm Springs Wildlife Management Area, Georgetown Lake, Mount Haggin Cross Country Ski Area.

Services: Food and lodging are available at the resort. Attractions include tennis, mountain biking, an exotic animal zoo, horseback riding, and an 18-hole golf course. The resort building features 152 guest rooms, a coffee shop, and a full-service dining room with a view of the outdoor pools. The resort often holds statewide conventions and meetings in its 7,000 square feet of conference facilities.

Camping: Tepee and tent camping is available, and an RV campground with 100 hookups is located adjacent to the resort. Nearby Lost Creek State Park has 40 camping/RV spots. To reach the park, go northwest from the hot springs on Montana Highway 441 to the intersection with Montana Highway 1. Turn west on MT 1 for about 2 miles to Montana Highway 48. Take MT 48 north, turning almost immediately onto Montana Highway 273. Follow MT 273 north for 2 miles, then turn west for 5 miles to Lost Creek State Park.

Map: Montana State Highways map.

Finding the springs: From Butte, drive west on Interstate 90 for 12 miles to Exit 211 (the Fairmont/Gregson exit). Take the exit and go 2 miles south on MT 441 to the hot springs.

Fairmont Hot Springs Resort
and Warm Springs

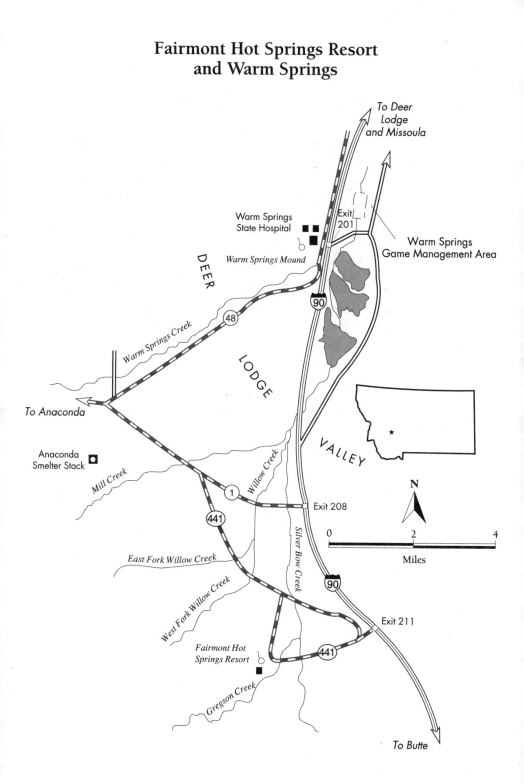

To Deer
Lodge
and Missoula

Warm Springs
State Hospital

Exit
201

Warm Springs
Game Management Area

DEER

Warm Springs Mound

Warm Springs Creek

48

90

LODGE

To Anaconda

Anaconda
Smelter Stack

Mill Creek

VALLEY

Willow Creek

1

Exit 208

441

East Fork Willow Creek

Silver Bow Creek

West Fork Willow Creek

90

Exit 211

N

0   2   4

Miles

Fairmont Hot
Springs Resort

441

Gregson Creek

To Butte

Outdoor pools and water slide at Fairmont Hot Springs Resort.

The hot springs: Fairmont Hot Springs Resort has some of the largest natural hot water pools in Montana. Guests and visitors have their choice of a variety of pools. The natural hot springs are enclosed in cedar-shingled holding tanks located near the wildlife zoo. Two swimming pools use hot water from a 160-degree-F geothermal well located about 1,700 feet north of the resort. Both the large indoor pool (measuring 45 feet by 128 feet) and the giant outdoor pool (59 feet by 164 feet) are heated to between 87 and 92 degrees F. Adjacent to the swimming pools are two soaking pools that are kept between 100 and 105 degrees F. The outdoor soaking pool, a 30-foot by 50-foot oasis of warmth, is especially popular in the winter, when hardy bathers make a quick dash to the outdoor swimming pool, then swim across it to reach the hot soaking pool out in the snow and steam. The less-adventurous winter visitor can stay in the 48-foot by 16-foot indoor soaking pool.

History: Early records show that a man named Hulbert settled at the hot springs in the 1860s. The brothers George and Eli Gregson purchased the land from Hulbert in 1869 and also claimed title to an additional 320 acres. The Gregsons built a small hotel and bathhouse at the hot springs, named the resort "Upper Deer Lodge Hot Springs," and ran a cattle and dairy operation on the surrounding acres.

Word spread of the healing powers of the hot water, and the bathhouse and hotel enjoyed a steady business from people who came to drink the water and to bathe in it. According to the 1886–1887 holiday edition of the *Butte Daily Miner:*

> The medicinal virtues of the waters cannot be disputed in the face of the large number of cures they have effected. Some of the most desperate cases of rheumatism, neuralgia, catarrh, kidney diseases, cutaneous affections and kindred diseases have been speedily and permanently cured by the use of these waters. For those suffering from nervous prostration or general debility, the springs are a certain benefit and if sufficient length of time is given to their use will effect a certain cure.
>
> The water has not an unpleasant taste to some, however it may taste to others. It is said that by seasoning it with pepper and salt it makes a very palatable soup. When drank as hot as can be borne, the taste of sulphur is pronounced enough to lead one to the conclusion that his Satanic majesty superintends the brewing in a branch kitchen just below.

The Gregsons sold the springs and surrounding land to Milo French in 1891. French had at one time been proprietor of Boulder Hot Springs between Butte and Helena. He and subsequent owner Con Hayes built two dance pavilions and a large two-story hotel, and the resort thrived during the early 1900s, especially in the summers. Miners and smeltermen from nearby

Gregson Hot Springs Hotel, Natatorium, 200 x 64, Boyce-Butte, 17 Miles from Butte, Mont.

The Gregson Hotel, circa 1914. PHOTO COURTESY OF WORLD MUSEUM OF MINING.

The Moorish-style Gregson Hot Springs resort, built in 1927.
PHOTO COURTESY OF WORLD MUSEUM OF MINING.

Butte and Anaconda were frequent guests. The 1870–1971 souvenir edition of the *Anaconda Leader* reported that the hot springs became "the resort for workers of Butte City, as well as for the thousands of toiling miners, a place of rest and recreation."

Some of the gatherings were boisterous. In August 1912, the Butte Miners Union hosted a picnic at the hot springs for 6,000 of its members and their families, the same day that the Anaconda Mill and Smeltermen's Union held their summer picnic at the resort. Some 14,000 people crowded into the area, and animosities ran high between the predominantly Irish miners from Butte and the Serbian smeltermen from Anaconda. A friendly tug-of-war between the two groups ignited passions when the losing Butte team cried foul. Fistfights broke out among the contestants, and soon hundreds of miners and smelterworkers were clashing on the hotel grounds. Littering the grounds from the afternoon's drinking, thousands of empty beer bottles provided handy weapons for the battle, and the next day's *Butte Daily Miner* reported that "the afternoon sun was hidden from sight by the clouds of flying bottles."

Despite such incidents (or perhaps in part because of them), the resort continued to thrive. In 1912, the hot springs were renamed Gregson Hot Springs in honor of the pioneering Gregson brothers. An advertisement in the 1913

Anaconda Standard noted that four trains left daily from Anaconda to the hot springs and that "electric orchestras" furnished the two dance halls with music.

The two-story Gregson Hotel was destroyed by fire in 1914, two days before Christmas. Another fire destroyed the remaining buildings on the property about a week later. Faulty wiring was blamed for both fires. A second hotel was built in 1915, but in 1926 it, too, burned to the ground.

A year later, the ever resilient owners constructed yet another hotel at the hot springs, this time a beautiful mission-style structure. A 1928 advertisement in the *Anaconda Standard* called Gregson Springs "The hottest hot springs in America" and referred to the new Gregson Hotel as "The Saratoga of the Northwest." The hotel included a 65-foot by 195-foot indoor hot water plunge. A cold water pool measuring 20 feet by 60 feet was built adjacent to the hot pool, "for the benefit of those who desire the invigorating effects of a cold plunge following the warm bath," according to the 1928 *Anaconda Standard*. The *Standard* also noted that the resort provided swimsuits and that between uses by guests the suits were "given a rigorous pine tar and sun drying treatment, insuring their perfect freshness to the wearer."

The resort continued to operate as Gregson Springs for the next 40 years, but the hotel fell into disrepair and was closed in 1971 when the walls threatened to collapse. In 1972 Lloyd Wilder, who owned a resort called Fairmont Hot Springs in British Columbia, purchased the Gregson property. Wilder invested over $5 million in the construction of the current resort and renamed it Fairmont Hot Springs Resort.

13

Warm Springs

(See map on page 55)

General description: A 40-foot-tall travertine mound created by a hot springs flowing from its peak. The rust-colored mound was once the most striking feature in the Deer Lodge Valley.

Location: Southwest Montana, 20 miles west of Butte.

Primitive/developed: Developed. A small observation deck sits atop the hot springs mound, and a locked metal plate now covers the springs. The springs were used in the past for resort plunges.

Best time of year: Because the hot springs mound must be viewed from a frontage road 0.5 mile away, the best time is probably in the winter, when foliage doesn't block the view.

Restrictions: The hot springs mound is located on the grounds of Warm Springs State Hospital. Visits by the general public are discouraged. No bathing is allowed.

Access: Any vehicle can make the trip along the frontage road for a distant view of the hot springs mound.

Water temperature: 172 degrees F at the hot springs mound.

Nearby attractions: Fairmont Hot Springs, Discovery Basin Ski Area, Anaconda-Pintler Wilderness, Georgetown Lake.

Services: Gas and food are available at a convenience store near the front entrance to Warm Springs State Hospital. All other services are available in Anaconda, 8 miles southwest.

Camping: Racetrack Forest Service Campground is located northwest of Warm Springs. Take Interstate 90 from Warm Springs north for 4 miles to the Racetrack exit. Take the Racetrack exit west for 1 mile, then south for 0.75 mile to Forest Service Road 169. Follow FS 169 west for 10 miles to the campground.

Map: Montana State Highways map.

Finding the springs: From Butte, head 20 miles west on Interstate 90 to the Warm Springs exit. Because visitors are discouraged from entering the grounds of the Warm Springs State Hospital, the best view of the mound is about 0.5 mile south of the hospital on the frontage road that parallels the interstate. Look north and west from the frontage road toward the back of the hospital property for the large hot springs mound, topped with a red-and-white observation kiosk. There are plans to construct a greenway that would pass behind the hospital and provide a much better view of the mound.

The hot springs: The 40-foot-tall carbonate mound located near the center of the otherwise level Deer Lodge Valley is an impressive site. The mound is about 30 feet in diameter. The hot springs bubbling from the peak of the mound produce about 50 gallons per minute of 172-degree-F water—one of the hottest geothermal resources in the state of Montana. Several other hot springs used to bubble near the base of the mound. The mound itself is a brownish color due to the high iron content in the mineral deposits. An observation kiosk and sitting benches surround the now-capped springs on the top of the mound.

History: Warm Springs was known to Native Americans and early settlers as "the deer lodge." The 1887–1888 edition of the *Holiday Miner,* published in Butte, explained the history of the name and suggests the flavor of perceptions about hot springs over a century ago:

The origin of the name is credited to the poetic imagery of the Indians. Captain Mills, himself an old settler, calls it an "old appellation," and states that it is derived from a large, sugarloaf mound, with a thermal spring on its summit. Situated near the center of the broad upper half of this valley, it is one of the most beautiful and interesting formations in the northwest, growing with the centuries, the waters building their throne slowly, imperceptibly, but steadily as the coral builds the ocean reefs, and in the coming years will attract many thousands to drink of its medicinal waters and find health and pleasure in the picturesque valley, mountain-circled and coursed by crystal streams.

The mound is over forty feet high. It stands in the midst of a perfectly level valley, and the hot springs on its summit, during the greater portion of the year, send up a heavy volume of vapor, rendering it a conspicuous object for from twenty to twenty-five miles in every direction. It bears in the distance a striking resemblance to an Indian lodge with the smoke ascending from it.

Because of the large number of deer that grazed near the mound, the local Indians called the hot springs mound "It Sooke en Car-ne," which literally meant "The lodge of the white-tailed deer."

Unfortunately, according to Mills, "the laconic Yankee pioneer came this way, and without remorse boiled down all its traditions and beauty and poesy into the practical appellation 'Deer Lodge,' by which is now known the valley, the river, the county and town."

Louis Belanger built the first bathhouse near the mound in 1865. In 1871, Belanger and his brother-in-law Elisha Gerard constructed a two-story hotel and summer bathhouse at the springs and began to promote the little resort in the local papers. Belanger's resort soon gained a reputation for great food. The *New Northwest* reported in September 1872 that "All that surprises us is that a six-horse coach is not required to carry guests to Belanger's. Think of the breakfasts. Coffee, clear, dark and fragrant, flanked with rich cream; biscuits, crisp and browned to artistic beauty; here a juicy steak and a plate-length trout, and there a broiled chicken, while in between the lesser-virtued dainties tempt a triumph; and all this sixteen miles from Deer Lodge, every morning."

The food was surpassed only by the holiday parties. A December 25, 1874, article in the *New Northwest* observed that "If anything is not done that could be done to make guests comfortable at Warm Springs, it is because the host and hostess forget it, and they have remarkably good memories. The dance only lasted until breakfast was announced, which was perhaps owing to the fact that it was the second or third successive evening that many of the party had

The "deer lodge" mound at Warm Springs.

danced till daylight. Something ought to be done by the legislature to encourage a love for dancing in Montana."

The little resort was sold in 1877 to Dr. Charles F. Mussingbrod who, along with his partner Dr. A. Mitchell, had recently acquired a contract to care for those residents of the Territory of Montana who were, in those days, called insane. For their services, Mussingbrod and Mitchell were paid a dollar per patient per day.

To better manage both the new mental asylum and the popular health resort, Mitchell and Mussingbrod built a two-story frame hotel with two parlors and twelve guest rooms for paying guests, a 20-foot by 25-foot two-story house for convalescent patients, and a separate dwelling for the most violent patients. Nearby they built a plunge bath for male patients, a second plunge for female patients, and a third for hotel guests. The new asylum opened in April 1877, accepting 13 mentally ill patients from throughout the Montana Territory.

The patients and the guests of the hotel shared the combined operation without incident, even as the number of patients steadily increased. The *Rocky Mountain Husbandman* wrote in 1885 that "So complete is the construction of the buildings and grounds that while sixty insane persons are accommodated in the asylum, visitors sojourning for health or pleasure are in no way disturbed."

In 1878 an observation deck was erected on the hot springs mound. The mound itself was a popular spot for hotel guests, according to an article in the

1885 *Rocky Mountain Husbandman*, since "water rises so that it may be reached with a dipper, but we believe does not flow over. It is the favorite spring for drinking. From the summit of this mound one has a fine view of the splendid valley. At the foot of the mound numerous small springs burst out, and it is from these that the baths are supplied."

Mussingbrod and Mitchell apparently succeeded in their dual roles of caring for the patients of a mental asylum and acting as genial hosts to the guests of a hotel, no doubt in large part because of the popularity of the hot springs. The restorative and revitalizing nature of the springs was publicized throughout the region, as evidenced by this glowing report in an unidentified 1880s news article cited in *History of Warm Springs State Hospital and the Division of Mental Health*, written by Richard Fanestil:

> The business man whose vital powers are impaired by constant labor at his desk, the overworked mechanic whose tired body calls for rest, the care-worn wife whose manifold household duties have overtaxed her weak form, the literary man whose wearied brain demands relaxation from toil, the day laborer who wants a holiday, and all others suffering from the ills to which flesh is heir can find no better place to recuperate and regain lost health and strength than at the deservingly popular Warm Springs of the Deer Lodge Valley.
>
> It would require a volume to enumerate all the cures effected by the use of the waters of these springs. Suffice it to say that in every instance where these springs have been given a fair trial, the patient has been restored to health. The unusually large percentage of insane persons who have regained their reason at the asylum speaks volumes of praise of this great sanitarium.

In 1912 the Montana legislature appropriated $533,000 to purchase the mental institution. At the time of the purchase the asylum housed 854 patients, and the hotel and health resort had closed. Under state ownership the mental institution was renamed the Warm Springs State Hospital. The hospital expanded through the first half of the twentieth century, caring for close to 2,000 patients at its peak in 1954. Currently the hospital houses fewer than 200 patients. A $16 million renovation of the hospital began in 1997. Some of the buildings constructed by Mussingbrod and Mitchell more than 100 years earlier, crumbling from lack of attention, were at long last torn down.

14

Boulder Hot Springs

General description: One of the last remaining grand hotels from the golden age of Montana's hot springs resorts. The thermal waters on the hillside behind the hotel feed indoor men's and women's plunges, as well as an outdoor pool with breathtaking views of the Boulder Valley. The hotel now serves the dual roles of a bed and breakfast inn and a peaceful center for workshops and retreats.

Location: Southwest Montana, 20 miles south of Helena.

Primitive/developed: Developed.

Best time of year: Open year-round.

Restrictions: Boulder Hot Springs is alcohol and tobacco free. The pools and plunges are open to the public for a small admission fee every afternoon and evening in the summer months and on Friday, Saturday, and Sunday afternoons and evenings during the winter months. Hot water plunges and pools are available free to all guests of the bed and breakfast. Rooms are available most times of the year unless a conference or retreat is scheduled.

Access: Any vehicle can make the trip.

Water temperature: The 32 hot springs flowing from the hillside behind the hotel range from 125 to 180 degrees F. The outdoor pool is kept at 95 degrees F, and the two indoor hot plunges average 104 degrees F.

Nearby attractions: Elkhorn ghost town, radon health mines, Deerlodge and Helena national forests.

Services: The bed and breakfast inn features antique-furnished rooms in the east wing of the hotel. Nourishing breakfasts are served to overnight guests, and lunch and dinner are available in nearby Boulder. An all-you-can-eat buffet with changing ethnic themes is offered to the public every Sunday, and buffet guests are invited to use the pools and plunges free of charge.

Camping: The Mormon Creek and Basin Canyon Forest Service campgrounds are located near Basin, 10 miles south of the town of Boulder on Interstate 15.

Map: Montana State Highways map.

Finding the springs: From Helena, drive south 27 miles on Interstate 15 to the Boulder exit. Take the Boulder exit and drive on Montana Highway 69 through the town of Boulder. Proceed 3 miles south of Boulder on MT 69. Turn at the sign to Boulder Hot Springs and drive about 0.5 mile on a gravel road to the old hotel. From Butte, take I-15 north 37 miles to the Boulder exit. From

Boulder Hot Springs

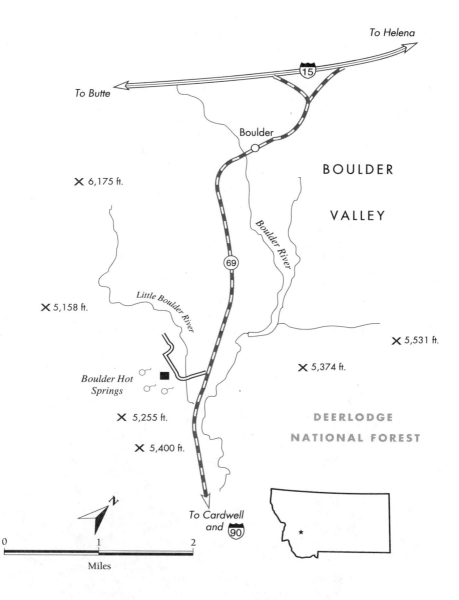

To Helena

15

To Butte

Boulder

BOULDER

VALLEY

✕ 6,175 ft.

Boulder River

69

Little Boulder River

✕ 5,158 ft.

✕ 5,531 ft.

✕ 5,374 ft.

Boulder Hot
Springs

✕ 5,255 ft.

DEERLODGE

NATIONAL FOREST

✕ 5,400 ft.

N

To Cardwell
and 90

0   1   2

Miles

Bozeman, take Interstate 90 to the Boulder/Cardwell exit, then follow MT 69 north for 30 miles to the hot springs.

The hot springs: There are 32 separate hot springs scattered across the hill behind the outdoor pool and hotel. Ten of these springs, with temperatures ranging from 150 to 175 degrees F, are collected in holding tanks near the pool. The water is then piped through the hotel's heating system, as well as directly into the plunges and steam rooms.

The 20-foot by 60-foot outdoor pool varies in depth from 3 to 5 feet and is kept at 95 degrees F. A 50-yard-long brick sidewalk connects the outdoor pool to a cozy sitting room. Just south of the sitting room are the women's plunges, with a 104-degree-F warm water plunge and a stimulating 75-degree-F cold water plunge. The smaller men's area north of the sitting room contains a single 104-degree-F plunge. Both plunge areas also contain steam rooms and showers.

The bed and breakfast guest rooms are in the hotel wing just west of the plunges. The old mission-style hotel is filled with history and is even said to have a resident ghost that occasionally appears in the lobby.

Boulder Hot Springs looks much the same today as in this 1910 photo.
PHOTO COURTESY OF MONTANA HISTORICAL SOCIETY.

History: Boulder Hot Springs was settled shortly after prospectors began searching for gold in the mountain streams of the area. A crude bathhouse and tavern were located on the property by 1866, and miners tired from days of back-breaking work came to the springs to soak away their aches and pains.

In the mid-1880s a rancher with the curious name of A. C. Quaintance purchased the springs. Quaintance built a new plunge at the hot springs, which was glowingly reported in the January 6, 1886, edition of the *Butte Miner.* "The plunge is filled with the health-giving fluid of the most ravishing temperature, into which the pleasure-seekers, regardless of sex, plunge and swim and float around in a heterogeneous mass and in perfect ecstasy."

Quaintance leased the property to C. W. Kerrick, a railroad contractor from Minneapolis. Kerrick constructed a sumptuous three-story hotel, complete with 52 guest rooms, a billiards room, and an amusement hall. The hotel opened on June 10, 1891. The announcement in the *Jefferson County Sentinel* on that day stated that the hot springs water at Boulder was an "absolute cure for rheumatism, dyspepsia, and all diseases of the digestive organs."

Riding on the resort's reputation as a focal point for health, Doctor George W. Archer opened a branch of the Keeley Institute at the hotel in 1893. According to an advertisement in the *Jefferson County Sentinel,* the institute used an unorthodox method to cure "liquor, opium, morphine, chloral, cocaine, cigarette and tobacco habits, and neurasthenia or nerve exhaustion." Dr. Leslie E. Keeley of Illinois had invented the controversial procedure, which involved injecting bichloride of gold into a patient's arm four times a day for three to six weeks. In 1909 Keeley claimed a 95 percent cure rate for his treatment of alcoholics. Keeley boasted that "if a new arrival needs whiskey, it is given to him in a bottle, and he can have more until his palate loathes it and he returns his unopened bottle to the doctor." One of Keeley's patients also noticed a beneficial side effect of the treatment, stating in a November 13, 1909, *Jefferson County Sentinel* article that he "found himself relieved of twenty pounds of superfluous flesh." The Keeley Institute also opened a franchise at nearby Alhambra Hot Springs.

In 1909, Butte millionaire James Murray purchased the springs and began a major renovation of the hotel. Murray added a new wing to the hotel and refurbished the interior of the old structure. The dining room featured numerous Tiffany lampshades, and the walls were decorated with hand-stenciled borders. Murray also commissioned custom-made china and silverware for the dining room. The 40-foot by 80-foot lobby was finished in dark oak and was furnished with massive mission oak chairs and couches.

"Pappy" Smith purchased the springs from James Murray in 1940, renamed the old resort the "Diamond S Ranchotel," and managed it until 1960. The resort had four more owners between 1960 and 1989, but they witnessed a steadily declining business. By 1989 most of the hotel had been closed, and the owner at the time defaulted on his mortgage payments. Rumors flew that the venerable old hotel was to be torn down and the land subdivided for private homes.

Fortunately, a well-known psychologist with local connections heard of the plight of the aging resort. Anne Wilson-Schaef, who grew up a few miles from Boulder, had developed a national reputation as an author and lecturer on addictions and recovery. When the hotel and hot springs were offered for sale in 1990, Wilson-Schaef, who was living in Colorado at the time, decided to purchase the resort and turn it into a teaching center. She and her business partners have since spent more than $1.2 million restoring much of the old hotel to its former glory, and there are plans to continue the renovation.

Barb Reiter currently manages Boulder Hot Springs.

15

Alhambra Hot Springs

General description: A medical and recreational resort that flourished from the gold mining days of the 1860s until the late 1950s. The hot water is now used to heat a retirement home.

Location: Southwest Montana, about 12 miles south of Helena.

Primitive/developed: Developed.

Best time of year: The source of the springs can be viewed year-round.

Restrictions: The privately owned hot springs are now used for space heating, and no public bathing is allowed. Visitors can see the source of the springs from a public road.

Access: Any vehicle can drive on the gravel road near the springs.

Water temperature: 138 degrees F at the springs.

Nearby attractions: Elkhorn ghost town, Boulder Hot Springs, Montana Historical Society (Helena).

Services: There are no services at Alhambra. Gas and food are available in Clancy, about 2 miles north, or in Helena, 12 miles north.

Camping: A private campground with spaces for tents and RVs is located about 0.5 mile north of Alhambra on the frontage road. Warm Springs Creek public campground is a few miles east of Alhambra.

Maps: Montana State Highways map, USGS Clancy MT.

Finding the springs: From Helena, drive south on Interstate 15 for 10 miles to the Clancy exit (Exit 182). Turn onto the frontage road on the east side of the

Alhambra Hot Springs

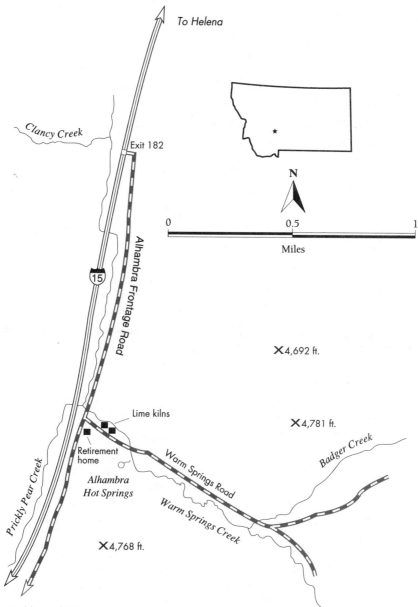

interstate, and head south for about 1 mile to the Evergreen Clancy Health and Rehabilitation Center. Turn east on the gravel road that heads up Warm Springs Canyon (on the north side of the rehabilitation center), and drive for approximately 0.25 mile. You'll see one of the hot springs seeps 100 yards south of the road next to Warm Springs Creek. Another seep is located on the hillside to the south of the creek and is covered by a small gazebo.

The hot springs: Alhambra Hot Springs consists of four main springs and a number of hot water seeps located along Warm Springs Creek. The water temperature averages 138 degrees F. The slightly radioactive hot water flows 0.25 mile downhill to the rehabilitation center, where the water is piped through the concrete floor for heating. In spite of its long history of therapeutic uses, Alhambra Hot Springs is not currently used for bathing.

History: Sylvenius Dustin homesteaded the property around Alhambra in the early 1860s. In 1866 Dustin sold the property and springs to Wilson Redding for $3,000 in gold dust. Redding had been a Confederate soldier during the Civil War, and after hostilities ended he left his native Missouri for the gold fields of Helena. Redding gave the name "Alhambra" to the mountain skyline around the hot springs, because of the similarity of its silhouette to the famous Alhambra Palace built by the Moors in Spain.

Redding built the first log hotel at the springs in 1866. In the early 1890s a larger hotel and several cottages were built at the site. Laborers enduring the harsh working conditions of the mines sought relief in the soothing hot waters at Alhambra. In 1891, *Northwest Magazine* made the startling claim that "workers in the mines and smelters of Montana have found the waters in some of the springs to contain the proper antidote against lead, arsenic and zinc poisoning, and even the worst stages of rheumatism and gout have been successfully treated where other remedies have repeatedly failed."

The new hotel at Alhambra also became a social gathering spot for the upper class from nearby Helena. "The hotel lawn is graced with queenly presence," stated the 1892 *Helena Weekly Herald*, "and melodious laughter accompanies the click of croquet, while the lords of creation loll and read or keep busy with their fishing tackle."

M. J. Sullivan purchased the resort from Redding's daughter in 1904. Sullivan proceeded to expand the hotel and medical facilities at Alhambra and aggressively marketed the health-giving properties of the mineral water. By the early 1920s, eight trains per day stopped at the resort. Alhambra Mineral Water was shipped via rail in large tank cars to Great Falls, where it was bottled and sold. Several mineral water fountains were available on the hotel grounds for guests to drink from, usually under instructions from the resident physician.

A picnic at Alhambra Hot Springs Hotel, circa 1910.
PHOTO COURTESY OF MONTANA HISTORICAL SOCIETY.

An "eminent chemist" hired by Sullivan to analyze the waters reported that "the drinking of this water is indicated and most beneficial in all kinds of stomach troubles, especially when such are due to the hyperacidity of the stomach. Its vigorous stimulation upon the skin makes the water especially fit for use in all skin and blood disease. At least one or two quarts should be drunk during the day and one or two baths a day used." The 1927 *Mineral Waters of the United States* noted that Alhambra mineral water was useful for treating "chronic rheumatism, rheumatic arthritis, sciatica and neuritis, renal and vesicle calculi, hepatic congestion, all gastric disturbances due to acidity, and general autointoxication."

Sullivan maintained a large public plunge in a main bathhouse, with separate vapor, mud, and plunge baths in the hotel. Beef, chicken, pork, and eggs produced on a nearby farm owned by Sullivan were served in the dining room. In local advertising, the hotel boasted of its incomparable chicken dinners.

The Alhambra Hotel was destroyed by a spectacular fire on the evening of April 24, 1959. The fire struck so quickly that the following day's *Great Falls Tribune* reported the only items saved were "a piano and a little beer."

In 1961, a one-story rehabilitation center was built on the site of the old hotel, and the hot water is currently used for heating this building.

Undated poem from an Alhambra Hot Springs brochure, published around 1910:

ALHAMBRA

If you're feeling rather tired and your nerves are all unstrung,
And you're thinking that a rest would do you good;
If you're crippled up with rheumatism, lumbago or the gout,
I would send you to Alhambra if I could.

Bubbling out upon the surface of the hillside just beyond
Are the "Hot Springs" that you ought to know about.
At some time they were placed there by the hands of Him who knows
All our sufferings and He wants to help us out.

Then one day Man was guided to this now called "Garden Spot"
And he builded there a home for such as need
Rest or recreation, health or "happiness complete"
Or for those who from their suffering would be freed.

The water has been tested and its healing powers are true,
The "Hot Baths" there will drive all pain away,
When you're sick and suffering and there's little chance to rest
Get ready for Alhambra—Don't delay.

With accommodations of the best and help efficient too,
With scenery there that is surpassed by none;
With lovely grounds and shaded walks and a charming little lake,
What could be more delightful than a trip like that to take?

All praises to Alhambra, the haven of sweet rest,
Where the plan of God was worked out by Man's skill.
Where saddened hearts may enter and from illness be relieved,
To scatter joy and gladness where they will.

16

Broadwater Athletic Club & Hot Springs

General description: A full-service athletic club with two warm water pools and both co-ed and single-sex Jacuzzis. In the 1890s, the thermal springs supplied Montana's largest and most elegant hot springs resort.
Location: Southwest Montana, on the west edge of the city of Helena.
Primitive/developed: Developed.
Best time of year: Open year-round.
Restrictions: The athletic club is privately owned. An admission fee is charged to use the health club facilities and pools.
Access: Any vehicle can make the trip.
Water temperature: The five springs on the property vary from 140 degrees F to 154 degrees F. The outdoor recreation pool is kept at 96 degrees F in the winter and 90 degrees F in the summer. The outdoor lap pool is maintained at 89 degrees F in winter and 85 degrees F in summer.
Nearby attractions: Montana State Capitol, Montana Historical Society, Helena National Forest, Great Divide Ski Area.
Services: Gas, food, and lodging are available in the city of Helena.
Camping: The Cromwell Dixon Forest Service Campground is 12 miles west of the hot springs on U.S. Highway 12.
Map: Montana State Highways map.

Finding the springs: From Helena, take US 12 west past the turnoff to Fort Harrison. Continue west for 1.5 miles on US 12 to the Broadwater Athletic Club & Hot Springs.

The hot springs: The two outdoor pools are heated with hot water from a well drilled near the natural hot springs just east of the athletic club. The larger of the pools is open to everyone, but the smaller lap pool on the south side of the building is for adults only. There's a large indoor co-ed Jacuzzi with a window overlooking the lap pool. Men's and women's dressing rooms each contain a smaller Jacuzzi. A large waterslide with its own small pool is located on the north side of the building. The club features weight rooms, racquetball and handball courts, and an indoor running track. There is also access to outdoor running trails.

History: The discovery of gold in Last Chance Gulch in 1864 brought a wave of prospectors to the Helena Valley. One of these gold seekers was Ferdinand Wassweiler, a German immigrant, who arrived in Helena in 1865. Wassweiler

Broadwater Athletic Club & Hot Springs

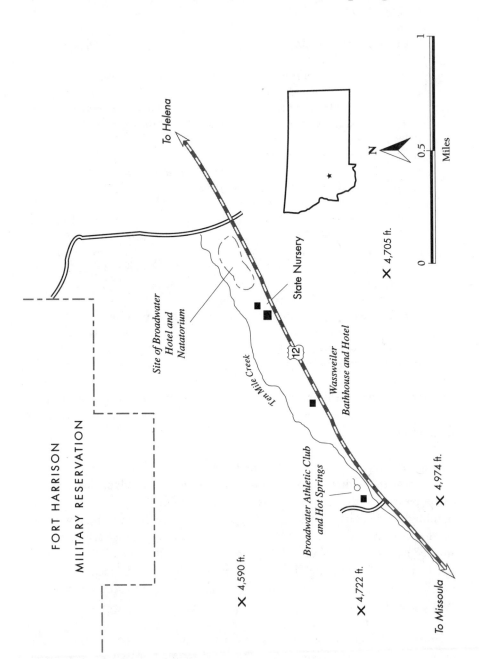

To Helena

Site of Broadwater
Hotel and
Natatorium

State Nursery

Ten Mile Creek

12

Wassweiler
Bathhouse and Hotel

Broadwater Athletic Club
and Hot Springs

FORT HARRISON

MILITARY RESERVATION

X 4,590 ft.

X 4,722 ft.

X 4,974 ft.

X 4,705 ft.

To Missoula

N

0.5

Miles

0

0.5

1

Wassweiler's Hot Springs, circa 1880. PHOTO COURTESY OF MONTANA HISTORICAL SOCIETY.

wasted little time in the gold fields. By 1866 he had built a covered plunge at the site of the hot springs near the current Broadwater Athletic Club & Hot Springs. That September Wassweiler enticed paying customers to the hot springs by advertising in the *Montana Radiator:* "These springs are the cure-all for the present age. It matters not what your disease is—after washing in these life-giving waters, you are bound to come out with a clean skin."

By October Wassweiler had also constructed a small two-story hotel at the springs. He continued to advertise in the *Montana Radiator,* boasting that he could "satisfy the most incredulous that a great number of cases of Inflammatory Rheumatism have been cured by the use of the Hot Springs."

Wassweiler welcomed guests until 1874, when he sold the portion of his land containing the bathhouse and hotel, along with the water rights, to Charles A. Broadwater. But Wassweiler didn't stay out of the hot springs business for long. In 1883 he opened a new hotel and bathhouse on the remaining portion of his land. He closed the plunge six years later but kept the hotel open until 1904, when failing health forced him to give up his career as a hot springs proprietor. Wassweiler's old stone bathhouse and brick hotel still stand and have been converted into an antiques mall. The buildings are 0.4 mile east of the present Broadwater Athletic Club & Hot Springs on US 12.

When Wassweiler sold a portion of his water rights to Charles A. Broadwater in 1874, he could scarcely have imagined that 15 years later those waters would nourish one of the world's most extravagant thermal resorts. Broadwater was a successful entrepreneur who in 1861 began a profitable freighting business in the boomtown of Bannack. Sensing even greater opportunity, he moved to Helena in 1864, shortly after the discovery of gold in Last Chance Gulch. Broadwater established himself as one of Helena's leading visionaries and tirelessly promoted the bright future he envisioned for the town.

By 1888 Helena was home to 14,000 people, and Broadwater was certain that it was destined to become a major population center. Never one to dream small dreams, he invested $500,000 to build one of the largest hotels and hot springs plunges constructed in the frontier West. Opening in the summer of 1889 on 40 acres of manicured grounds, the Broadwater Hotel and Natatorium fulfilled Charles Broadwater's ideals of elegance and refinement.

The *New Northwest* described the giant natatorium in its June 1890 issue as "a lofty and picturesque structure of Moorish architecture, covering with its huge vaulted roof a bathing pool 300 feet long and 100 feet wide, at one end of which is a twin waterfall, pouring over great granite rocks, one cascade being of natural hot mineral water and the other of pure cold water. The two falls mingle their waters to produce a temperature in the enormous bath of agreeable warmth." Half of the 12,000 square feet of windows in the natatorium were made of stained glass. A hundred dressing rooms lined the sides of the giant pool.

The huge plunge was an immediate success with residents of Helena. The *Helena Weekly Herald* described a weekend in June 1890: "5,000 is a moderate estimate of the number of people who visited the famous resort. The great plunge was crowded with bathers, and at all times presented the appearance of a pool covered with heavy raindrops, so thickly was it studded with heads."

Many tests of skill were held in the natatorium, including a greased pole walking contest in which eight men tried to walk on a slippery log laid across the plunge and grab a pig tethered at the opposite end. The winner received five dollars (and presumably the pig). Other contests included a walking race in the shallow end of the pool, a tub race, and an exhibition of trick dives from a pedestal rising high into the natatorium dome.

The new Broadwater Hotel, located a few hundred feet west, was equal to the elegance and size of the natatorium. The building measured 200 feet by 400 feet and had a large verandah stretching around the front. Persian rugs covered the floors and French wallpaper lined the walls. After meals of up to ten courses served in the elegant dining room, guests could repose in parlors filled with Victorian furniture.

The Broadwater Hotel featured a variety of therapeutic treatments using the natural hot water. Forty private bathrooms had silver-trimmed marble tubs

The elegant Broadwater Natatorium, circa 1890. PHOTO COURTESY OF MONTANA HISTORICAL SOCIETY.

imported from Paris. The "needle bath" gave stimulating shocks to the skin of guests entering a circle of pipes spraying pinpoint streams of hot and cold water.

Unfortunately, the lavish hotel and plunge faced financial problems from the start. Helena's small population was insufficient to support such a grand resort, and the anticipated influx of out-of-state tourists never materialized. Charles Broadwater died three years after the grand opening, and without his visionary direction the resort foundered. Three years after his death, Broadwater's hotel closed its doors, partially reopening briefly in the 1930s until Prohibition and the threat of the coming world war permanently shut it down. The natatorium operated until 1935, when a severe earthquake irreparably damaged the building. The giant plunge, called by the May 26, 1892, *Helena Weekly Herald* "the finest specimen of Moorish architecture on the American continent," was demolished in 1946.

The Broadwater Hotel and Natatorium was located 1.2 miles east of the current athletic club (0.2 mile east of the State Nursery) on the north side of US 12. Remnants of beautiful landscaping with towering windbreaks and parklike clearings are all that remain of what was once described as "the grandest resort of s'em all."

17

Spa Hot Springs Motel

General description: A geothermally heated motel with an attached warm water outdoor pool and a hot indoor soaking pool. The high sulfur content of the thermal waters leaves bathers with a silky feeling on their skin. The owner is a licensed chiropractor and acupuncturist whose medical clinic is located adjacent to the pools.

Location: Southwest Montana, within the city limits of White Sulphur Springs.

Primitive/developed: Developed.

Best time of year: Open year-round.

Restrictions: An admission fee is charged to use the pools. Overnight guests at the motel swim for free.

Access: Any vehicle can make the trip.

Water temperature: The hot water well supplying the pools is 130 degrees F. The outdoor pool averages 98 degrees F in the winter and 96 degrees F in the summer. The indoor pool is kept around 105 degrees F year-round.

Nearby attractions: Smith River, the ghost town of Castle, Lewis and Clark National Forest, Showdown Ski Area, Kings Hill Scenic Byway, Silver Crest Nordic Ski Area.

Services: The Spa Motel has 21 guest rooms. Perhaps a reflection of the owner's interest in chiropractic, each room is furnished with top-of-the-line mattresses and pillows to ensure a great night's sleep after an evening soak. There are several restaurants in the surrounding town of White Sulphur Springs.

Camping: Grasshopper Creek Campground, Richardson Creek Campground, and Lake Sutherlin Campground are located west of White Sulphur Springs on U.S. Highway 12. Newlan Creek Campground is located on Newlan Creek Reservoir north of White Sulphur Springs on U.S. Highway 89.

Map: Montana State Highways map.

Finding the springs: The Spa Motel is located in the town of White Sulphur Springs on Main Street, across from the First National Bank.

The hot springs: Thermal water for the pools and motel is provided by a 130-degree-F geothermal well drilled near the site of the original springs. The outdoor pool is kept at 98 degrees F in the winter and 96 degrees F in the summer. A 105-degree-F indoor soaking pool is located a few feet west of the main pool.

Spa Hot Springs Motel

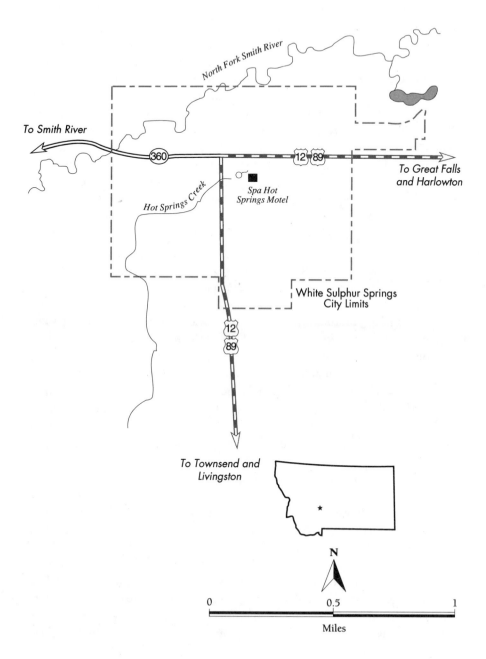

North Fork Smith River

To Smith River

360

12 89

To Great Falls
and Harlowton

Spa Hot
Springs Motel

Hot Springs Creek

White Sulphur Springs
City Limits

12
89

To Townsend and
Livingston

N

0   0.5   1

Miles

Hot water pipes in the deck surrounding the outdoor pool keep ice from forming in the winter, "even when the temperature is 40 below zero," according to Dr. Gene Gudmundson, owner of the motel.

Gudmundson wears several hats besides proprietor of the hot springs and motel. In addition to his training in chiropractic and acupuncture, Gudmundson is a yoga teacher and a specialist in Chinese medicine and holds a black belt in Hapkido. He is a true believer in the healing effects of his hot springs and is convinced that the high sulfur content is responsible for much of its benefit.

Gudmundson's passion for natural hot springs extends beyond his own resort. In 1994 Dr. Gudmundson spearheaded the creation of the Montana Mineral Hot Springs Association, uniting hot springs resort owners to look at issues of common interest. The impetus for forming the association was an attempt by state officials to force hot springs resort owners to chlorinate their natural hot water pools in the same manner required of municipal swimming pools. Many bathers come to hot springs specifically because of the mineral content in the water. Artificial chlorination would have destroyed the mineral balance they sought, doing away with one of the key attractions—and pleasures—of natural hot springs.

Gudmundson and others introduced a bill in the Montana legislature to distinguish hot mineral pools from municipal swimming pools, and in 1995 the bill became state law. All natural hot springs resorts in Montana may now operate without chlorinating their water, provided all of the hot water is exchanged at least once every 8 hours and the pools are drained and cleaned every 72 hours. Water temperature and pH must also be monitored.

Dr. Gudmundson and other resort owners in Montana are satisfied with the new law, which Gudmundson described as "the best hot springs law in the country." A sign near the Spa Motel's outdoor pool expresses Gudmundson's belief in natural hot water: "This pool is proudly drained and cleaned every single night, then refilled with the finest natural hot mineral spring water to be found anywhere in the world. We are not presumptuous enough to add chemicals of any kind to what is already the best water that nature has to offer."

History: James Brewer built a 12-foot by 12-foot plunge at the springs in 1872. This early plunge at what was then known as Brewer's Springs was popular with gold miners from the surrounding hills. This fact was noted in the January 24, 1878, edition of *Rocky Mountain Husbandman:* "In the early days of the opening of the gulch mines of the country, many a decrepit miner has passed over to these springs, tired, sore, and stiffened, aching with rheumatic pains, brought on from the effects of laboring in the wet mines, and after a short season of bathing, returned again to his labor feeling as well, nimble and fresh as if ten years younger."

The outdoor pool at the Spa Hot Springs Motel.

Brewer sold the bathhouse and springs to Dr. William Parberry in 1877, who renamed the area "White Sulphur Springs" after the snowy white mineral deposited by the thermal waters on the surrounding rocks and gravel. Parberry renovated the little resort, adding an office building, dressing room, and two hot pools.

Despite its new buildings, the White Sulphur Springs resort was still on the edge of the frontier. In the late 1870s few other neighbors lived in the Shields River Valley, and attacks by Native Americans were still a concern to the new settlers. A reporter for the *Rocky Mountain Husbandman* visited the springs in September 1877 and described the preparations that Parberry had made to ensure the safety of bathers: "Persons who have contemplated visiting the springs need not be deterred from doing so on account of the Indian troubles, as Dr. Parberry has provided a dozen stands of arms and plenty of ammunition, and there are always a number of guests to 'hold the fort' against the hostiles."

In 1882 Parberry and some business partners formed a corporation to build a new town in the area surrounding the resort. The group acquired not only the hot springs and 17 surrounding acres but also 1,000 city lots to resell to arriving settlers.

The hot springs remained popular with locals, although it never became a major resort. For a time the hot water was bottled and shipped throughout the region, where its healthful properties were praised. The *Helena Independent* reported on October 20, 1906, about one particular benefit of the bottled mineral water: "Along the line of the Montana Railroad and in Lewistown the water is in great demand as an anti-intoxicant. When the Fergus County sheepherders go on a tear and want to kill the after effects, they drink the White Sulphur water and it acts as an immediate bracer."

The Spa Motel was built in the 1950s but has undergone extensive renovation in the past few years.

> Oh! Fountain of perpetual youth,
> We hail with joy the evincing truth:
> That in thy magic water is rife;
> A balm for all the ills of life;
> And nowhere in this world is found,
> Save on this very hallowed ground—
> Of pharmacist's or Nature's compound—
> A remedy, in which there doth abound
> A healing power that can compare
> With thy boiling fluid, pure and fair.
>
> In thee, is beauty for the faded cheek.
> An appetizer for the faint and weak;
> The lame to leap and the blind to see,
> The old rheumatic from pain set free;
> Dyspeptic's life in thee is saved,
> Old age snatched from verge of the grave;
> Eternal youth and beauty divine,
> To the sons and daughters of every clime,
> Who, in thy crystal pools do dip,
> Or from this sparkling fountain sip.
>
> —*Rocky Mountain Husbandman*
> January 7, 1886

18

Renova Hot Springs

General description: Two hot water seeps located on the banks of a side channel of the Jefferson River. Volunteers have constructed rock-lined pools that allow cooler river water to mingle with the thermal water, providing a variety of soaking temperatures.

Location: Southwest Montana, about 15 miles south of Whitehall.

Primitive/developed: Primitive, although the downstream pools have had concrete applied to strengthen the natural rock walls.

Best time of year: High water levels on the Jefferson River (usually in the late spring and late fall) can flood the pools, so midsummer and early fall are probably best for soaking.

Restrictions: None. The springs are located on public land.

Access: The road is accessible year-round to most passenger vehicles, although winter snows may limit access at times. The road gradually worsens as you approach the springs, so low-clearance passenger vehicles may not do well on the trip.

Water temperature: The seeps vary from 110 to 122 degrees F. Temperature in the constructed pools varies drastically, depending on the amount of river water mixing with warm water. Some pools may be ice-cold during high water flows, but others may be too hot for soaking if the river level is insufficient for mixing.

Nearby attractions: Tobacco Root Mountains, Lewis and Clark Caverns State Park, Missouri Headwaters State Park.

Services: None; gas, food, and lodging can be found 10 miles away in Whitehall.

Camping: The nearest public campground is at Lewis and Clark Caverns State Park, about 10 miles east of Whitehall on Montana Highway 10. A private campground and RV park, Pipestone Campground, is located about 6 miles west of Whitehall at Exit 241 on Interstate 90. Camping may also be possible on public land near the fishing access located about 200 yards south of the springs.

Map: USGS Vendome MT.

Finding the springs: From Whitehall, take Montana Highway 55 south for 10 miles to the Waterloo turnoff. Drive southeast on this road for about 0.5 mile, crossing a bridge over the Jefferson River. About 0.1 mile past the bridge, turn east on a gravel road marked with a sign pointing to Perry Canyon Ranch. Continue east on this road for about 2.2 miles until you reach an intersection with Point of Rocks Road (which runs north-south). Turn north on this gravel

Renova Hot Springs

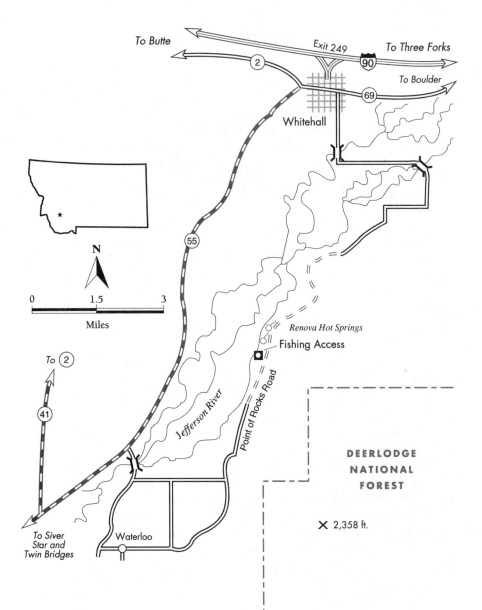

To Butte

Exit 249

To Three Forks

2

90

To Boulder

69

Whitehall

55

N

0   1.5   3

Miles

To 2

41

Renova Hot Springs

Fishing Access

Jefferson River

Point of Rocks Road

DEERLODGE
NATIONAL
FOREST

X 2,358 ft.

To Siver
Star and
Twin Bridges

Waterloo

Renova Hot Springs on the banks of the Jefferson River.

and dirt road for 3.6 miles to the springs. About 200 yards before the springs you will see a turnoff for a fishing/boating access. The road past this access hugs a side channel of the Jefferson River. The springs themselves are located on the west side of the road about 10 feet below the road bank at the edge of the river channel (sniff the air for the smell of sulfur from the springs). There is a turnout on the roadside above the springs big enough to park one or two cars, or you can backtrack and park at the fishing access and walk 200 yards north to the springs.

The hot springs: Renova Hot Springs consists of two areas of hot water seeps 15 yards apart on a side channel of the Jefferson River. Volunteers have built rock pools around the seeps in the river channel, and river water flows through and over the rock walls of the pool to mix with the 110- to 122-degree-F thermal water. The two hot water pools farthest downstream are the nicest for soaking; one will comfortably hold three to four people, while the second pool is perfect for solo soakers. A third pool 15 yards upstream is often washed out by the river but can comfortably hold two or three if the river level isn't too high.

You take your chances with Renova Hot Springs, because the river level determines whether the springs are submerged, are mixed just right for a nice soak, or are too hot to enjoy. Heavy irrigation draws from late July until mid-September have the most dramatic impact on water levels in the Jefferson, but often this is when Renova Hot Springs is best for soaking. The surrounding scenery of the Jefferson River and the Tobacco Root Mountains make this hot springs definitely worth a visit, even if you hit a season when the soaking is less than perfect. This is a great spot to visit after a day of fly-fishing or floating on the Jefferson River, and you'll often have the hot springs to yourself.

19

Pipestone Hot Springs

General description: An abandoned hot springs with decaying resort buildings easily seen from a public road.
Location: Southwest Montana, about 17 miles east of Butte just off Interstate 90.
Primitive/developed: Developed, but in ruins.
Best time of year: Open year-round.
Restrictions: Pipestone Hot Springs is privately owned. You can observe the old ruins and the steaming hot water runoff channel from the public road that bisects the property, but please don't trespass.
Access: Any vehicle can make the short drive from I-90 along the asphalt road that leads to the old resort.
Water temperature: 135 degrees F at the source.
Nearby attractions: Homestake Pass and Delmoe Lake on the Continental Divide, World Museum of Mining in Butte.
Services: No services are available at Pipestone Hot Springs. Pipestone Campground, about 1 mile west of the springs, has snacks and drinks available from April to October. Gasoline, food, and lodging are available in Whitehall, about 6 miles east on I-90, or in Butte, about 17 miles west on I-90.
Camping: Pipestone Campground, a private facility with 20 tent spaces and 55 RV hookups, is located about 1 mile west of Pipestone Hot Springs on the frontage road paralleling I-90 (just west of Exit 241). The campground is open from April 1 to October 15. Delmoe Lake Campground, operated by the Forest Service, is open from late May until early September. Drive 10 miles west of Pipestone on I-90 to Homestake Pass, then 10 miles north on Forest Service Road 222 to Delmoe Lake.
Maps: Montana State Highways map, USGS Dry Mountain MT.

Finding the springs: Take Exit 241 off I-90 and turn east on the Pipestone frontage road that parallels I-90. Go about 0.8 mile east to an intersection with a gravel road to the south. Take this southern road about 50 yards and pull off

Pipestone Hot Springs

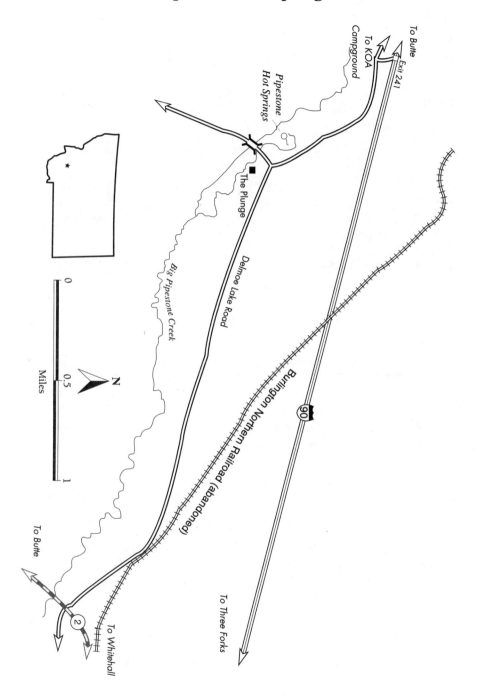

Ruins of the old resort at Pipestone Hot Springs.

to the side of the road. The ruins of the old resort and pool are visible on both sides of the road.

The hot springs: A large quonset hut about 200 yards east of the road contains the swimming pool, which for a time was an open-air facility. A steady stream of hot water can be seen flowing from the pool building area, past the old guesthouse, under a footbridge, and then under the gravel road where you are standing. To the west of the road stand an old wooden dancing pavilion and a smaller drinking pavilion located over one of the springs. About a hundred yards southeast of the hotel, along the banks of Pipestone Creek, you might catch a glimpse of the 19 remaining guest cabins hidden downstream among tall cottonwoods.

History: Legal title to the land around Pipestone Hot Springs was first acquired in 1868 by prospectors who admired the hot water resource and its sheltered location, as well as its proximity to gold mining, which was taking place in the area in the 1860s and 1870s. The land was sold in 1870 to John Paul, who built public accommodations at the springs in 1878. In 1912, John Alley, an attorney for Butte's powerful Anaconda Company, purchased the resort. The Alley family still owns Pipestone Hot Springs.

Stories of wonderful cures to be had by bathing at Pipestone Hot Springs were told in the local press. According to the 1887–1888 *Butte Holiday Intermountain*, invalids "suffering from rheumatism, neuralgia, dyspepsia, paralysis, kidney and liver complaints, impure blood, lead poisoning, etc. experienced speedy and permanent relief after a course of bathing and drinking." Another article reported that Pipestone Hot Springs "makes ancient kidneys new."

At its peak in the early 1900s the resort attracted spa visitors from throughout the region. The resort owners especially enticed nearby Butte citizens, urging them to leave the air pollution caused by the copper smelters in Butte and "get out of the smoke for a day or two."

Stagecoaches traveled to the springs from Butte three times a week. Once rail lines were available, trains brought vacationers to the hot springs four or five times a day during the peak summer season. About 100 canvas-roofed guest cabins dotted the resort grounds. Vapor bathhouses, hot mud bathing facilities, and a 25-foot by 100-foot swimming pool were available for the pleasure of the resort guests, some of whom stayed for the entire summer.

While Pipestone Hot Springs was well known for hot soaks, its hotels were known for their tendency to burn to the ground. One large hotel burned in 1913, when a lit candle was left in a woman's dressing room. News articles reported that five wooden buildings including the hotel burned to the ground in 15 minutes, with only the water tank surviving. A new hotel was built a short time later, but this hotel was destroyed by fire in 1918, with only a player piano and some furniture being saved. Finally, a smaller building, with only nine guest rooms, lobby, and dining room, was built near the pool, where it remains today.

Like many hot springs resorts in Montana, the popularity of vacationing and "taking the waters" at Pipestone declined with the passing decades. The Alley family closed the resort to the public in 1963.

20

The Lodge at Potosi Hot Springs

General description: A secluded private guest ranch with a natural warm water pool and soaking tub. This exclusive mountain resort with its gourmet meals and variety of outdoor activities is especially popular with out-of-state guests.

Location: Southwest Montana, 53 miles west of Bozeman in the Tobacco Root Mountains.

Primitive/developed: Developed.

Best time of year: Open year-round.

Restrictions: The resort facilities and soaking pools are for the exclusive use of lodge guests. No public bathing is allowed. Advance reservations for lodging and meals are required.

Access: Any vehicle can make the trip in the summertime. The mountain road between Pony and the lodge is plowed in the winter, but high-clearance vehicles or four-wheel-drive vehicles are still a good idea during the snowy months.

Water temperature: 93 degrees F at the springs; 85 degrees F in the pool and enclosed soaking tub.

Nearby attractions: Upper Potosi Hot Springs, Tobacco Root Mountains, Madison River, Norris Hot Springs.

Services: Food and lodging are available at the resort.

Camping: Tepee camping is available for lodge guests desiring more rustic accommodations.

Maps: Montana State Highways map, USGS Harrison MT.

Finding the springs: From Three Forks, drive 19 miles south on U.S. Highway 287 to Harrison. Turn southwest onto Pony Road and drive 6 miles to Pony. Just before you enter Pony, turn left (southeast) onto South Willow Creek Road (look for the Forest Service sign pointing to Potosi Creek Campground). Follow this road for 7 miles to The Lodge at Potosi Hot Springs.

The hot springs: The 25-foot by 50-foot swimming pool is located in a narrow canyon behind the main lodge on the same site as the original 1892 pool. Concrete walls enclose three sides of the pool, with the fourth consisting of a granite cliff from which the hot springs flow. Farther up the canyon is a fully enclosed hot water soaking tub, with windows facing the creek. The pool and soaking tub are rarely crowded, because only registered guests of the resort have access.

The main lodge, a 3,600-square-foot log building set near the canyon road, contains a large Western-style dining room where lodge guests gather for

Potosi Hot Springs

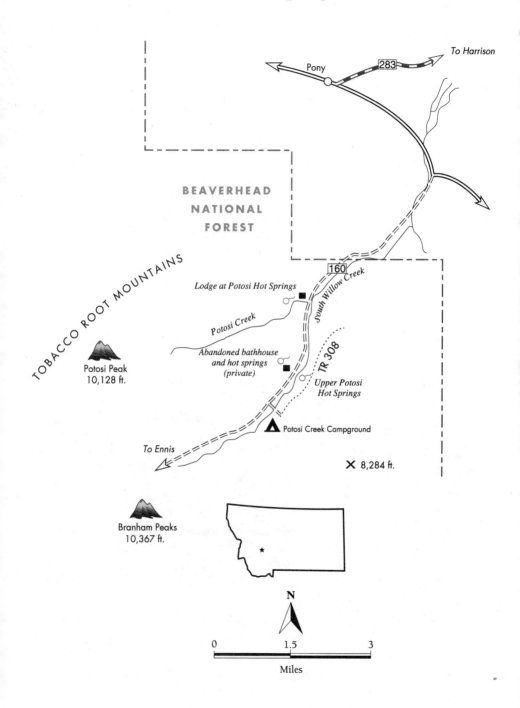

To Harrison

Pony

283

BEAVERHEAD
NATIONAL
FOREST

160

South Willow Creek

Lodge at Potosi Hot Springs

Potosi Creek

Abandoned bathhouse
and hot springs
(private)

TR 308

Upper Potosi
Hot Springs

TOBACCO ROOT MOUNTAINS

Potosi Peak
10,128 ft.

Potosi Creek Campground

To Ennis

✕ 8,284 ft.

Branham Peaks
10,367 ft.

N

0   1.5   3

Miles

gourmet meals. Family-style three-course dinners are served during the week, and five-course meals are featured on the weekends. Co-owner Patti Trapp wears the chef's hat and puts her Parisian and Seattle culinary training to good use. The dinners at Potosi Lodge are considered "as good as any you'll find in the Rockies," according to a review in *Condé Nast Traveler*.

Four luxurious guest cabins are located a few hundred yards from the main lodge. Hidden in the trees on the banks of South Willow Creek, the cabins come with fully equipped kitchens, comfortable rustic furniture, and a fireplace lined with river rock. Each cabin comfortably sleeps up to six guests.

The secluded outdoor activities and relaxing surroundings lure harried executives from big cities to the resort. A substantial number of lodge guests come from out of state, filling the guest book with addresses ranging from Manhattan and Los Angeles to Seattle. Summertime guests can enjoy hiking, mountain biking, and horseback riding, as well as fly-fishing in the creek a few steps from their cabin doors. Winter activities include snowshoeing, dog sledding, and cross-country skiing (the lodge grooms several miles of ski trails).

History: Horace Walter, a carpenter from Indiana, took claim to Potosi Hot Springs in 1892. Walter built a swimming pool, bathhouse, geothermally heated greenhouse, and large hotel near the springs. Walter sold the property in 1902 to William Young from Butte. The hotel continued to operate until 1909, when

The Lodge at Potosi Hot Springs.

the resort was abandoned. Ten years later the buildings had fallen into ruin, leading the *Anaconda Standard* to report in 1919 that the old resort had turned into a "deserted village." The owners of the property never rebuilt the log hotel, but for many years they did allow vacationers to camp near the hot springs, and it became a popular summer getaway.

Ownership of the springs passed through several hands until the 1960s, when it became a popular destination for the counterculture movement. Squatters took up residence in shacks built near the hot water, discouraging local Montanans from using the springs. By 1971, rumors of drug use and naked frolicking in the woods filtered down to the ranching communities in the Madison Valley and a court order was issued to the sheriff to clean up the springs. The sheriff and a posse of several locals drove to the old resort and announced that the squatters had two hours to vacate the premises. After everyone had gathered their belongings, the sheriff burned all of the shacks and dynamited one of the concrete walls of the swimming pool.

Potosi Hot Springs remained fairly quiet for the next two decades. In 1979, Pete Gross purchased the property and built a large, geothermally heated lodge on the site of the old hotel. Gross sold the property to Dale and Patti Trapp in 1991. The Trapps remodeled the lodge, added new cabins, and converted the property into a private guest ranch.

21

Upper Potosi Hot Springs

(See map on page 91)

General description: Two primitive high-country hot springs pools with outstanding views of the surrounding Tobacco Root Mountains. This is one of the few hot springs in Montana on public land.
Location: Southwest Montana, 55 miles east of Bozeman.
Primitive/developed: Primitive.
Best time of year: Summer and early fall.
Restrictions: None. Swimsuits are optional.
Access: Any vehicle can make the trip in the summertime. The last 2 miles of the road to the Potosi Creek Campground are unplowed in the winter, making the road impassable until late spring. It is possible to cross-country ski or snowshoe to the campground and hot springs from The Lodge at Potosi Hot Springs, because the road is plowed to this guest ranch in the winter.

Water temperature: The upper pool is 104 to 110 degrees F. The lower pool is a few degrees cooler.

Nearby attractions: The Lodge at Potosi Hot Springs, Tobacco Root Mountains, Madison River, Norris Hot Springs.

Services: No services are available. Gas, food, and lodging are available in Harrison and Three Forks.

Camping: Tent and RV camping is available at the Potosi Creek Forest Service Campground at the trailhead to Upper Potosi Hot Springs.

Maps: Montana State Highways map, USGS Harrison MT.

Finding the springs: From Three Forks, drive 19 miles south on U.S. Highway 287 to Harrison. Turn southwest onto Pony Road and drive 6 miles to Pony. Just before you enter Pony, turn left (southeast) onto South Willow Creek Road (watch for the Potosi Creek Campground Forest Service sign). Follow this road for 8 miles to the Potosi Creek Campground. Park your car near the creek bisecting the campground. Ford the creek and walk about 50 yards to a trailhead in the southeast corner of the campground. Take Forest Service Trail 308 east parallel to a barbed-wire fence and South Willow Creek. Follow this level trail for about 1 mile until you see the creekbed widening and an aspen grove on your left. Fifty yards past the aspens, look to your left toward the creekbed. The hot springs are located about 10 yards off the trail in a 10-foot by 20-foot lodgepole pine enclosure.

The author soaking in Upper Potosi Hot Springs.

The hot springs: The two primitive soaking pools and the great view of the surrounding mountains make Upper Potosi well worth the easy hike. Surrounding the pools is a lodgepole pine fence built to exclude the cattle that occasionally graze in the creekbed surrounds the pools. You'll need to climb over or through the fence to reach the hot water. The kidney-shaped upper soaking pool is about 6 feet by 10 feet and comfortably holds three or four bathers. The hot water enters from the uphill side of the pool and from seeps in the pool's bottom. Two to three gallons per minute of hot water flow through a plastic pipe from the upper to the lower pool. The smaller lower pool can host one or two soakers. Water temperatures in the pools vary from 104 to 110 degrees F. Swimsuits are optional.

While you're steeping in the hot springs, look across the creek to the Forest Service road. The small building on the hillside behind the road is an old bathhouse on yet another hot spring. Located on private property, this hot spring is closed to the public but is indicative of the extensive thermal activity in the area.

22

Norris Hot Springs

General description: An open-air wooden pool that has changed little since the 1880s.
Location: Southwest Montana, about 35 miles west of Bozeman.
Primitive/developed: Developed.
Best time of year: Open year-round.
Restrictions: An admission fee is charged to use the pool. Bathing suits are required.
Access: Any vehicle can make the trip.
Water temperature: 127 degrees F at the springs, 105 degrees F in the pool.
Nearby attractions: Madison River, Madison Buffalo Jump State Park, Tobacco Root Mountains.
Services: None at the springs. Gas and food are available in Norris, 0.5 mile west of the springs. Lodging is available in Ennis, 17 miles south of the springs, and in Bozeman, 35 miles east.
Camping: There are 10 tent sites and 15 RV sites available at the hot springs. Red Mountain Bureau of Land Management Campground is located 9 miles northeast of Norris. Other campgrounds are located at fishing access points along the Madison River.
Map: Montana State Highways map.

Norris Hot Springs

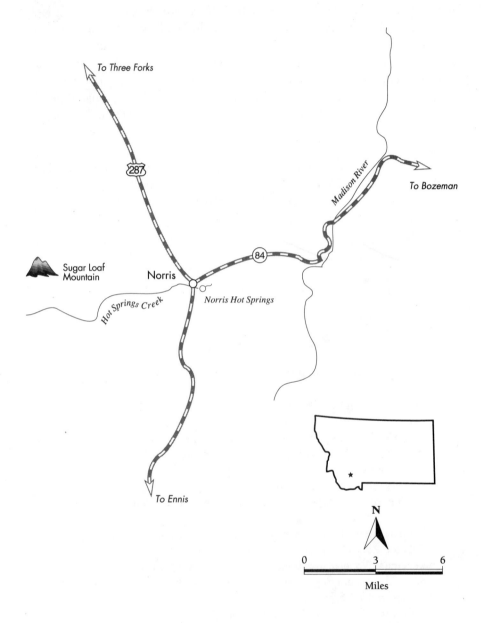

To Three Forks

287

Sugar Loaf
Mountain

Norris

Hot Springs Creek

Madison River

To Bozeman

84

Norris Hot Springs

To Ennis

N

0   3   6
Miles

Norris Hot Springs.

Finding the springs: From Bozeman, take U.S. Highway 191 west for 7 miles to the junction with Montana Highway 84. Take MT 84 west 29 miles to Norris Hot Springs. The springs are located about 0.5 mile before the junction of MT 84 with U.S. Highway 287 at the town of Norris. From Three Forks, head southwest on Montana Highway 2 to the junction with US 287, then travel south on US 287 about 18 miles to the town of Norris. Turn east on MT 84 and go about 0.5 mile to Norris Hot Springs.

The hot springs: Soaking at Norris Hot Springs is like stepping back in time. The old 30-foot by 40-foot soaking pool looks much as it must have 100 years ago. The pool is constructed completely of wood, including a wooden deck, an old wooden changing room, and a weathered wooden fence surrounding the pool.

Eight to ten separate springs with an average temperature of 127 degrees F feed the pool. The hot water is air-cooled by forcing it through a small vertical pipe at one end of the pool. Natural artesian pressure shoots the water out of the pipe in a graceful 12-foot arc above the pool, creating a constant hot water shower on the bathers below. Close to 500,000 gallons of water a day flow through the pool. There is no detectable sulfur smell in the water.

History: Alex Norris founded the town of Norris in 1865. The town prospered for a few decades from gold mining until area gold deposits were depleted. Many of the original buildings in Norris were moved to ranches in the area, and the population gradually dropped to around 50 people, where it remains today.

The hot springs were originally used to power a water wheel and to supply water for nearby mining operations. Homesteaded by Charles Hapgood, the springs soon became a popular bathing spot. In the 1930s, the springs were known as "Norris Plunge" and were managed by a local community club. The springs had several owners through the years, but the pool itself was little changed. For many years the springs were named Bear Trap Hot Springs, after nearby Bear Trap Canyon on the Madison River, but the name has recently reverted to the original Norris Hot Springs.

Doris Zankowsky currently owns the hot springs. Doris's husband Frank was passing through the area in 1972 on his way to Idaho when he stopped for a soak at Norris and decided to buy the property. Zankowsky sold the springs in 1988 to Arne Cohen on a long-term mortgage. When Cohen relinquished ownership of the springs in 1997, Doris Zankowsky returned to take over the operation.

Norris Hot Springs had a wild reputation in the late 1980s and early 1990s. The hot springs were known for swimsuit-optional "buff nights" on Sundays. A selection of more than 150 types of beer was sold to thirsty soakers. Locals turned up in droves on buff night, packing the small pool "like sardines," according to Zankowsky's son. When Doris Zankowsky regained ownership of the hot springs in 1997, the beer and the buff nights were eliminated to attract a more varied clientele.

The hot springs remain popular, especially with summer tourists, college students from Bozeman, and floaters from the nearby Madison River. The springs are also popular in the winter; Zankowsky's son recalls a New Year's Eve when the outside temperature was 23 degrees F below zero, but the Norris pool was still filled with holiday soakers.

23

Bozeman Hot Springs

General description: A comfortable older resort offering a variety of soaking opportunities in seven separate pools.

Location: Southwest Montana, 8 miles west of Bozeman, 70 miles north of West Yellowstone.

Primitive/developed: Developed.

Best time of year: Open year-round.

Restrictions: An admission fee is charged for using the pools. The pools are closed from dusk on Friday until Saturday evening.

Access: Any vehicle can make the trip.

Water temperature: 131 degrees F at the source. The five small soaking pools range from a brisk 58 degrees F to a toasty 105 to 110 degrees F. The larger indoor and outdoor pools are kept at around 90 degrees F.

Nearby attractions: Gallatin River, Gallatin Gateway Inn, Lee Metcalf Wilderness, Big Sky Ski Resort.

Services: A snack bar is available by the pools. Gas, food, and lodging are available at several places between the hot springs and Bozeman, 8 miles east.

Camping: Adjacent to the springs is a KOA campground with tent camping and RV parking. Several Forest Service campgrounds are available in Gallatin Canyon about 20 miles south of the springs.

Map: Montana State Highways map.

Finding the springs: From Bozeman, head west on U.S. Highway 191 for 7 miles. Turn south at the intersection with Montana Highway 85. The hot springs are located 0.75 mile south of the intersection. A bright blue school bus with "Bozeman Hot Springs" painted on its side marks the turnoff.

The hot springs: Bozeman Hot Springs offers a smorgasbord of soaking opportunities. The main building houses six different pools, each kept at a different temperature. The large 30-foot by 60-foot indoor swimming pool is kept near 90 degrees F. Next to the main pool are five smaller soaking pools, each about 10 feet square. These pools range in temperature from a chilly 58 degrees F to a hot pool kept at between 105 and 110 degrees F. It's easy to slip over the top of one pool into the next. Really adventurous soakers alternate between the hottest and the coldest pools.

A seventh pool is located just outside the main entrance. This open-air pool is usually kept at around 90 degrees F and has several lounge chairs around its edges for sunbathing.

Bozeman Hot Springs

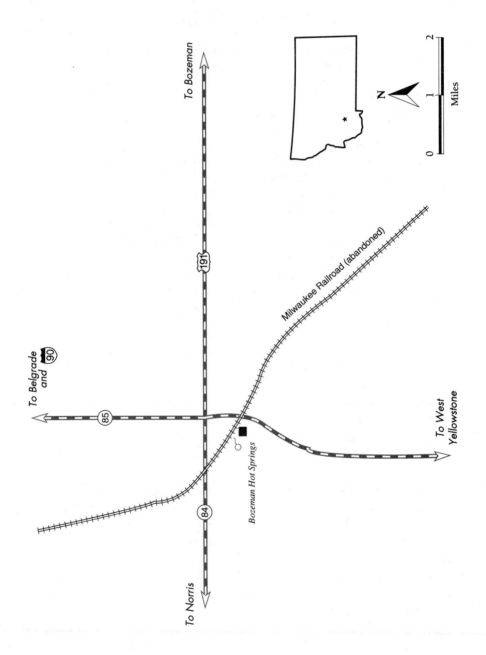

To Bozeman

191

To Belgrade
and 90

85

84

To Norris

Milwaukee Railroad (abandoned)

To West
Yellowstone

Bozeman Hot Springs

N

Miles

0   1   2

The open-air "herdic" used to transport guests to Ferris (now Bozeman) Hot Springs. Photo courtesy of Montana State University.

History: Jeremiah Mathews, a local wagon and carriage maker, purchased the springs in 1879. Mathews built a bathhouse near the springs with five private bathing rooms and a 14-foot by 18-foot plunge bath. The water at Mathews' Warm Springs was described in the April 17, 1890, edition of the *Bozeman Avant-Courier* as being "remarkably soft, pure and delightfully refreshing for both beverage and bathing purposes." The *Avant-Courier* further stated that "the water is a cure-all for all the diseases to which human flesh is heir, but for rheumatic affections, skin diseases, dyspepsia, impurity of the blood, chronic constipation, etc. it has come to be considered almost an infallible specific."

E. Myron Ferris purchased the springs from Mathews in 1890 for $25,000. Ferris changed the name to Ferris Hot Springs and immediately set about transforming the sleepy spa into a major recreation center for the Gallatin Valley. He built a two-story hotel, a large plunge, and private baths. The hotel grounds featured lawn tennis and croquet. Resort guests were transported from Bozeman to the springs in a horse-drawn "herdic," a fancy coach with open sides.

Ferris wasted little time in promoting his new resort. An 1891 advertisement in the *Avant-Courier* declared Ferris Hot Springs to be "The Great Pleasure and Health Resort of America." Ferris boasted that "a chemical analysis shows that the water resembles in its chemical composition the water of Carlsbad in Europe, although the temperature is lower." An 1891 *Avant-Courier* article stated that "the Springs and hotel come as near as filling the wants of those who

It's hard to miss the turnoff to Bozeman Hot Springs.

wish a quiet spot to rest, recuperate and get rid of rheumatism, gout, dyspepsia, kidney trouble and kindred ills as any we know of."

After World War I, Ferris decided to sell the springs and surrounding land. Finding no single buyer, Ferris divided the land into parcels, then held a widely publicized raffle at $100 per chance with the winners getting whatever parcel was drawn. The grand prize was a parcel containing the hotel, hot springs, and ten acres. Seven hundred raffle tickets were sold. A restaurant worker in Bozeman won the hot springs and hotel parcel, and many others won new homesteads.

Little new activity occurred until the early 1920s, when Sam Collett purchased the springs. Collett expanded the bathhouse and plunge and built a beautiful maple-floored ballroom next to the springs, declared to be "one of the best dance halls in the state." Dances were held in the ballroom every weekend throughout the summer season in the 1920s and 1930s. Over time the popularity of ballroom dancing declined, and the structure was more often used for roller skating than for waltzing. Today the hotel is gone, but the abandoned ballroom can still be seen in the large building attached to the pools.

24

Hunter's Hot Springs

General description: Formerly the site of the elegant Hotel Dakota, these thermal springs were one of Montana's major social and recreational centers in the early 1900s. Little remains of the old resort, although the steaming springs still flow through a windswept valley just north of the Yellowstone River.

Location: Southwest Montana, 19 miles east of Livingston.

Primitive/developed: The hot springs have been used in past years in crude bathhouses, luxurious plunges, drinking water kiosks, and in a bottled water plant, but all of those structures have long since vanished. Some of the thermal water now heats commercial greenhouses.

Best time of year: The road past the site of the old hotel is open year-round. Spring, summer, and early fall are best for observation.

Restrictions: The hot springs and hotel site are on private land. Stay on the public road that bisects the property, and don't cross the fences onto private land.

Access: Any vehicle can make the trip.

Water temperature: The hot springs temperature averages 139 degrees F according to measurements taken in the 1980s, although earlier reports record a range of temperatures from 138 to 168 degrees F.

Nearby attractions: Crazy Mountains, Absaroka-Beartooth Wilderness, Greycliff Prairie Dog Town State Park, Natural Bridge State Park, Chico Hot Springs.

Services: None are available at the hot springs. Gas, food, and lodging are available in Livingston and Big Timber.

Camping: A small camping area managed by the Montana Department of Fish, Wildlife, and Parks is located at the Springdale Bridge Fishing Access, approximately 2 miles south of Hunter's Hot Springs on the south side of the Yellowstone River.

Maps: Montana State Highways map, USGS Livingston MT.

Finding the springs: From Livingston, drive 20 miles east on Interstate 90 to Exit 354 (the Springdale exit). Take the exit west for 1 mile along Montana Highway 563 (the frontage road) to the small town of Springdale. The highway turns into Hunter Avenue, the main road bisecting Springdale. Continue north on Hunter Avenue (the paved road will turn into a gravel road), crossing the bridge over the Yellowstone River, for 1.5 miles until you reach a Y in the road. You'll see some geothermally heated greenhouses in the valley to the west. Take

Hunter's Hot Springs

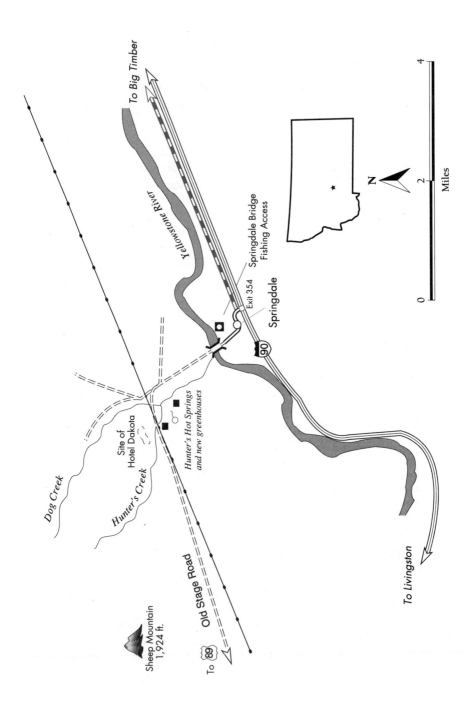

To Big Timber

Yellowstone River

Springdale Bridge
Fishing Access

Exit 354

Springdale

90

To Livingston

Dog Creek

Site of
Hotel Dakota

Hunter's Creek

Hunter's Hot Springs
and new greenhouses

Sheep Mountain
1,924 ft.

Old Stage Road

To 89

N

Miles

0   2   4

the west fork of the Y, and continue for 0.3 mile northwest (you are now on the old Yellowstone Trail Road).

Pull over to the side of the road where you see the remains of an old stone fence on the road's south side. The majestic Hotel Dakota and the hot water plunge were located in the large flat area on the north side of the road opposite the stone fence. After you've looked at what few relics can be seen from this spot in the road, continue west for 0.3 mile past a modern greenhouse on the road's south side. The road now begins to rise out of the valley. Pull off to the side of the road, get out of your car, and look back to the southeast. The open valley in front of you contains the several hot springs that fed the Hotel Dakota and the bathing plunges. Most of the springs are now capped, but you may see some steam escaping from a few of the springs.

The hot springs: Hunter's Hot Springs produces one of the largest flows of hot water in Montana. More than 1,300 gallons per minute of 139-degree-F water flows from three principal springs and up to a dozen smaller springs. The springs are scattered over several hundred yards in the rolling foothills south of the site of the old hotel.

History: Hunter's Hot Springs was first claimed by Dr. A. J. Hunter, a Kentucky physician who had served as a surgeon for the Confederate army during the Civil War. Enthralled by the stories of fortunes to be made in the gold fields of the Montana Territory, Dr. Hunter packed up his family and headed west. As they neared the end of their journey in the spring of 1864, the party camped near the Yellowstone River 45 miles east of the new town of Bozeman. Dr. Hunter left his family near the river and set off for the nearby foothills to hunt for the evening's dinner. Coming over a small rise, Dr. Hunter discovered an encampment of Crow Indians near a hot springs. The Crows were friendly to Hunter, and he observed several sick and elderly tribal members bathing in the hot water. Having visited the famous spas in Hot Springs, Arkansas, Dr. Hunter recognized the potential business opportunity in these unnamed springs. Dr. Hunter staked a claim around the springs (which he named after himself) and then proceeded on with his family to Bozeman.

For the next four years Dr. Hunter tried to make his fortune mining for gold in Virginia City and Helena, but he had little success. In 1869 he returned to Bozeman to practice medicine and to plan for the development of his hot springs claim. A year later Dr. Hunter realized his dream of developing the hot springs. He built a log cabin for his family near the springs, then dammed the hot creek runoff, creating a large bathing pool.

The Crow Indians continued their friendship with Dr. Hunter, and the hot water pool was shared both by new settlers and Crows alike. An 1898 brochure

The elegant Hotel Dakota at Hunter's Hot Springs, circa 1920.

promoting Hunter's Hot Springs described Dr. Hunter's life at the springs in the frontier days of the 1870s: "During the early years when the Indians were his chief visitors, he had witnessed at least 1,000 tepees around these springs, containing Indians who had come to be cured of diseases which had baffled the skill of the great medicine men of many tribes."

The peaceful members of the Crow Tribe helped keep the hostile Sioux from causing trouble for the fledgling resort. However, the Crows would travel away from the area in the summer to hunt buffalo, leaving the hot springs vulnerable to Sioux attack. Lieutenant James A. Bradley, who camped near the hot springs in 1876, recorded the concerns of the Hunter family in his journal: "Dr. Hunter's family is now at the springs, but full of dread of the Sioux. His house is, in the summer season, something of a resort for the afflicted, but the Sioux frequently appear in the vicinity and once attacked the house—facts which do not attract custom." Over the next decade Dr. Hunter improved the bathing and lodging facilities at the hot springs, constructing a two-story hotel in 1883.

Although many bathers surely received relief from arthritic pain and other ailments, some of the medical claims ascribed to the thermal water must have raised a few eyebrows. The *Bozeman Avant-Courier* carried a story about the wondrous power of Hunter's Hot Springs in its April 18, 1872, edition: "Judging from the hirsute appearance of those who had been there, we opine that the legion of 'baldheaded Bachs' who waste time and money on bogus hair restorers, would find a few weeks' sojourn at the warm springs more conducive to the rejuvenation of their capillary adornments."

An 1889 promotional brochure for the resort attributed some of the miracle cures to a particularly shocking property of the thermal water. A Dr. W. T. Collins reportedly discovered "electricity" in the springs on October 1, 1887. The brochure proclaimed that "A rare element, one only found in three or four hot mineral springs of the Old World—electricity—exists in these springs in a strong and quite perceptible current. . . . The foremost specialists of the Old World on mineral springs, rank springs possessed of the element of electricity in the fore rank of all mineral springs."

By the time "electricity" had been discovered in the springs, Dr. Hunter had retired to Bozeman and sold the resort to a business consortium, which built a new frame hotel on the property. The new owners had trouble keeping the resort profitable, and in 1886 they sold it to James A. Murray of Butte, who also owned the hotel at Boulder Hot Springs.

Murray's designs for the property were far more grandiose than the simple log hotel and plunge built by Dr. Hunter more than a decade earlier. Murray developed plans for a hotel and plunge that would be matched only by the Hotel Broadwater in Helena in its size and elegance.

The Hotel Dakota opened in November 1909. The 454-foot-long hostelry had five separate wings and could easily accommodate 300 guests. The stucco-covered building was Moorish in design, with a two-story verandah that stretched for more than 400 feet.

The main lobby featured beamed ceilings and wood-paneled walls, with mission-oak furniture strategically placed for the comfort of weary travelers. The dining room, paneled in natural pine, occupied one of the five wings of the hotel.

The east wing of the Hotel Dakota contained the "bathing department," complete with a solarium, swimming pool, gymnasium, and vapor baths. The 103-foot by 50-foot swimming pool had an assortment of diving boards, swings, and ropes provided for the entertainment of the bathers. Private plunges and a vapor bath were adjacent to the pool. A "sweat room" was also available, where guests were wrapped in warm blankets after a hot plunge bath, then laid on cots to sweat out the impurities from their bodies.

Besides its recreational use, the thermal water from Hunter's Hot Springs was also popular as a beverage and for therapeutic purposes. A mineral water bottling plant was built south of the new hotel, and Hunter's Hot Springs Mineral Water (available in both plain and lemon flavors) was shipped throughout the region. Wooden gazebos were built next to some of the hot springs, and hotel guests would wander along a boardwalk to the springs, dipping the hot

Label from mineral water bottle, Hunter's Hot Springs.

mineral water from the springs with drinking ladles hung from posts in the center of the gazebos. A golf course and two tennis courts were featured outdoor attractions, and the Montana Tennis Association held its annual meeting and state tennis tournament at the resort.

Hotel Dakota's reputation as one of the leading social centers of Montana lasted a scant 20 years. With the coming of the automobile, guests no longer felt obliged to schedule an extended stay at the resort. Also damaging to business was the relocation of the road to Yellowstone National Park. Where once the main road to Yellowstone had passed through the resort property (it's the gravel road you'll be driving on to look at the resort), a new tourist road was built south of the Yellowstone River parallel to what is now Interstate 90. This greatly reduced the number of visitors to the hot springs.

The coming of Prohibition dealt another serious blow to the Hotel Dakota. The hotel bar had long been a gathering place for sportsmen and businessmen, and liquor flowed freely when the hotel hosted the state Republican and Democratic conventions. Mr. and Mrs. Harold Johnson, who owned the hot springs years after the hotel bar was closed, have an undated newspaper story in their mementos about the antics of one of the hard-drinking guests of the hotel. Apparently the guest had consumed a few too many drinks one night in the hotel bar. Deciding to take a walk outside, the man mistakenly entered the plunge building and stumbled into the deep pool. Dripping from head to toe and confused by what had happened, he eventually found his way back to the bar. His drinking companions, noticing the man's soggy predicament, asked if he was all right. "Yes," he replied, "but don't go outside—it's raining like hell!"

The fatal blow to the resort came on November 3, 1932, when fire destroyed the Hotel Dakota in less than two hours. The plunge building survived the fire and was reopened as a public swimming pool a short time later. The swimming pool was run by a series of owners until 1974, when it was closed for the last time.

For the next 20 years the abandoned plunge building stood as the sole reminder of the once great resort. The plunge was finally razed in the mid-1990s, and today only a few lonely fire hydrants mark the bare field where once stood the queen of Montana's elegant hotels.

25

Chico Hot Springs Lodge

General description: A romantic turn-of-the-century resort that combines Victorian refinement with easy-going Western hospitality. The hot springs feed a large sheltered soaking pool and an adjacent outdoor swimming pool. Gourmet meals are served in what is consistently rated one of the best restaurants in Montana.

Location: Southwest Montana, 31 miles north of Yellowstone National Park, 22 miles south of Livingston.

Primitive/developed: Developed.

Best time of year: Open year-round.

Restrictions: Chico Hot Springs Lodge is privately owned. An admission fee is charged to use the hot pools. Overnight guests soak for free.

Access: Any vehicle can make the trip, including small airplanes. The blacktop road leading to the resort is often used as a runway by airborne visitors. Approaching planes radio the resort (unicom frequency 122.8). Chico staff then block both ends of the 5,300-foot asphalt "runway" with cars or trucks. After landing, planes taxi to the lower lodge to be tied down for the night, not unlike horses at an old hitching post.

Water temperature: 113 degrees F at the springs; 104 degrees F in the sheltered outdoor soaking pool; 96 degrees F in the adjacent open-air swimming pool.

Nearby attractions: Yellowstone National Park, Absaroka-Beartooth Wilderness, Yellowstone River.

Services: Food and lodging are available at the resort. All other services are available in Livingston, 22 miles north, or Gardiner, 31 miles south.
Camping: Two Montana Department of Fish, Wildlife, and Parks campgrounds are located north of Chico just off U.S. Highway 89. Mallard's Rest Campground is about 9 miles north of Chico, and Loch Leven Campground is 13 miles north.
Map: Montana State Highways Map.

Finding the springs: From Livingston, head south on US 89 for 22 miles to the small town of Emigrant. Turn east onto Murphy Road, immediately crossing the Yellowstone River. Continue about 0.5 mile to East River Road (County Road 540). Turn left on East River Road and follow it about 1 mile until it intersects with Chico Road. Turn south on Chico Road for another 1.5 miles to the resort. If you're approaching from Gardiner or Yellowstone National Park, drive north 31 miles on US 89 to the turnoff at Emigrant. It's really much easier to find than it sounds; just follow the Chico Hot Springs signs from US 89 at Emigrant.

The hot springs: Tucked beneath towering 10,921-foot Emigrant Peak on the border of the Absaroka-Beartooth Wilderness, Chico Hot Springs Lodge offers the perfect escape from modern civilization. The 113-degree-F hot springs are piped into a 10-foot by 30-foot soaking pool, which is kept at around 104 degrees F year-round. The soaking pool is partially enclosed but connects with a large open-air swimming pool that maintains a 96-degree-F temperature. The outdoor pool was actually indoors until 1957, when the roof over the pool collapsed. Swimmers seemed to prefer the crisp air and the sparkling stars, and the pool has been kept open to the elements ever since. The pools can be entered either through the Chico saloon or from the white-clapboard main lodge.

The main lodge contains 44 guest rooms, simply furnished with period antiques. The comfortable lobby is lined with mementos from the resort's past, and the dark floors creak with history. No jangling telephones or blaring televisions break the Victorian mystique of the old building. Most of the rooms in the main lodge have shared bathrooms, although a few deluxe rooms offer private baths. The new 16-room lower lodge lies west of the main lodge. Also available are a honeymoon cottage, a small motel, and a five-bedroom log house. On the hill behind the main lodge are two chalets, often rented by families, that comfortably sleep six to ten people each.

Although it offers superb hot water soaks, Chico is one of the few hot springs resorts in the region that is worth visiting solely for its great food. Hungry guests have their choice of three restaurants at the resort: the Chico Inn, the House of Ribs, and the Poolside Grille.

Chico Hot Springs Lodge

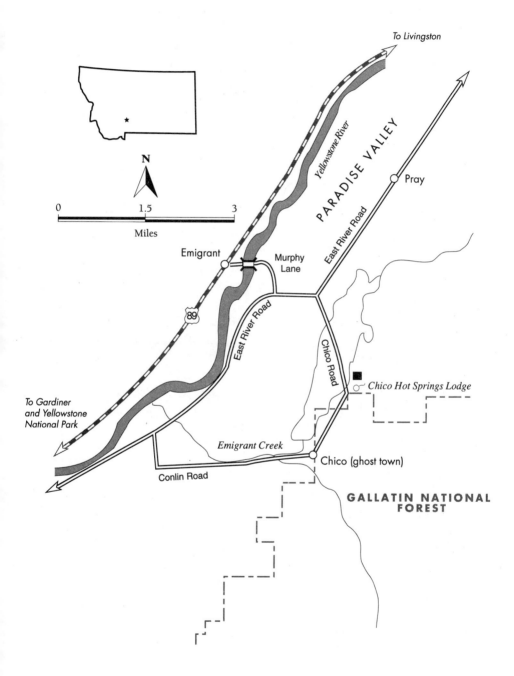

The barnwood-paneled Chico Inn, the resort's most popular dining option, serves gourmet cuisine on par with the finest big city restaurants. Dinners start with fennel-studded breadsticks and an appetizer of steamed artichokes with garlic butter. The entrees usually include a seafood dish (flown in fresh daily), prime rib, beef tenderloin, and other regional specialties. Most of the vegetables served in the restaurant are grown in Chico's own geothermally heated greenhouse. If there's room left after the main course, guests can enjoy Chico's signature orange flambé, a mixture of orange pulp and two liqueurs served in a chocolate-lined orange shell, doused with rum and set ablaze at tableside. Advance reservations for dinner are strongly recommended, especially on the weekends and holidays.

Everyone is treated like an old friend at Chico, where pretentiousness is checked at the front door. Dinner guests may be seated next to famous residents of nearby Paradise Valley, who have included Peter Fonda, Jeff Bridges, Dennis Quaid, and Meg Ryan. Artist Russell Chatham, whose paintings hang on the restaurant walls, has been known to stop by occasionally, and so have writers Tom McGuane and Jim Harrison.

Thanks to its proximity to some of Montana's best outdoor resources, Chico offers great activities during any season of the year. Cross-country skiing on nearby Forest Service trails and dogsleds pulled by teams of Siberian huskies are popular with many winter guests. Summer pastimes include horseback riding, raft trips, and fly-fishing on the Yellowstone River, hiking and mountain biking in the nearby mountain ranges, and scenic airplane flights.

History: The history of settlers in the Chico area dates back to 1862, when gold was discovered by Thomas Curry in nearby Emigrant Gulch. Three years later, on a cold day in January, an unknown gold miner recorded in his diary that he "went out to the hot springs and washed my dirty duds." In 1866, six adventurers stopped near the springs on their return from the area that would soon become Yellowstone National Park. The Emigrant Gulch miners listened in awe as the six men told of the wonders they had seen in the Yellowstone area. One of the storytellers, a Mexican named Chico, left a lasting impression on the miners, and his name became associated with the mining camp and eventually with the hot springs themselves.

The hot springs were frequented by locals throughout the late 1800s. A reporter from the *Livingston Enterprise* visited the springs in 1883, where he "enjoyed himself in the temporary bath house there, the water being just the right heat to bathe in and lots of it."

Chico Hot Springs Lodge.

The 40-room Chico Warm Springs Hotel opened in 1900 and quickly became a social center of the region. The newspaper in the town of Bozeman, some 50 miles away, often carried lists of Chico guests in its social column. More guest rooms and a large indoor plunge were added in 1902 to handle the increasing popularity of the resort. Dances were held on the weekends, concert bands played on the hotel grounds, and a saloon built next to the hotel slaked the thirst of many a visitor.

Many hot springs resorts in Montana alternated between serving as a social center and as a health resort, and Chico was no exception. In 1910 the saloon closed and a 24-bed hospital was opened. Dr. George Townsend, a prominent surgeon, was hired to attract patients to the new hospital. Area newspapers noted Dr. Townsend's spectacular surgical successes, including a brain operation he performed in 1921.

Chico's popularity declined in the late 1920s, and the resort and hospital struggled to survive through the 1930s and 1940s. In 1950 a new owner of Chico closed the hospital and changed the theme of the resort, making it a Western dude ranch. The rebirth of Chico worked, and the resort gradually regained its popularity as a Western vacation resort.

In 1976 Mike and Eve Art purchased Chico and remain its proprietors today.

Chico Hot Springs

You may talk about the wonders
Mid the busy marts of trade,
Such as railway legislation
And great discoveries made.

You may speak of all that's famous
In this world from pole to pole;
Think of all the tons of mineral
And the brilliant mines of gold.

There are marvels in old Dixie,
Where the cotton blossoms grow;
There are many great discoveries
Where ocean waters flow.

But here in old Montana,
In "Emigrant Gold Creek"
Is a pool of sparkling water
That will cure the lame and sick.

Chico Springs, among the mountains,
With its water pure and hot,
Will supply both health and vigor
That for money can't be bought.

If you're troubled with rheumatics,
Or with other ails unknown,
Spend a month at Chico Hot Springs,
And you'll find it "home sweet home."

—Ed. Edwards
circa 1918

(From an undated postcard published in *Photo History of Chico Lodge*, by Doris and Bill Whithorn. Used with permission of Doris Whithorn.)

26

Corwin Springs–La Duke Springs

General description: Scalding hot springs that flow down a steep bank into the Yellowstone River. A bathhouse was built near the springs in the 1900s. In early times the water was piped 2 miles down the river to the elegant Corwin Springs Hotel and Sanitarium, which burned in 1916.

Location: Southwest Montana, about 7 miles north of Gardiner and the northern entrance to Yellowstone National Park.

Primitive/developed: Primitive at the springs, with the ruins of the old resort building about 2 miles north.

Best time of year: The hot water holding tank and the old mission-style plunge can be seen year-round. Soaking in La Duke Springs is possible only when the Yellowstone River is low enough to permit an acceptable mix of cold river water with the hot springs water (late summer and fall). Even when the Yellowstone River is low, its swift current makes this a potentially dangerous soak. A much better soaking spot is available at Boiling River in Yellowstone National Park, 10 miles south of La Duke Springs.

Restrictions: None. The hot springs and runoff channel leading to the Yellowstone River are on Forest Service land.

Access: Any vehicle can make the trip. The springs and old resort ruins are located adjacent to U.S. Highway 89.

Water temperature: 154 degrees F at the springs.

Nearby attractions: Yellowstone National Park, Chico Hot Springs, Absaroka-Beartooth Wilderness.

Services: Food is available at a restaurant in Corwin Springs. All other services are available in Gardiner, 7 miles to the south.

Camping: The Carbella Bureau of Land Management Campground is located about 13 miles north of Corwin Springs off US 89. The Forest Service campground at Eagle Creek is located 2 miles northeast of Gardiner on Jardine Road.

Map: Montana State Highways map.

Finding the springs: From Livingston, head south on US 89 through the Paradise Valley for 50 miles to the town of Corwin Springs. The La Duke Springs Picnic Area is about 2 miles farther south on US 89 (look for the Forest Service sign). From Gardiner, drive about 5 miles north on US 89 to La Duke Springs, and another 2 miles north to Corwin Springs.

La Duke Springs is located about 150 yards south of the picnic area on the east side of the highway. You'll have to walk alongside the highway to take a closer look, so watch for traffic. The hot springs are enclosed in a cement tank

Corwin Springs–La Duke Springs

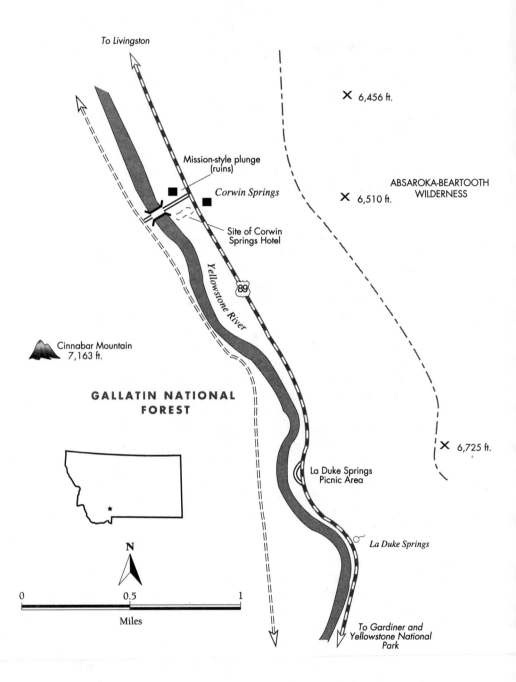

To Livingston

✕ 6,456 ft.

Mission-style plunge
(ruins)

Corwin Springs

ABSAROKA-BEARTOOTH
WILDERNESS

✕ 6,510 ft.

Site of Corwin
Springs Hotel

Yellowstone River

89

Cinnabar Mountain
7,163 ft.

**GALLATIN NATIONAL
FOREST**

✕ 6,725 ft.

La Duke Springs
Picnic Area

La Duke Springs

N

0   0.5   1

Miles

To Gardiner and
Yellowstone National
Park

partially covered with weathered wooden boards. The water in this tank is extremely hot, so don't soak here. The old concrete foundation adjacent to the holding tank may have been the site of a bathhouse built by Julius La Duke in 1902.

From the holding tank the hot water flows underneath US 89, down a steep bank, and into the Yellowstone River. You'll have to cross the highway again to see the steaming water flowing into the river. It's a steep rocky scramble to get down to the area where the hot water mixes with the river.

After you've visited La Duke Springs, head north 2 miles to the little town of Corwin Springs. Just north of the Ranch Kitchen Restaurant is a gravel road leading west to an iron bridge that crosses the Yellowstone River. The open flat area on the south side of the gravel road just before you cross the iron bridge is where the Corwin Springs Hotel once stood. Just to the north on the other side of the gravel road stands the mission-style plunge from the 1920s. You'll recognize it by the square turrets with red-tiled roofs in the corners of the stucco-covered building. The plunge is currently used for storage and is surrounded by mobile homes. Stay on the gravel road when observing this area—both sides of the road are private property.

The hot springs: Both the La Duke Springs bathhouse and the Corwin Springs Hotel depended on the same source of hot water, which collects in the holding tank south of the La Duke Springs Picnic Area. The springs emerge at a steamy 154 degrees F, flow into the holding tank, and then travel under the highway and into the Yellowstone River.

History: In 1902 Julius La Duke took claim to the hot springs, constructing a small plunge and boarding house. The only access in the 1900s was via a narrow road between Livingston and Yellowstone Park on the opposite side of the river from the springs. La Duke ferried guests across the Yellowstone River to his bathhouse and later installed a suspension bridge.

Tragedy struck the little resort in 1905, when La Duke's four-year-old son Lester fell into the hot springs and was scalded to death. In its story about the accident, the *Livingston Enterprise* described La Duke Springs as "one of the hottest in eastern Montana."

In 1908 La Duke Springs came to the attention of Dr. F. E. Corwin, the resident physician at Chico Hot Springs, 25 miles to the north. Corwin had become restless working for the Chico resort and dreamed of building his own palatial spa modeled after the ones in Bavaria. He visited La Duke Springs and shortly thereafter purchased the rights to the hot water. Within a few months Corwin had formed the Electric Hot Springs Company and raised over $100,000 to construct his dream.

Steaming water from La Duke Hot Springs entering the Yellowstone River.

To build his spacious hotel and plunge, Corwin needed a much larger area of land than the narrow canyon surrounding La Duke Springs could provide. He purchased land about 2 miles downriver from the springs and planned to transport the hot water through wooden pipes to his new resort.

By the summer of 1909, the Corwin Springs Hotel and Sanitarium was ready for business. The 86-room hotel was built in an alpine style reminiscent of resort hotels in Switzerland. Hot and cold running water was piped into every room, and the grand parlor and sweeping front porch were a joyous site to weary travelers. Corwin hired a landscape gardener from Kansas City to design the hotel grounds, and he built an electric plant nearby. At night the resort twinkled with lights. The *Livingston Enterprise* rhapsodized that "tourists passing by would think they had passed through fairyland."

Wooden pipes transported water from La Duke Springs to a 50-foot by 80-foot plunge adjacent to the new hotel. The hot water flowed continuously through the plunge, providing a complete change of water every six minutes. The resort also featured vapor baths, private plunges, and tub baths.

Corwin paid $18,000 to have a sturdy iron bridge built across the Yellowstone River to connect with the Northern Pacific Railway. Guests embarking from the trains were taken by horse-drawn coach across the bridge to the front door of the hotel. The hotel featured the latest in fire safety. According to a 1909 *Livingston Enterprise* article, "Fire protection is obtained from

The Corwin Hot Springs Hotel and Plunge, circa 1914.
Photo courtesy of Montana Historical Society.

hydrants installed at the four corners of the hotel, from any of which a stream can be thrown over the top of the structure."

Visitors thronged to the new resort during its opening summer of 1909. The nearby town of Gardiner was practically emptied on weekends, with locals flocking to Corwin Springs to soak in the hot water and enjoy the magnificent vistas. Despite the initial flurry of guests, the hotel began to have financial troubles within six months of its opening. Due, perhaps, to the small local population base and to competition with nearby Chico Hot Springs, the hotel operation lost money. A bank in Livingston foreclosed on the property and appointed its own management team to run the hotel.

On Thanksgiving Day in 1916, Corwin Hot Springs Hotel was destroyed by fire. The vaunted fire protection system installed seven years earlier proved to be insufficient, and the hotel and plunge buildings went up in flames.

In the 1920s the Corwin Springs property was sold to Walter J. Hill, son of James J. Hill, the wealthy president of the Northern Pacific Railroad. In addition to the old hotel site, Hill purchased over 20,000 surrounding acres. On this sprawling acreage he built the Eagle Nest Ranch, which included a clubhouse, dance hall, dining hall, nine-hole golf course, and, near the old iron bridge, a mission-style hot water plunge. The 70-foot by 115-foot plunge building, which still stands, contained 30 changing rooms surrounding the open-air pool.

Welch Brogan managed the resort for Hill in the 1930s and eventually bought the resort. In time, Brogan's interests turned to other business endeavors, and he closed the plunge and dude ranch in the 1940s. Nothing much happened for the next 40 years until 1981, when a religious group called the Church Universal and Triumphant purchased the land and 12,000 surrounding acres, renaming it the Royal Teton Ranch. The east gate to the Royal Teton Ranch is now located by the old mission-style plunge.

NORTHEAST MONTANA

Characterized by wide expanses of wheat fields and oil patches, northeast Montana is the least-populated area of the state. The region features many federally protected areas, including the Charles M. Russell National Wildlife Refuge, the Bowdoin National Wildlife Refuge, the UL Bend National Wildlife Refuge, and the National Wild and Scenic portion of the Missouri River. The Fort Peck Dam, one of the world's largest earthen structures, is located south of Glasgow. The region also contains the Fort Belknap and Fort Peck Indian reservations.

The few natural hot springs in northeast Montana are located in the foothills of the Little Rocky and North Moccasin mountains. Deep wells have also tapped hot water aquifers along the Montana Highline just south of the Canadian border, although only one commercial resort uses this thermal water for public bathing.

27

Gigantic Warm Springs

General description: One of the world's largest natural warm springs, located on an isolated ranch in the foothills of the North Moccasin Mountains.

Location: Central Montana, 14 miles north of Lewistown.

Primitive/developed: The hot springs are natural, but an artificial dam forms a large swimming pool.

Best time of year: Open June to September or October, depending on the weather.

Restrictions: Privately owned. An admission fee is charged. No alcohol is allowed.

Access: Following paved and gravel roads, almost any passenger car can make the trip to the springs.

Water temperature: 68 degrees F.

Nearby attractions: James Kipp State Park, Big Spring Creek and Trout Hatchery, Crystal Lake.

Services: None; gas, food, and lodging can be found in Lewistown, 14 miles south.

Camping: Limited tent and RV camping is available near the springs for a small fee. No trash services or RV hookups are available.

Maps: Montana State Highways map, USGS Lewistown MT.

Gigantic Warm Springs

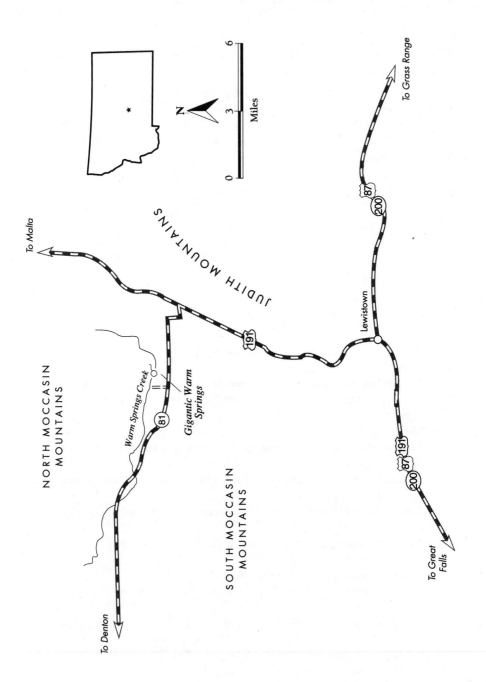

Finding the springs: From Lewistown, travel north on U.S. Highway 191 about 10 miles. Turn west on Montana Highway 81. Travel 3 miles until you see a large green-and-white sign that says "Gigantic Warm Springs." Turn north at the sign onto a gravel road for about 1 mile until you come to a farmhouse. There will probably be someone at the small stand by the road who will take your admission fee. If no one is there, go up to the farmhouse and knock on the door. Once you've paid your admission, drive through the gate for another 0.2 mile to the springs.

The hot springs: This is a monster of a spring—almost 50,000 gallons per minute of crystal-clear, 68-degree-F water emerges from dozens of bubbling vents, forming a pool more than 100 yards in diameter. A 1927 USGS report, titled *Large Springs in the United States,* called Gigantic Springs "a spring of the first magnitude." A sign posted by the pool in the 1980s boasted that Gigantic Springs was "considered to be the largest warm spring in the world, and the third largest spring of any size in the world." Regardless of its true stature in the world battle for the title of largest spring, Gigantic Springs certainly ranks near the top.

Gigantic Springs is a great family recreation spot. The relatively cool water temperature makes the springs especially popular on hot days. "The hotter it is outside, the more visitors we have," says rancher and springs owner David Vaneck.

Gigantic Warm Springs.

The pool itself, which has a sparkling clean gravel bottom, is about 5 feet deep in the center. A 20-foot by 90-foot wading area occupies one side of the pool. A wooden deck surrounds much of the pool, and a lifeguard stand is kept occupied during the summer season. At the far end of the pool an old rock and log dam tries in vain to contain the springs, which pour over the top of the dam to form Warm Springs Creek. The creek is a major fishery in central Montana, containing smallmouth bass as well as rainbow and brook trout.

A long windbreak of narrow-leaf cottonwoods was planted near the springs in the 1950s. These trees now shade a dozen picnic tables, creating a parklike atmosphere. Weddings and family reunions are occasionally held by the springs, and guests enjoy the beauty of the surrounding North Moccasin Mountains. A 20-foot by 40-foot open-air shelter can be used for rainy-day gatherings.

History: Gold miners in the early 1900s recognized the economic potential in the massive flow of water from Gigantic Springs. By 1910, an undershot water wheel and pump had been installed at the springs. A 200-horsepower water turbine generated electricity for the new Kendall Mine, 6.5 miles to the northeast, while a piston pump supplied spring water for mining and milling operations in Kendall.

After the heyday of gold mining in Kendall had passed, the power plant and pumping facilities at Gigantic Springs were abandoned. In the late 1930s the Vaneck family purchased the springs and surrounding land for back taxes. Generations of Lewistown residents have relaxed and had fun at Gigantic Springs, which today is managed by David Vaneck.

28

Landusky Plunge

General description: A deep, crystal-clear warm springs pool in the southwest foothills of the Little Rocky Mountains. The quintessential swimming hole.

Location: Central Montana, about 88 miles northeast of Lewistown, 65 miles southwest of Malta.

Primitive/developed: Primitive.

Best time of year: Summer and early fall.

Restrictions: Landusky Plunge and the surrounding area are managed by the Square Butte Grazing Association. According to Gary Casebolt, manager of the association, there are no restrictions on access to the swimming hole. Landusky Plunge is a popular summer recreation spot for Native Americans from the nearby Fort Belknap Indian Reservation.

Access: High-clearance vehicles are advised, because the last 3 miles of the dirt road are quite rough. If the road is muddy it may be impassable without a four-wheel-drive vehicle.

Water temperature: 77 degrees F at the source; 68 degrees F to 70 degrees F in the plunge (may be cooler in winter).

Nearby attractions: C. M. Russell National Wildlife Refuge, Landusky ghost town, Kid Curry's hideout.

Services: None. Gas, food, and lodging are available in Lewistown, 88 miles southwest, or Malta, 65 miles northeast.

Camping: Montana Gulch Campground is located about 5 miles north of Landusky Plunge, just south of the ghost town of Landusky.

Map: USGS Hays SE MT.

Finding the springs: From Lewistown, take U.S. Highway 191 north 79 miles to Montana Highway 66. If you're coming from Malta, take US 191 south 55 miles to MT 66. Go north on MT 66 for about 6 miles to the Landusky turnoff. Take the Landusky road for 1.2 miles until you see a sign for the Little Rockies Christian Camp. Don't take the road to the camp—instead, go about 50 yards farther north, cross a cattleguard, and take the dirt road to the east (you will be parallel to the Christian camp road for a bit). Stay on this dirt road for 2.5 miles until you reach a fork in the road. Take the south (right-hand) road for another 0.5 mile. This road ends in a clearing about 20 yards above the plunge.

The hot springs: If you wax nostalgic for the old swimming hole of simpler times, Landusky Plunge is for you. The 77-degree-F springs emerge from a rock wall about a foot above the plunge and flow into a narrow channel that quickly widens into the deeper pool. Volunteers have constructed rock dams in the narrow channel to form pools that are slightly warmer than the plunge itself. The shallow pools are great for relaxing soaks on a hot day. If you're more adventurous, slip out of the shallow pools and into the deeper, clear waters of the main plunge. An old earthen dam and irrigation headgate are responsible for this pristine pond, which is more than 100 feet across and about 10 feet deep. A limestone peninsula about 20 feet wide juts into the pool and is a perfect spot for jumping into the deepest part of the plunge.

History: Landusky Plunge and the sleepy town of Landusky were named after Pike Landusky, who discovered gold in the Little Rockies in 1893. Although Landusky tried to keep the discovery quiet by packing out the gold-rich quartz ore by the light of the moon, word soon got out and other miners rushed to

Landusky Plunge

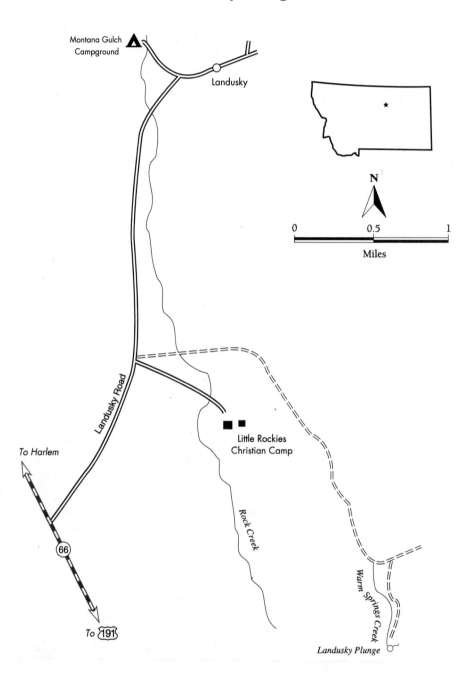

Montana Gulch
Campground

Landusky

N

0   0.5   1

Miles

Landusky Road

To Harlem

66

Little Rockies
Christian Camp

Rock Creek

Warm Springs Creek

To 191

Landusky Plunge

stake their claims. In 1894 a town was organized, and Pike Landusky built the first saloon. Not only was Landusky a saloon owner, he was also the town constable, which may help explain the wild reputation the town acquired. Many a miner drank freely at Pike's saloon, then whooped it up with his six-shooter in the street. After one particularly wild night of gunplay, a local gambler remarked that "he could go outside with a pint cup and gather a quart of bullets."

Although Pike Landusky had a reputation as a violent man, the Curry brothers, whose ranch was nearby, were equally nasty. Led by Harvey "Kid" Curry, the brothers liked nothing better than to terrorize the town of Landusky, riding their horses into stores and filling the streets with gunfire. After one such incident in December 1894, Kid Curry and his brother Johnny were arrested and placed in the custody of saloon owner and constable Pike Landusky, who wasted no time verbally and physically abusing the Curry brothers before he finally released them.

Seeking revenge a few days later, Kid Curry returned to the saloon, knocked Landusky to the ground, and shot him dead. Realizing he had killed a lawman, Curry and his brothers headed to the hills and began their infamous reign as the Curry Gang. The culmination of their lawlessness came seven years later on July 3, 1901, when they held up a Great Northern passenger train near Malta. The gang escaped with more than $40,000 in currency and rode back to a hideout a few miles from Landusky Plunge. Kid Curry eventually went south,

Warm springs water entering the shallow end of Landusky Plunge.

but he was captured two years later in Tennessee. He escaped from prison shortly thereafter and was never seen again.

The town of Landusky was almost deserted when the easily accessible gold played out, but it revived for a time in the 1930s when new deposits were found. Large mining activities ceased from 1936 until 1979, when Pegasus Gold Company opened the giant Zortman and Landusky open-pit mines, which can easily be seen from the town of Landusky.

29

Sleeping Buffalo Resort

General description: A prairie spa built on the site of a hot water well along the sparsely populated Montana Highline.
Location: Northeast Montana, 17 miles east of Malta.
Primitive/developed: Developed resort.
Best time of year: Open year-round.
Restrictions: Private resort. Admission fee charged to use pools.
Access: Any vehicle can make the trip.
Water temperature: 108 degrees F at the well; 106 degrees F in the mineral pool; 90 degrees F in the inside swimming pool; 100 degrees F in the outside pool.
Nearby attractions: Nelson Reservoir, Bowdoin National Wildlife Refuge.
Services: Food and lodging available at the resort. All other services available in Malta, 17 miles east, and Saco, 10 miles west.
Camping: Several tent sites and RV spots (20 with full hookups) available at the resort. A public campground administered by the U.S. Bureau of Reclamation is located at Nelson Reservoir, about 1 mile north of the resort.
Map: Montana State Highways map.

Finding the springs: From Malta, drive 17 miles east on U.S. Highway 2. From Glasgow, drive 53 miles west on US 2. Watch for the state highway marker by Sleeping Buffalo Rock. Turn north on County Road 243 for 1.5 miles to the resort.

The hot springs: The only hot springs along Montana's northern tier, Sleeping Buffalo Resort has attracted bathers from North Dakota, Saskatchewan, and Montana since the 1920s. The term "hot springs" is actually a misnomer, because the source of Sleeping Buffalo's hot water is a 3,500-foot-deep well that produces more than 700 gallons per minute of 108-degree-F water.

Sleeping Buffalo Resort

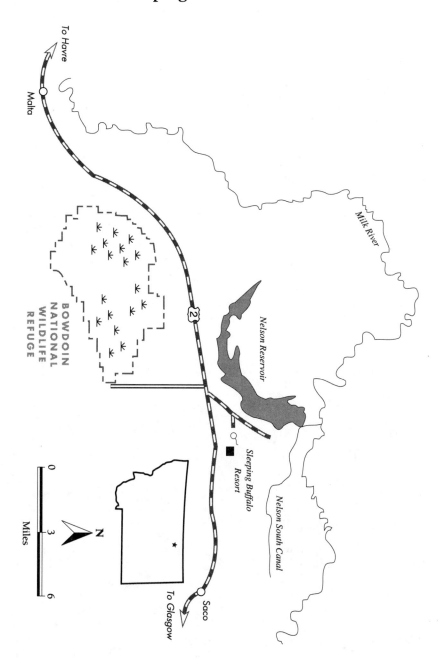

The artesian well pressure forces the hot water into three separate pools. The 8-foot by 26-foot indoor hot soaking pool is kept at a toasty 106 to 110 degrees F, perfect to warm chilly bones on a cold December day. A larger indoor pool (about 45 feet by 60 feet) stays close to 90 degrees F year-round.

The Olympic-sized outdoor pool is normally maintained at 100 degrees F but may be closed in the winter. Two water slides exit into the shallow end of the pool, which is 4 to 5 feet deep. A concrete barrier bisects the outdoor pool, separating the deeper end from the shallower area adjacent to the water slides.

Other amenities at the resort include a poolside restaurant and gift shop, baseball fields and volleyball courts, and a nine-hole golf course. Aggressive mosquitoes are legendary in this region, so be prepared to do battle with the pesky critters in the summer months.

History: The story of the Sleeping Buffalo Resort began in 1924, when a wild-cat oil driller struck a highly pressurized mix of hot water and natural gas. The drill rig was removed, and the artesian water was left to spill onto the prairie. Locals would often visit the well to see the hissing mixture of hot water and gas. Visitors sometimes threw lit matches into the well, igniting the gas and sending a blue flame dancing across the surface of the water. The nighttime glow from this "burning well" could be seen for quite a distance until a strong wind or the roiling water itself doused the flame.

The indoor hot mineral pool at the Sleeping Buffalo Resort.

In 1927 a local rancher built wooden walls around the well to form a crude swimming pool. Suffering from polio, the rancher's son found relief by taking frequent baths in the hot pool. Word spread about the therapeutic nature of the water, and soon a larger pool was constructed of railroad ties.

Noting the recreational potential of the well, the American Legion posts of Saco, Malta, and Hinsdale sought federal funding in 1930 to develop a new resort. Within a few months the U.S. Congress had appropriated money to use the water for "curative and recreational purposes." The "American Legion Health Plunge" was born. One of the first actions taken by the Legion was to shut off the natural gas from the rest of the hot water flow.

When Franklin Roosevelt became president in 1933, his own enthusiasm for hot springs soaks gave another boost to the young resort. Roosevelt was often photographed swimming in the pools of Warm Springs, Georgia, where he found relief for his polio-damaged limbs. Local businessman H. L. Lance was aware of Roosevelt's love for hot water and of the "New Deal" work programs being developed to employ men who were jobless because of the Depression. Lance approached federal sources about building a large resort complex at the Legion Plunge, boasting that the Montana hot water well was chemically similar to Roosevelt's favorite thermal pool in Georgia. Soon the Legion Health Plunge swarmed with workers paid by the federal Works Progress Administration. An accomplished stone mason named Bruno Parpzsch took charge of most of the WPA construction, and today his beautiful stonework can still be seen on the outside of many of the buildings at the resort.

The American Legion Health Plunge thrived until the spring of 1957, when the resort closed abruptly because a hot water well casing collapsed about 1,000 feet below the surface. The hot water simply stopped. The plunge pools were bone dry, and hundreds of bathers were turned away. The resort was closed for 18 months until a new well was drilled and the hot water again flowed into the pools.

In 1965 a group calling itself the Sleeping Buffalo Recreation Association acquired the resort. The resort has had several owners since the 1960s and is presently managed by Roger Ereaux.

Sleeping Buffalo Rock, for which the present resort is named, can be seen at the turnoff on US 2. Stranded on a nearby ridge by retreating glaciers, the rock resembles a buffalo sleeping on the prairie. It was held sacred by Native American tribes in the area, who often left offerings of beads and food in the depression on top of the rock. Even today you will often see offerings of food, cigarettes, and money placed on Sleeping Buffalo Rock by those seeking good fortune.

SOUTHEAST MONTANA

Best known for its cowboy heritage, southeast Montana is a land of rolling hills and plains, endless horizons, and isolated small towns. Miles City and Glendive, the region's largest cities, lie along the banks of the Yellowstone River, which bisects this region. The Little Bighorn Battlefield, site of Custer's Last Stand, is located here. Some of the buildings from old Fort Keough, which served as a cavalry outpost in the late nineteenth century, still stand near Miles City. Grazing cattle, oil wells, and wheat fields dominate the arid landscape.

A limestone aquifer called the Madison Formation underlies most of this region, and it contains an abundance of hot water. However, this geothermal resource is several thousand feet deep, and hot water comes to the surface only when the aquifer has been penetrated by drilling, as is the case at Angela Well.

30

Angela Well

General description: One of the hottest and most isolated geothermal resources in Montana. The spectacular white terraces around this hot water well look like a miniature version of Mammoth Hot Springs in Yellowstone.
Location: Southeast Montana, 38 miles north of Miles City, 67 miles south of Jordan.
Primitive/developed: Primitive, with the remains of an old bathhouse near the well.
Best time of year: Spring, fall, and early winter. According to the postmistress in the nearby town of Angela, locals avoid visiting the hot water well in the summer because the "horseflies are so bad you can't even get out of your car."
Restrictions: The well is on private property owned by Charles and Linda Moore of Angela, but they have no restrictions on letting the public visit or soak in the hot water. Please respect the owners' hospitality by keeping the area free of trash.
Access: High-clearance vehicles are recommended. The last 4 miles of the trip are on gumbo roads that may be impassable after a rainstorm. Although this area receives little snow in the winter, drifts may at times block the road.

Water temperature: 185 degrees F at the wellhead, with a variety of cooler temperatures in the runoff channel and the pool below the travertine terrace.

Nearby attractions: Range Riders Museum, Yellowstone River (both near Miles City).

Services: None. Gas, food, and lodging are available in Miles City, 38 miles south.

Camping: None available near the springs. Camping is allowed on Bureau of Land Management land located in the area (call the BLM field office in Miles City for more information on camping regulations). A private campground is also available in Miles City, 38 miles south of Angela Well.

Map: BLM Angela MT topo map.

Finding the springs: From Miles City, drive 28 miles north on Montana Highway 59 to the town of Angela (the town consists of a post office and a couple of houses). About 100 yards north of the Angela post office, turn west onto County Road 203. Go 6.2 miles west on this gravel road. You'll see a dirt road on your left (south). This road is sometimes marked in the summer by a bullet-ridden "No Hunting" sign on a four-foot steel fence post with an old cowboy boot jammed on top of it. (The sign is erected to guide cattle trucks to nearby grazing areas). Take this dirt road for about 1 mile until you cross a cattle guard.

Cast-iron bathtubs on the mineral terrace near Angela Well.

Angela Well

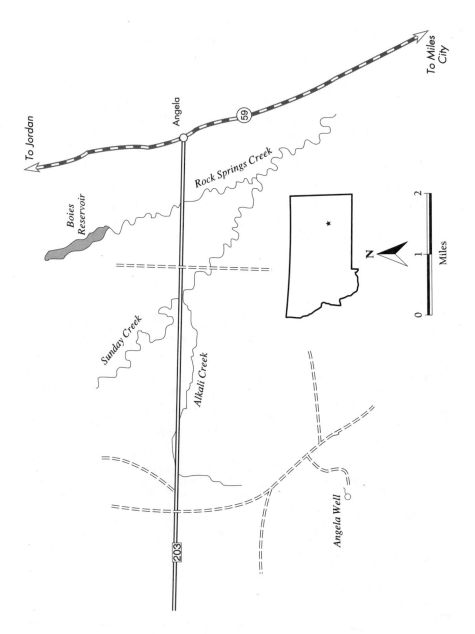

Past the cattle guard are some forks in the road to the left and right, but keep on the most traveled dirt road for another 3 miles to the well.

The hot springs: Montana's easternmost geothermal resource is also one of its most remarkable. More than 1,200 gallons per minute of 185-degree-F water discharge from a horizontal pipe connected to a mineral-encrusted wellhead. There's a strong sulfur smell here, indicative of the large amount of minerals in the water. The torrent of hot water pours onto a snow-white terrace about 50 feet in diameter and 4 feet high. Older dry terraces to the south of the active terrace attest to the rapid mineralization effects of the water in past decades. The water on the terrace exceeds 150 degrees F.

Hot water running down the face of the terrace enters a pool about 100 feet long, varying from 6 to 20 feet wide. The pool is only a foot or so deep, and the bottom is quite muddy. Determined bathers can ease into the pool's far end and move toward the terrace until a comfortable soaking temperature is found.

Because of its isolated location, Angela Well is rarely visited. Linda Moore, daughter of current owner Charles Moore, recalls significantly more visitors in the past than today, with older residents of Miles City sometimes driving to the well to soak their feet and fill drinking jugs with the mineral water.

The concrete foundation of an old bathhouse lies about 10 yards north of the well. Two cast-iron tubs rest on the old foundation, and another tub lies half-submerged in a hot pool next to the bathhouse. All of the water in the pools near the well and the bathhouse is much too hot for soaking. The bathhouse at one time was a schoolteacher's house, which was moved to the hot water well by Bob and Dan Moore. According to Linda Moore, the steam from the hot springs "ate the nails out of the walls of the building." Only the concrete foundation and the mineral-encrusted tubs remain today.

USE EXTREME CAUTION AT ANGELA WELL: You can get into serious trouble if you take a wrong step onto the terrace by the wellhead. The water on the terrace is as hot as the pools in Yellowstone National Park, but there are no rangers or signs to warn you to be careful. The deep mud just beneath the terrace encircling the lower pool is encrusted with white minerals, which makes it appear more solid than it really is. Stay away from this area. If you're in doubt about the temperature or safety of any of the pools, it's better just to enjoy the scenery and marvel at the mineral terraces.

The rolling prairies around Angela Well stretch endlessly in all directions, with only the occasional cow or meadowlark breaking the silence. It's easy to imagine dusty cowboys taking a hot bath here on a Saturday night, enjoying a well-deserved soak in one of those old cast-iron tubs.

YELLOWSTONE NATIONAL PARK

With more than 10,000 thermal anomalies, Yellowstone National Park contains the greatest concentration of hot springs and geysers in the world. The vast majority of these features are hot springs, mud pots, or steam-emitting fumaroles, but Yellowstone is most famous for the more than 800 geysers concentrated within the park's boundaries.

Why does such an amazing concentration of hot springs and geysers exist in this particular place in the world? The answer lies in a combination of an abnormally high underground heat source, plentiful rainwater, and particular minerals in the rocks.

The earth's crust is normally about 90 miles thick, but under Yellowstone its thickness is only about 40 miles. This shallow area creates a "hot spot" where molten rock (magma) is much closer to the earth's surface than it is in most other places. As rainwater seeps through porous rock layers above the magma, it gradually becomes hot. The immense pressure exerted by the upper layers of rock prevents this hot water from boiling, and water temperature may exceed 500 degrees F when it is closest to the magma. When the superheated water finds its way into fissures in the overlying rock, it rises to the surface.

Most of the thermal water reaching the surface in Yellowstone flows quietly into a hot spring or mud pot, but under special circumstances the water can remain trapped in silica-lined chambers beneath the earth, where pressure builds as more water pushes up from below. A cap of cooler water may delay the pressurized, superheated water from boiling, but when the pressure becomes great enough, the superheated water will suddenly push through the cooler water cap. This rapidly reduces the pressure on the superheated water; it turns to steam and erupts on the surface as a geyser. After a few minutes the upward force of the steam usually declines and the geyser subsides. The emptied rock chamber begins to fill with superheated water again, and the cycle starts anew.

HISTORY OF THERMAL WATER USE IN YELLOWSTONE

In 1871, Dr. Ferdinand Hayden, the director of the U.S. Geological Survey, set out from Utah with a party of 34 men to explore the Yellowstone region. Hayden's 500-page report opened the eyes of the nation to the wonders of the area and led to the creation of Yellowstone National Park in March 1872. During Hayden's explorations he noted that several settlers had already discovered the therapeutic nature of a few of the hot springs, including Boiling River just north of

Yellowstone National Park

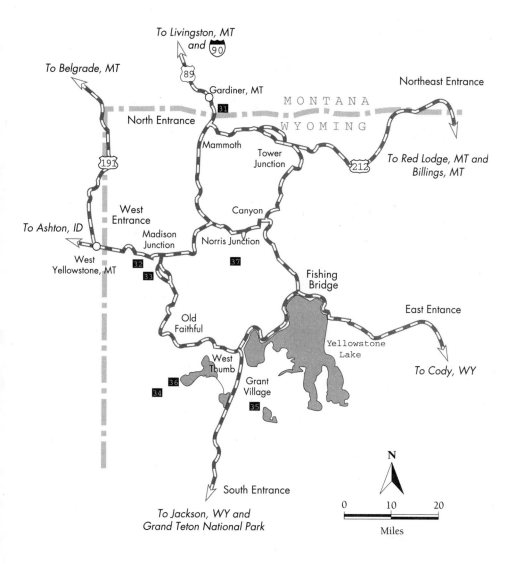

To Livingston, MT and 90

To Belgrade, MT

89

Gardiner, MT

Northeast Entrance

MONTANA

WYOMING

31

North Entrance

Mammoth

Tower Junction

To Red Lodge, MT and Billings, MT

212

191

West Entrance

Canyon

To Ashton, ID

Madison Junction

Norris Junction

West Yellowstone, MT

32

33

37

Fishing Bridge

East Entrance

Old Faithful

Yellowstone Lake

To Cody, WY

West Thumb

36

34

Grant Village

35

N

South Entrance

To Jackson, WY and Grand Teton National Park

0   10   20

Miles

Bathhouse on the Hymen Terrace at Mammoth Hot Springs, circa 1884.

Mammoth Hot Springs. In his 1871 expedition diary, Hayden wrote, "Around [Boiling River] had already gathered a number of invalids, who were living in tents, and their praises were enthusiastic in favor of the sanitary effects of the springs. Some of them were used for drinking and others for bathing purposes."

By 1872, a house and barn had been built near Boiling River by Matthew McGuirk. McGuirk claimed the Boiling River as private property and charged visitors to take treatments at "McGuirk's Medicinal Springs." But his entrepreneurial venture was short-lived. In 1874 McGuirk was evicted from the Boiling River area by the superintendent of the newly created Yellowstone National Park, and the buildings were torn down.

Thermal water was also used for bathing and drinking at Mammoth Hot Springs, where Harry R. Horr constructed a rustic bathhouse in 1871.

One of the most popular recreational uses of thermal water occurred at Bath Lake, a natural warm water pool near the Mammoth Hot Springs terrace. Nude bathing was common. A waiter named George Thomas, who worked at the hotel restaurant in Mammoth in 1883, recalled one perfect summer day at Bath Lake:

It was a wonderful swimming hole and had a long plank floating in the water and a swimmer could lie full length at one end of the plank and still be deep enough in the water to paddle around and be happy. One afternoon I and three other young fellows from the Hotel Waiters force, went to this lake for a swim. We had no bathing suits on, and the lake was surrounded by a growth of shrubbery that hid the water from sight, so we figured that we would not be disturbed by any passers-by. We had been in the water about an hour when we were surprised by a shower of stones that were being thrown by four young women who wanted their turn in the lake. As we were reasonable gentlemen, we left the water, grabbed our clothes and took to the brush, leaving the victorious women to enjoy their bath.

For several years nude bathing flourished at Bath Lake, with both sexes taking turns swimming in the naturally warm water. Apparently this collegial sharing of the lake was too much for park officials, and in 1885, women were banned from swimming in the lake. The *Livingston Enterprise* reported its dismay at the restriction: "It is to be regretted that both sexes cannot share this delightful bath. Ladies cannot even see it, for in pleasant weather [a] large number of male bathers occupy it exclusively. The government ought to regulate this matter by either constructing or permitting the construction of dressing rooms in which both sexes could have bathing suits and together 'bask in the glare and swim the tepid water.'"

Tolerance for nude bathing at Bath Lake eventually declined, and by 1912 swimsuits were required (by that time women had been granted permission to again share Bath Lake with men, albeit clad in swimsuits as well). A bathhouse was constructed close to Bath Lake by 1919 but was removed in 1925 when the nearby Mammoth swimming pool was opened.

The new swimming pool built at Mammoth wasn't the only officially sanctioned warm water pool constructed in Yellowstone. Another swimming pool was built a few hundred yards from Old Faithful in the Upper Geyser Basin in 1914. It was remodeled in 1934 and served park visitors through the summer of 1950.

Other portions of Yellowstone were also popular bathing and washing spots in the early days of the park. An area called Old Bath Lake served as a collecting basin for hot springs water in the Lower Geyser Basin. Old Bath Lake was probably used for bathing as early as the 1900s, and a bathhouse was constructed on its shores. (As a result of the number of times that park rangers have had to arrest tourists violating regulations by bathing in undiluted thermal pools such as this one, Old Bath Lake is now called Ranger Pool.)

Many of the early soakers in Yellowstone were people hired to help build the park infrastructure. Observing the construction of a road in 1880 near what is now called the Queen's Laundry Hot Spring in the Lower Geyser Basin, Park Superintendent P. W. Norris described how the activities of construction workers led to the naming of the springs: "[D]uring a Sabbath's rest and bathing recreation, some of the boys crossed from our camp to the attractive bordered pools below this great boiling fountain, and in one cool enough for bathing discovered its matchless cleansing properties, and from the long line of bright-colored clothing soon seen drying upon the adjacent stumps and branches, while their owners were gamboling like dolphins in the pools, the envious cooks dubbed it the Laundry."

The National Park Service eventually adopted a new policy prohibiting the commercial use of thermal water in Yellowstone, and all swimming pools and bathhouses were removed from within the park boundaries.

REGULATIONS ON SOAKING IN YELLOWSTONE

With its thousands of hot springs, you might think Yellowstone National Park is a paradise for those in search of a soak. Certainly, early settlers and park visitors used natural hot pools for decades. But today, however, as tempting as they may appear, all of the thermal pools and geysers are off-limits to bathers.

Yellowstone National Park falls under the supervision of the federal government, which has issued legal guidelines on bathing in the park's hot springs. The basic soaking rule for Yellowstone is found in the fine print of the U.S. Code of Federal Regulations, Title 36, Part 7.13(m): "The swimming or bathing in a natural, historical, or archeological thermal pool or stream that has waters originating from a thermal springs or pool is prohibited."

Why the restrictions? It boils down to the fundamental reason for which Yellowstone National Park was created: to protect the park's natural resources for the enjoyment of future generations and to provide for the safety of the public who come to enjoy those natural wonders.

Yellowstone's wild appearance belies the fragile nature of much of its beauty. Many of the geysers and hot springs contain remarkable deposits of silicon dioxide (geyserite) and calcium carbonate (travertine). Some of these formations developed with agonizing slowness—it may take more than 30 years for a single inch of snow-white geyserite to deposit at the edge of a hot springs. A single misstep by a bather could destroy decades of deposition.

Indiscriminate bathing can also inflict subtler but still damaging results. Foreign objects such as clothing, rocks, or soda cans that are left in the springs

Bathhouse near Old Faithful Geyser, circa 1920.

can alter the complex underground plumbing system, reducing the temperature of the hot pools. As the temperature cools, the thermally adapted algae and bacteria responsible for the beautiful colors of the springs may die. Without the algae and bacteria, the brilliant hues fade and disappear, usually forever.

Swimming in Yellowstone hot springs may also stir up sediment, which prevents the color-producing algae and bacteria from getting enough light for photosynthesis. If enough organisms die, the hot springs again may lose their color.

Restricting bathing in Yellowstone hot springs also helps fulfill the second goal of the park: to ensure the safety of park visitors. The majority of Yellowstone's thermal features are scalding hot. Most of the park's springs and geysers are near boiling, which at these high mountain elevations is around 198 degrees F or about 100 degrees above the safe temperature for soaking.

Unfortunately, injuries and deaths have occurred when visitors have fallen into, or attempted to swim in, Yellowstone's hot springs. One of the earliest victims was explorer Truman Everts, who became separated from the Washburn Expedition in 1870. Everts wandered through Yellowstone for 37 days and sought refuge from the cold by attempting to soak in a hot springs near Heart Lake. Everts burned his hip in the hot water, perhaps the first recorded error of judgment by a bather in what would eventually become Yellowstone National Park.

At least 19 people have died in Yellowstone's hot springs since the 1880s. Most of the deaths were accidental, and at least two fatalities occurred when individuals tried to soak in hot pools. There have also been hundreds of injuries incurred when individuals attempted to test the scalding water with their hands or to wade in the runoff channels from the hot springs.

A less common but still serious danger results from the unstable geologic nature of Yellowstone itself. Placid warm springs pools in the park have been known suddenly to increase in temperature after an earthquake, a relatively common event in Yellowstone. Bathers in hot pools would be in for a rude shock if they happened to be in those pools when the earth moved.

LEGAL SOAKS IN YELLOWSTONE

With all of the dangers and regulations against soaking in the park's hot springs and geysers, it might seem that the only way to get a hot soak in Yellowstone is to take a bath in a hotel room at the Old Faithful Inn. But fortunately the federal regulations on thermal soaking have a loophole just big enough to squeeze a towel and swimsuit through.

Although it is illegal to swim in a totally self-contained hot spring or geyser, it is legal to soak where the thermal water mixes with water from a "nonthermal" source such as a freshwater river or stream. But be aware that the park rangers still have the authority to close any area to bathing at any time (even if it appears to meet the regulatory standard) if there is a need to protect the natural resource or the public. These closures may occur during high spring runoff on rivers adjacent to a spring or if a bear has been spotted roaming near a spring.

Several areas in Yellowstone National Park currently meet the legal requirements for soaking. Three of the most popular soaking areas are close to roads: the runoff from Boiling River where it mixes with the cold water of the Gardner River, the Firehole Swimming Area, and the hot springs that mix with the Madison River near Madison Campground. Several legal backcountry soaks are also popular, including an area near the Ferris Fork of the Bechler River, Witch Creek, Violet Springs, and an area near the Shoshone Geyser Basin. These soaking areas are described in more detail in the following sections.

SOAKS CLOSE TO ROADS

31

Boiling River

General description: Yellowstone National Park's most popular soaking area. A 6-foot-wide stream of hot water plunges over travertine rocks into a 50-yard-long band of thermal soaking pools along the Gardner River.
Location: Northwest Wyoming in Yellowstone National Park, 2 miles south of the park's north entrance.
Primitive/developed: Primitive.
Best time of year: Late summer, fall, and winter. The bathing area may be closed in the spring and early summer due to high water in the Gardner River. Wintertime soaks are magical, with immense clouds of steam rising from hot springs into the frigid mountain air.
Restrictions: The bathing area is open from dusk till dawn (usually 5:00 A.M. to 9:00 P.M. in the summer and 6:00 A.M. to 6:00 P.M. in the winter). No alcohol, pets, or nudity are allowed. Unlike many areas of Yellowstone, Boiling River is accessible year-round.
Access: Any vehicle can make the trip.
Water temperature: 140 degrees F in the undiluted hot water channel; 50 to 120 degrees F in the soaking pools where the thermal water mixes with the cold Gardner River.
Nearby attractions: Mammoth Hot Springs, Tower Falls, Norris Geyser Basin, Corwin Springs.
Services: Gas, food, and lodging are available in the town of Gardiner, Montana, and at Mammoth in Yellowstone National Park.
Camping: The nearest campground is located at Mammoth, 1 mile south of Boiling River.
Maps: Trails Illustrated (Mammoth Hot Springs), USGS Gardiner MT.

Finding the springs: From Mammoth, drive 2 miles north toward the town of Gardiner and the North Entrance. Parking lots are located on both sides of the road, just past the sign marking the 45th parallel (halfway between the Equator and the North Pole). The parking lot on the east side of the road is closer to the trailhead. Walk south along the well-used trail on the banks of the Gardner River for 0.5 mile to Boiling River (note that "Gardner River" and the nearby town of "Gardiner" are spelled differently). There are no changing areas near

Soaking area where Boiling River mixes with Gardner River.

Boiling River, and swimsuits are required, so it's best to put on your swimsuit before you leave the parking area (the small outhouse there will serve the purpose). Be sure to take a towel. In the winter bring along plenty of warm clothes, as it can be a frigid walk back to your car if you're not prepared.

The hot springs: The largest discharge of thermal water in Yellowstone, Boiling River is also the park's most popular soaking location, at times accommodating 150 people in the warm water. The attractiveness of this soak is no doubt attributable to its easy access from the North Entrance Road, its beautiful location, and the awesome soaking opportunities.

Geologists suspect that the Boiling River's 100-yard channel of 140-degree-F hot water is the underground flow from Mammoth Hot Springs, some 2 miles to the south. The 6-foot-wide stream pours over travertine ledges into the swift-flowing Gardner River, where it mixes with cold river water. The water level in the Gardner River determines the temperature of your soak. You may encounter a blast of hot water on your back, while at the same time your toes are shivering in the icy river water, but most bathers eventually find just the right spot for their thermal tastes.

Boiling River had a wild reputation during the 1960s and 1970s, culminating in 1982 with the drowning of two men who had been drinking during a nighttime soak. The men ventured too far out into the strong current of the Gardner River and were swept downstream in the darkness. In February 1983, park officials tightened regulations on use of the soaking area. Nudity, alcohol consumption, and nighttime soaks were prohibited.

The swift current of the Gardner River is nothing to take lightly. Stay close to the riverbank (which you'll naturally do, since this is where the hot water mixing occurs) and hold onto rocks and fellow bathers to keep yourself near the shore. Park officials usually deem that soaking is far too dangerous during periods of high water runoff in the Gardner, and the area is often closed in the springtime. In 1997 the water level in the Gardner River was so high that the bathing area was closed until early August.

In spite of the strong river current, Boiling River is still one of the outstanding natural soaking opportunities in the Northern Rockies. The tremendous volume of hot water pouring over ledges into the river below provides an abundance of memorable soaking opportunities. You may even see a buffalo or an elk grazing on the far banks of the Gardner River, yet another reminder of the wisdom of preserving this wild country for all to enjoy.

32

Madison Campground Warm Springs

General description: A group of warm water seeps in a side channel of the Madison River, located in the shadow of National Park Mountain.

Location: Northwest Wyoming, I mile from Madison Junction in Yellowstone National Park.

Primitive/developed: Primitive.

Best time of year: Early May to late October. Madison Campground and the road to Madison Junction are closed in the winter. Warmer days in the summer and fall are best, because the water temperature in the seeps rarely exceeds 95 degrees F.

Restrictions: No alcohol or pets are allowed. Check at the Madison Campground registration office for current information on nudity and nighttime soaking.

Access: Any vehicle can make the trip.

Water temperature: The seeps emerge from the ground at 100 degrees F, but the Madison River dilutes the temperature in the soaking area to 80 to 90 degrees F.

Nearby attractions: Firehole River Swimming Area, Lower Geyser Basin, Norris Geyser Basin.

Services: Gas, food, and lodging are available in West Yellowstone, 14 miles west, and at Old Faithful, 16 miles south.

Camping: Madison Campground is located about 100 yards north of the Madison River and the warm springs.

Maps: Trails Illustrated (Yellowstone National Park), Madison Campground map (available at Madison Campground registration office).

Finding the springs: Drive into Madison Campground (14 miles east of the West Entrance to Yellowstone) to the farthest loop of campsites (Loop H), and park your car along the road near Campsite 273. There's a faint trail behind the campsite that leads 100 yards to the banks of the Madison River. (Don't worry if you can't find the trail—the open meadow between the campsite and the river makes it unnecessary.) Once you reach the riverbank, look for a side channel that cuts off a small, grassy island from the rest of the river. Two or three hot springs seeps are located along the north bank of the 100-yard-long side channel.

The hot springs: Although they aren't the warmest soaks available in Yellowstone, the Madison Campground Warm Springs provide a nice place to relax when the air temperature is mild. The river channel itself makes for an enjoyable summer day soak, but most bathers prefer sitting as close as possible to the seeps for hotter temperatures. The thermal water bubbles out of the banks at around 100 degrees F, and the cold water of the Madison River keeps the soak-

Family fun at Madison Campground Warm Springs.
PHOTO COURTESY OF JESSIE O'CONNER, JACKSON HOLE CHAMBER OF COMMERCE.

ing area a bit cooler (between 80 and 90 degrees F). Like all thermal areas in Yellowstone, it's illegal to dig deeper pools in the river channel or to dam the natural flow of hot water with river rocks. Respect these restrictions and enjoy the water in its natural state.

A few hundred yards to the southeast, on the opposite side of the Madison River, is the spot where the idea for America's first national park was conceived. On September 19, 1870, a group of explorers were camped in the meadow below what is now called National Park Mountain. Struck by the beauty of the surrounding area, the men decided that the wild territory was too unique to be developed by private interests. They pledged themselves to promote the idea of a national preserve for the benefit and enjoyment of all Americans. Nathaniel Langford, one of the men sitting around the campfire that evening, traveled to the East Coast to promote the idea, and when Yellowstone National Park became a reality in 1872, Langford was appointed the first superintendent of the park. National Park Mountain, which rises over the Madison River just south of the warm springs, was named in honor of the historic campfire discussion that sparked the idea to preserve this land for generations to come.

33

Firehole River Swimming Area

General description: An old-fashioned swimming hole warmed by the runoff from distant hot springs and geysers.

Location: Northwest Wyoming, 2 miles from Madison Junction on Firehole Canyon Drive in Yellowstone National Park.

Primitive/developed: Primitive.

Best time of year: The swimming area is open from May to October. Firehole Canyon Drive, as well as most of the other roads in Yellowstone, are closed in the winter. Warmer days in the summer are best for swimming, because the water in the Firehole River Swimming Area averages 80 degrees F.

Restrictions: No pets or glass containers are allowed. In the 1960s and 1970s, diving off 80-foot cliffs into the deep pools of the Firehole River was popular, but cliff diving is now prohibited. Swimsuits seem to be the norm.

Access: Any vehicle can make the trip.

Water temperature: The swimming areas of the pools and adjacent Firehole River average 80 degrees F.

Nearby attractions: Madison Campground Warm Springs, Lower Geyser Basin, Norris Geyser Basin.

Services: Gas, food, and lodging are available in West Yellowstone, Montana, 16 miles west, and at Old Faithful, 14 miles south.
Camping: Madison Campground is located about 3 miles northwest of the Firehole River Swimming Area.
Map: Trails Illustrated (Yellowstone National Park).

Finding the springs: Drive to Madison Junction, 14 miles east of the West Entrance to Yellowstone. Turn south on the road to Old Faithful, and then almost immediately turn west onto Firehole Canyon Drive. Drive about 1.5 miles south, paralleling the Firehole River, until you see the signs and parking area for the Firehole River Swimming Area. Park your car and descend the steep stairway to the swimming hole in the river below.

The hot springs: The Firehole River Swimming Area has long been a popular summer recreation spot for visitors to Yellowstone, especially on those few days in July and August when the air temperature pushes over 90 degrees F. The tall cliffs along the Firehole River surround a deep warm water pool between swift-flowing rapids. Some bathers enter the current above and float down into the calm water of the pool. The hills surrounding the swimming area are covered with the burned skeletons of lodgepole pine trees, mute evidence of the fires that swept through Yellowstone in the summer of 1988.

Heed the Park Service restrictions at Firehole River Swimming Area.

History: The famous explorer Jim Bridger was partially responsible for naming the Firehole River. Bridger was known for his tall tales about the Yellowstone region, and a classic example is his explanation of why there is warm water in the Firehole River. Captain William F. Raynolds, who documented some of Bridger's tales, recounted Bridger's story in his 1868 report to the U.S. Congress. Bridger told Raynolds that water in the Firehole River "flowed so fast down the side of the hill that the friction of the water against the rocks, heated the rocks."

BACKCOUNTRY SOAKS

Yellowstone National Park offers some marvelous soaking opportunities near major roads and is also home to some great thermal bathing areas far from the recreational vehicle crowd. Some of these backcountry hot pots are well-known to hot springs aficionados, but there are also some spots that are known only to those who have personally explored Yellowstone's most isolated areas. Longtime park employees sometimes whisper of perfect hot soaking spots deep in the heart of Yellowstone, but they usually keep the details to themselves, much like old prospectors hiding knowledge of their latest gold strike.

Visiting the backcountry soaking areas in Yellowstone requires careful preparation and an understanding of the park's unique hiking and camping regulations. You can't just hop out of your car and meander down a gentle trail to most of these backcountry springs. Yellowstone is wild country, and hiking

A Yellowstone native enjoys a soak in a backcountry pool.
PHOTO COURTESY OF GALLATIN COUNTY HISTORICAL SOCIETY.

and camping here demand awareness of the special conditions you may encounter. Yellowstone's wild country is home to unmarked thermal areas, grizzly bears, rapidly changing weather conditions, and other natural phenomena. Overnight camping in Yellowstone also requires a special backcountry permit that will assign you to a designated site.

To prepare yourself for backcountry travel in Yellowstone, refer to Bill Schneider's *Hiking Yellowstone National Park* (Falcon Press, 1997). It contains comprehensive information on hiking and camping in Yellowstone's bear country, as well as detailed maps and descriptions of over 100 hikes, including those that lead to most of the backcountry soaks described below.

Park regulations prohibit soaking in undiluted thermal water, and that includes hot springs in the backcountry. As tempting as a hot pool may appear in an isolated Yellowstone setting, it's illegal to soak in any pool or runoff channel that isn't mixing with a natural cold water source such as a river or creek. Before starting your trip be sure to check with the Backcountry Office to see if there are any special soaking restrictions in the area you intend to visit, as backcountry closures may occur at any time. (Contact the Yellowstone National Park Backcountry Office by dialing 307-344-2160 or 307-344-2163.)

An in-depth discussion of all of Yellowstone's backcountry soaking areas is beyond the scope of this touring guide. There is also something to be said for keeping a few backcountry soaking areas unadvertised, leaving them to be discovered by modern-day Jim Bridgers. What follows are brief descriptions of a few of the most well-known, a starter set to begin your own explorations of Yellowstone's backcountry soaking opportunities.

34

Ferris Fork Hot Springs

This is the most popular backcountry soaking area in Yellowstone, and with good reason. Located near Three River Junction on the Bechler River Trail in the southwest corner of the park, this soaking area usually requires a two-day hike just to reach it. Hikers can either take the Bechler River Trail northeast from the Bechler River Ranger Station or head southwest from the Lone Star Trailhead 3.5 miles east of Old Faithful. Ferris Fork Hot Springs is midway along the trail, so it's about 15 miles from either trailhead to reach the soaking area. Make sure you're well prepared for the long hike, and obtain your campsite assignments from the Backcountry Office before you head for the trail.

Ferris Fork Hot Springs, also known as Ferris Pool, is a truly amazing thermal phenomenon. The hot springs is located in the center of the river and erupts with such force that it forms a dome of hot water a foot higher than the normal river level. The river, usually about 4 feet deep, forms a 40-foot-diameter pool around the hot springs. Thermal runoff enters the pool from other nearby springs as well. The pool's temperature is determined by the amount of cold river water in the mix, and the temperature may vary within a few feet from a brisk 40 degrees F to over 100 degrees F. During some very dry years when river levels are low, there may not be enough cold water in the mix to keep Ferris Pool at a tolerable soaking temperature. Swimsuits tend to be the exception rather than the rule here.

Overnight campers may be tempted to hike in the evening from their campsites to Ferris Pool for a nighttime soak, but park officials strongly discourage this. There are several very hot thermal springs near the hiking trail to Ferris Pool, and a wrong step in the dark could mean serious trouble, especially given the distance to medical assistance.

35

Witch Creek

Witch Creek is heated by the runoff water from numerous hot springs along its banks. Witch Creek is located along the trail to Heart Lake. To reach the trailhead, drive 5.2 miles south of Grant Village Junction to the Heart Lake Trail parking area on the east side of the road. It's about an 8-mile hike from the trailhead to Heart Lake. The last 3 miles of the trail follow Witch Creek, which empties into the lake. There are some warm water channels in Witch Creek about 1 mile north of Heart Lake where the cold creek water mixes with the runoff from nearby hot springs. A fact sheet issued by park officials in 1983 described an incident in which a bather at Witch Creek was "covered with painful welts from a warmwater larva." As with all thermal bathing in Yellowstone, you assume your own risks when you soak in Witch Creek.

36

Shoshone Creek and Shoshone Geyser Basin

The scenic hiking trail along Shoshone Creek provides access to several thermal soaking areas in Shoshone Geyser Basin. To reach the trail, drive east of Old Faithful for 3.5 miles to the Lone Star Trailhead. It's a long 9-mile hike to the Shoshone Geyser Basin, so be sure to get your backcountry camping permits and assigned campsite ahead of time. There are many unmarked thermal springs and geysers in this area and few established trails. What appears to be solid ground can actually be a thin crust over extremely hot water, so use great caution if you decide to soak along the creek.

37

Violet Creek

This thermally heated creek is located on the Mary Mountain Trail at the northwestern edge of the Hayden Valley. Reach the trailhead by driving 11.6 miles north of Fishing Bridge Junction. A hike of 4 miles brings you to mile-long Violet Creek. Hot springs scattered along the banks of the waterway create a number of warm pools in the creek. Be extremely careful where you walk, as there are some very hot thermal areas on the banks of Violet Creek. The Hayden Valley is prime grizzly bear country, and overnight camping is not allowed. Visitors must plan to either hike back to their cars or continue another 16 miles to the west trailhead of the Mary Mountain Trail on the road to Old Faithful.

OTHER BACKCOUNTRY SOAKS

A number of other locations deep in the heart of Yellowstone may offer nice thermal soaks, but you'll have to explore these for yourself to see if there's any truth to the rumors. Areas with good soaking potential include Dunanda Falls, Union Falls, Silver Scarf Creek, Mountain Ash Creek, and Snake River Hot Springs. Even if you don't discover a mix of thermal and cold water appropriate for bathing, you'll always return with great memories of hiking in this unique preserve of geothermal wonders.

NORTHWEST WYOMING (OUTSIDE YELLOWSTONE)

Best known for Yellowstone National Park, northwest Wyoming also contains many less frequently visited but equally spectacular scenic areas, including the Wind River Mountain Range and the Wind River Indian Reservation. The Targhee, Bridger-Teton, and Shoshone national forests border Yellowstone National Park, and the Bighorn National Forest lies just west of Sheridan. Northwest Wyoming echoes with the footsteps of explorers, fur trappers, and cowboys, including John Colter, the Astorians, and Buffalo Bill Cody.

Although Yellowstone contains the vast majority of northwest Wyoming's hot springs, there are over a dozen other thermal spots in the area. Hot Springs State Park near Thermopolis is the most well-known. DeMaris Hot Springs near Cody, Chief Washakie Plunge on the Wind River Reservation, and the several hot springs south of Jackson Hole are also popular soaking spots.

38

Huckleberry–Polecat Hot Springs

General description: A beautiful series of hot springs pools located in a mountain meadow 2 miles south of Yellowstone National Park. Unfortunately, high radiation levels and the presence of potentially deadly amoebae in the water make soaking inadvisable.

Location: Northwest Wyoming, between Yellowstone and Grand Teton national parks.

Primitive/developed: Primitive.

Best time of year: Late summer and fall are best for taking the short hike and fording Polecat Creek, although the hot springs are visited year-round. Mosquitoes can be a problem in early summer. The trail is a favorite cross-country ski trip from nearby Flagg Ranch.

Restrictions: None, but the National Park Service strongly advises against bathing in the hot springs because of the radioactive water and the presence of a deadly microorganism.

Access: Any vehicle can make the trip to the trailhead.

Water temperature: 130 degrees F at the springs; 100 to 110 degrees F in the various pools and the waterfall.

Nearby attractions: Yellowstone National Park, Grand Teton National Park, Snake River, Bridger-Teton National Forest.

Services: None. The nearest gas, food, and lodging are available at the Flagg Ranch Resort, 2 miles east of the hot springs.

Camping: RV and tent camping is available at the Flagg Ranch Resort Campground. Lizard Creek Campground is located 9 miles south of Flagg Ranch on the shore of Jackson Lake. Camping is also allowed near the hot springs, but you must camp at least 200 yards away from any water source.

Map: USGS Flagg Ranch WY.

Finding the springs: From the south entrance of Yellowstone National Park, drive 2 miles south on the John D. Rockefeller Memorial Parkway (U.S. Highway 89/191/287). Turn west at Flagg Ranch/Grassy Lake. From the town of Jackson, drive north for 55 miles on US 89/191/287 to the Flagg Ranch/Grassy Lake turnoff.

At the Flagg Ranch headquarters, turn north for 0.5 mile, and then follow Grassy Lake Road west for 1 mile. About 50 yards after crossing a small bridge, park your car on the north side of the road. Nearby you'll see an abandoned road blocked off with a "No Vehicles" sign. Walk north along the abandoned road until you reach Polecat Creek (about 0.4 mile). You now

Hot waterfall at Huckleberry Hot Springs.

Huckleberry–Polecat Hot Springs

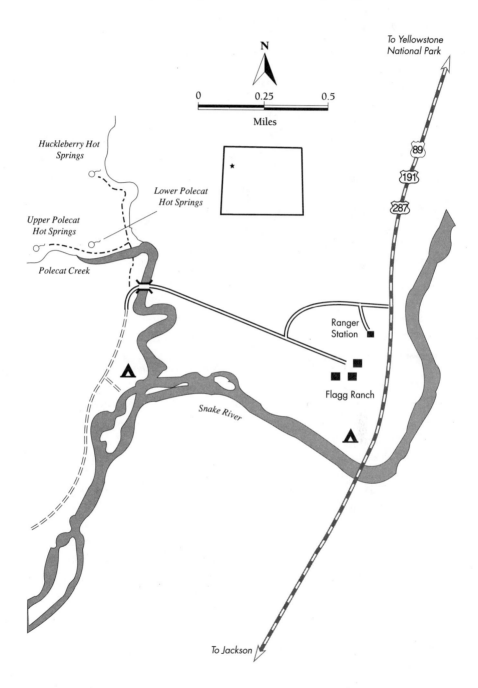

Lower Polecat Hot Springs.

have to ford Polecat Creek. The ford is usually not difficult, but high water in the spring might warrant extra caution when crossing. (A bridge at one time spanned the creek but was removed in the 1960s when the commercial swimming pool at Huckleberry Hot Springs was abandoned.)

Immediately after crossing the creek, find a trail that veers away from the road and heads west (left) along the north bank of Polecat Creek. Follow this trail for about 200 yards to Lower Polecat Hot Springs. Continue upstream along the banks of Polecat Creek for another 0.25 mile until the creek curves to the south. Near some pine trees you'll see Upper Polecat Hot Springs in a marshy area on the edge of the creek.

Huckleberry Hot Springs is a bit easier to find. Instead of turning west on the trail to Polecat Hot Springs after you ford Polecat Creek, continue north along the abandoned road for another 200 yards. The road eventually diminishes into a trail that parallels a small creek formed by runoff from the several pools and springs that make up Huckleberry Hot Springs. The water in the creek increases in temperature as you move upstream until you reach the steaming pools and waterfall.

The hot springs: Upper and Lower Polecat springs are both situated on the north side of Polecat Creek, with fabulous views of a high mountain meadow stretching to the south toward Jackson Lake and the Grand Tetons. Lower Polecat Hot Springs consists of a couple of warm pools about 6 feet across, formed by makeshift dams across the warm water flowing from a hillside into Polecat Creek. Water temperature is around 105 degrees F. Upper Polecat Hot Springs, a short walk farther along Polecat Creek, consists of a series of seeps in a marshy area next to the creek. Temperature here is also around 105 degrees F.

The hot water pools of Huckleberry Hot Springs lie along a small creekbed about 0.5 mile north of Polecat Hot Springs. Hot water flows from a 130-degree-F pool over an 8-foot-ledge into a series of pools in the creekbed below. Other hot pools lie above the waterfall in the creekbed.

Due in part to their proximity to the highway, Huckleberry and Polecat hot springs are very popular for soaking. Some holiday weekends in the winter will find several dozen soakers vying for space in the pools below the waterfall. Nude bathing tends to be the rule rather than the exception.

CAUTION: In spite of their popularity, Huckleberry and Polecat hot springs are unsafe for soaking. In addition to high radiation levels, the hot springs water contains amoebae that can cause death within ten days of infecting a bather. Microscopic amoebae (*Naegleria fowleri*) thrive in stagnant thermal pools with temperatures between 104 and 108 degrees F. Such pools are common on the plateau above the Huckleberry Hot Springs creekbed and Polecat Creek, and researchers from the University of Wyoming are fairly certain that the dangerous amoebae are found in the area (check the Flagg Ranch Campground for a fact sheet on the amoebae research). If *Naegleria fowleri* amoebae get into the nasal passages of an unfortunate bather, they can eventually work their way into the brain, where they can cause primary amoebic meningoencephalitis (PAM), a severe inflammation of brain tissues that can lead to death.

Although there have been no known fatalities from the amoebae in Wyoming or Montana, a hot springs bather did die in 1986 of an amoebic infection contracted from a hot springs near the Arizona-New Mexico border, and four others died that same year from amoebae they encountered in stagnant warm water ponds in Louisiana and Georgia. The same kind of amoebae have also been found in the famous hot springs pools built by the Romans in Bath, England, where, in the late 1970s, a bather died after becoming infected.

If lethal amoebae weren't reason enough to avoid soaking here, the high radiation level of the water should give soakers pause. Radiation measured at the waterfall at Huckleberry Hot Springs is 10 to 100 times higher than normal background levels, and prolonged exposure to the radioactive water is not recommended.

While bathing is not prohibited, the National Park Service strongly advises against soaking in these hot springs. If you decide to soak anyway, at least keep your head above water at all times, and avoid getting water droplets into your eyes and nose. But given the other great hot springs south of nearby Jackson, it's just not worth the risk to soak in Huckleberry or Polecat. Think of these hot springs as a fine destination for a day hike to enjoy spectacular views and to see—but not sample—the steaming water.

History: No known development of Huckleberry or Polecat hot springs occurred until 1962, when Slim Linville and John and Jess Wort were granted permission to construct a commercial swimming pool at Huckleberry Hot Springs. The trio built a 40-foot by 80-foot outdoor pool along with a trailer park, campground, picnic area, laundromat, and a general store that advertised, among other things, elk horn souvenirs. The little resort was quite popular but was closed in 1983 when the National Park Service decided to let the area revert to its natural state. Park Service personnel bulldozed the pool and buildings and removed the Polecat Creek bridge. Today nothing remains of the old resort.

39

Kelly Warm Springs

General description: A large warm pool, perfect for summer swims, located in Jackson Hole in the shadow of the Grand Tetons.
Location: Northwest Wyoming, 18 miles north of Jackson.
Primitive/developed: Primitive, with an adjacent parking lot.
Best time of year: Summer and fall. The relatively cool water temperature is best for soaking and swimming on warmer days.
Restrictions: None.
Access: Any vehicle can make the trip.
Water temperature: 81 degrees F.
Nearby attractions: Grand Teton National Park, Teton Wilderness, Bridger-Teton National Forest.
Services: None at the springs. A general store 1.5 miles south of the springs offers a modest selection of goods. Gas, food, and lodging are available in Jackson, 18 miles south.
Camping: The Gros Ventre Campground is located west of Kelly in Grand Teton National Park. Red Hills, Crystal Creek, and Atherton Creek Forest

Service campgrounds are located east of Kelly Hot Springs on Forest Service Road 30400, above Lower Slide Lake.

Map: Wyoming State Highways map.

Finding the springs: From Jackson, drive north 10 miles on U.S. Highway 26/89/191 to the Gros Ventre Junction. Turn east and drive 6 miles to the little town of Kelly. Turn north at Kelly, and drive 1.1 miles north to the turnoff to Gros Ventre Road (Forest Service Road 30400). Turn east onto Gros Ventre Road for 0.4 mile to the parking lot and warm springs.

The hot springs: Although not a particularly hot soak or swim, Kelly Warm Springs is perfect for those blue-sky summer days when the Grand Tetons shimmer on the horizon. The large gravel-lined pool is more than 100 yards long and 50 yards wide, varying in depth from 1 to 8 feet. Numerous springs bubble on the edges of the pool, keeping the water at a constant 81 degrees F. The warm pool is a favorite hangout for kayakers practicing their paddling techniques.

History: The peaceful town of Kelly and the meandering Gros Ventre River that passes near the warm springs are in stark contrast to the geologic cataclysm and subsequent human tragedies that befell the area in the 1920s. Heavy rain had fallen for several days in June 1925, saturating the ground. Without warning on the morning of June 23, a huge section of earth more than 1 mile long

Kelly Warm Springs, with the Grand Tetons in the distance.

Kelly Warm Springs

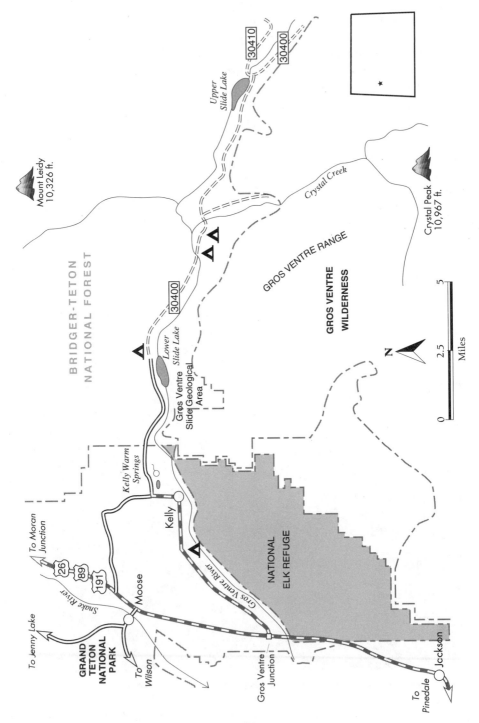

and 0.5 mile wide slid down a mountainside into the canyon of the Gros Ventre River just east of Kelly Warm Springs. Fifty million cubic yards of earth formed a dam more than 250 feet high. The swollen Gros Ventre River pooled behind the natural dam, eventually forming a lake more than 7 miles long; although the rising lake flooded several homesteads, no lives were lost.

Residents of the town of Kelly, which stood a few miles downstream from the new lake, worried that the earthen dam could break as the waters continued to rise. State geologists tested the dam's integrity and assured the residents of Kelly that the dam was secure. The lake behind the dam was renamed Slide Lake, and it became a popular tourist attraction during the two years following the landslide.

Unfortunately the assurances that the dam was safe proved to be tragically wrong. On June 13, 1927, water broke through the dam, sending an 8-foot wall of water, rocks, and mud racing toward the town of Kelly. A Forest Service ranger who had witnessed the dam breaking galloped on horseback to warn the Kelly townsfolk. Most of the people ran to higher ground before the flood hit the town, but six people drowned when they tarried too long trying to pack a few valuables before leaving their homes. Today all that remains of the town of Kelly are a few residential buildings and a general store, which is a good place to stop for a soda after soaking in the warm springs and contemplating the ways of nature and of man.

40

Astoria Hot Springs

General description: A scenic, family-oriented RV and tent campground with two hot springs pools, located on the banks of the Snake River near Jackson Hole.

Location: Northwest Wyoming, 17 miles southwest of Jackson.

Primitive/developed: Developed.

Best time of year: Late spring and summer. The resort opens in mid-May and closes in early October.

Restrictions: Astoria Hot Springs is privately owned. The pools are available to overnight campers and, for a fee, to day visitors.

Access: Any vehicle can make the trip.

Water temperature: 104 degrees F at the springs; 90 to 95 degrees F in the swimming and wading pools.

Nearby attractions: Grand Teton National Park, Granite Hot Springs, Bridger-Teton National Forest, Gros Ventre Wilderness.

Services: A snack bar is available at the resort. Gas, food, and lodging are available at Hoback Junction, 3 miles east, or Jackson, 17 miles north.
Camping: Over 100 RV and tent camping sites are available at the resort. The RV sites have full or partial hookups. The secluded tent camping sites are located in cottonwood groves on the bank of the Snake River. Additional camping is available at several Forest Service campsites east of the hot springs along U.S. Highway 26/89.
Map: Wyoming State Highways map.

Finding the springs: From Jackson drive 14 miles south on U.S. Highway 26/89/191 to Hoback Junction. Turn west at Hoback Junction onto US 26/89. Astoria Hot Springs is located 3 miles west of Hoback Junction on the opposite side of the Snake River from the highway. Look for a bright blue bridge crossing the river; a sign atop the bridge is emblazoned with "Astoria Hot Springs" in red letters on a white background. Turn onto the bridge and cross the Snake River. The hot springs are about 200 yards past the bridge. If you are coming from the west, Astoria Hot Springs is located about 20 miles east of Alpine on US 26/89. You'll see the bridge just after you exit the narrow gorge known as "The Grand Canyon of the Snake River."

The hot springs: Located at 6,100 feet, Astoria Hot Springs offers great swimming and camping for summer visitors on their way to Grand Teton or

Astoria Hot Springs.

Astoria Hot Springs

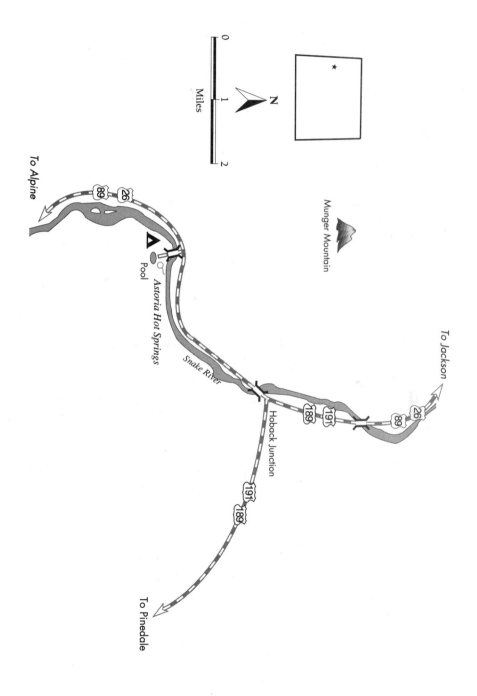

Yellowstone national parks. The 40-foot by 80-foot outdoor pool varies in depth from 2 to 8 feet and is kept at a comfortable 90 to 95 degrees F. An adjacent triangular "kiddie pool" is 12 to 18 inches deep, and is the same temperature as the bigger pool. A narrow building nearby contains eight small rooms with private soaking tubs, but they have been closed for several years.

In addition to excellent camping facilities available at the resort, there are a number of day-use activities including volleyball, horseshoes, a playground, and a picnic area. Mountain biking, hiking, fishing, and rafting are all available on the nearby Snake River or in the surrounding mountains.

History: Astoria Hot Springs derives its name from the Astor Expedition of 1811, the first transcontinental party to venture westward after Lewis and Clark's journey six years earlier. John Jacob Astor, founder of the American Fur Company, sent 61 men and 118 horses west from St. Louis with orders to establish a trading post at the mouth of the Columbia River. The "Astorians," as the men of the expedition came to be known, took a more southerly route than Lewis and Clark to avoid hostile bands of warriors reported in the Upper Missouri River country. In September 1811 the Astorians reached Hoback Junction, 3 miles east of Astoria Hot Springs. Here they turned north through Jackson Hole and crossed Teton Pass on their way to the Pacific Ocean.

It's unknown whether any of the Astorians actually saw Astoria Hot Springs. A description of the springs was not put down on paper until the spring of 1871, when a member of the Hayden survey party that had been exploring Yellowstone National Park wrote of "a small cluster [of springs] which escapes among the gravel on the south side [of the Snake River]." In 1886 a survey of mineral water resources in the United States reported that nearby residents would arrive at the springs by horseback and bathe in the warm water to treat rheumatism.

Although visitors used a small log bathhouse at Astoria Hot Springs in the early 1900s, the springs remained relatively undeveloped until the late 1960s, when the present resort was built.

41

Granite Hot Springs

General description: A picturesque soaking pool located at an elevation of 7,000 feet in the Gros Ventre Mountains. The hot springs are increasingly popular with winter visitors.

Location: Northwest Wyoming, 35 miles southeast of Jackson.

Primitive/developed: Developed.

Best time of year: Summer and fall for those in cars and RVs, winter for those willing to ski, snowmobile, or mush on a dogsled.

Restrictions: A full-time caretaker maintains the pool. There is an admission fee. Pool hours are 10:00 A.M. until dusk, which can range from 4:00 P.M. to 9:00 P.M., depending on the time of year. Swimsuits are required.

Access: Any passenger vehicle can make the trip in the summer and early fall. The last 10 miles, a gravel Forest Service road from the highway, is closed by snow in the winter, and travel is limited to dogsleds, snowmobiles, and cross-country skis. The road and hot springs pool are usually closed for a week or two in the fall when the snow isn't yet deep enough for skiing, snowmobiling, or mushing. The road and hot springs may also be closed for a week or two in the springtime when snowmelt makes the road too muddy for travel.

Water temperature: The pool temperature varies depending on the season. In the springtime, cold water from the more than 400 inches of yearly snowfall percolates into the ground to mix with the hot springs water. At the height of snowmelt, the temperature in the pool may dip to the mid-80s F. The pool temperature steadily increases after the snowmelt has ceased, reaching a peak of 110 to 112 degrees F by midwinter, perfect for cold weather soaks.

Nearby attractions: Bridger-Teton National Forest, Jackson Hole Ski Resort, Grand Teton National Park, Snake River, Astoria Hot Springs.

Services: There are no services at the hot springs. Gas, food, and lodging are available at Hoback Junction, 23 miles to the southwest.

Camping: Granite Creek Campground is 0.7 mile south of Granite Hot Springs. The area is known grizzly bear habitat, so be sure to take proper precautions with food.

Map: Wyoming State Highways map.

Finding the springs: From Jackson, head south for 12 miles on U.S. Highway 26/89/189/191 to Hoback Junction. Turn east onto Wyoming Highway 189/191, and follow the Hoback River for 13 miles to the turnoff to the Granite Recreation Area (Forest Service Road 30500). Turn north on the Forest Service

Granite Hot Springs

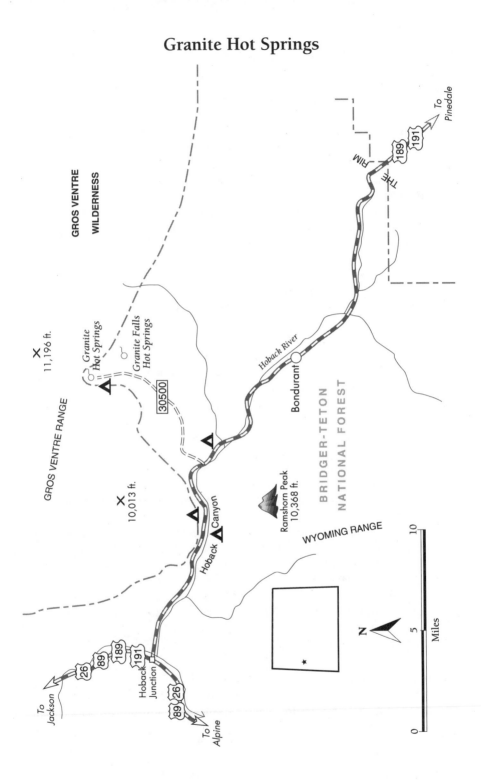

GROS VENTRE
WILDERNESS

GROS VENTRE RANGE

× 11,196 ft.

Granite Hot Springs

Granite Falls Hot Springs

30500

× 10,013 ft.

Hoback Canyon

Hoback River

Bondurant

Ramshorn Peak
10,368 ft.

WYOMING RANGE

BRIDGER-TETON
NATIONAL FOREST

THE RIM

189 191

To Pinedale

26 89 189 191

Hoback Junction

89 26

To Jackson

To Alpine

N

0   5   10
Miles

road as it parallels Granite Creek, and follow it for 10 miles to Granite Hot Springs.

The hot springs: Tucked into a pristine valley in the Gros Ventre Mountains, the warm water pool at Granite Hot Springs offers one of the most picturesque soaks in the Rocky Mountains. The west side of the 45-foot by 75-foot pool juts up against large granite boulders often covered with snowdrifts in the winter. Bathers have great views to the east and south down the Granite Creek Valley. The pool depth varies from 2 to 3 feet at the shallow end to almost 8 feet at the deeper end. The changing house, a spartan log cabin, is located 50 yards north of the pool; after soaking, wintertime bathers will have a bracing dash back to their clothes.

History: Fur trappers probably visited the hot springs as early as the 1820s. Fur-bearing animals were plentiful in Granite Creek, and you can still see beaver dams on your drive up the canyon. Early settlers built a rough dirt road to the springs and dug a pool to collect the hot water for bathing.

In 1935 the Civilian Conservation Corps constructed the present swimming pool, the nearby campground, and the gravel road leading to the highway. From 1935 until the early 1950s the pool was popular during summer months but received only an occasional winter visitor.

Granite Hot Springs.

Rampant algae growth in the early years of the warm water pool was recalled in an untitled 1981 history of Granite Hot Springs written by Dr. Donald MacLeod: "Algae had accumulated in a mat 4 to 6 inches thick over the entire pool, and swimmers used to roll it up like a carpet and push it over the outlet." In 1951 the pool was painted with algae-resistant paint, greatly reducing the problem.

During the 1960s Granite Hot Springs was largely unsupervised. Problems arose as the pool's popularity increased, culminating in three alcohol-related deaths of soakers who trespassed into the hot springs late at night. The Forest Service clamped down on use of the pool, hired a full-time caretaker, and enforced a nighttime curfew.

Winter use of Granite Hot Springs increased during the 1970s, and today the pool is almost as popular in the winter as it is in the summer. Several outfitters around Jackson provide snowmobile and cross-country ski trips to Granite Hot Springs, and dogsled treks are also becoming popular. Since the winter temperature of the pool can exceed 110 degrees F, those hardy enough to brave the 10-mile trek up the snowy access road are rewarded with one of the steamiest and most scenic soaks in Wyoming.

42

Granite Falls Hot Springs

(See map on page 166)

General description: Several shallow soaking pools and a hot waterfall located just below beautiful Granite Falls in the Gros Ventre Mountains. Hard-core soaking enthusiasts can combine a morning of steamy immersion in the primitive Granite Falls hot pools with an afternoon of bliss in the more developed Granite Hot Springs pool 0.5 mile to the north.
Location: Northwest Wyoming, 35 miles southeast of Jackson.
Primitive/developed: Primitive.
Best time of year: Summer and fall for those with cars and RVs; winter for those willing to ski, snowmobile, or mush on a dogsled. In springtime, the soaking pools are washed out by the high waters of Granite Creek.
Restrictions: None. Swimsuits are optional.
Access: Any passenger vehicle can make the trip in the summer and early fall. The last 10 miles, a gravel Forest Service road from the highway, are closed by snow in the winter and travel is limited to dogsleds, snowmobiles, and cross-country skis.

Water temperature: 120 to 130 degrees F in the hot waterfall; 95 to 115 degrees F in the soaking pools.

Nearby attractions: Granite Hot Springs, Bridger-Teton National Forest, Jackson Hole Ski Resort, Grand Teton National Park, Snake River, Astoria Hot Springs.

Services: There are no services at the hot springs. Gas, food, and lodging are available at Hoback Junction, 23 miles to the southwest.

Camping: Granite Creek Campground is 0.5 mile south of Granite Falls Hot Springs. The area is known grizzly bear habitat, so be sure to take proper precautions with food.

Maps: Wyoming State Highways map, USGS Granite Falls WY.

Finding the springs: From Jackson, head south for 12 miles on U.S. Highway 26/89/189/191 to Hoback Junction. Turn east onto US Highway 189/191, and then parallel the Hoback River for 13 miles to the turnoff to the Granite Recreation Area (Forest Service Road 30500). Turn north on the Forest Service road as it parallels Granite Creek, and follow it for 9 miles to Granite Creek Campground.

Continue on the gravel road for another 0.5 mile until you see the sizable waterfall on Granite Creek. Take the dirt road that forks to the east toward the creek, then park your car just below the falls. The rock-lined pools of Granite Falls Hot Springs are on the opposite side of Granite Creek, about 50 yards downstream from Granite Falls. If the water level is low enough, you can ford

Granite Falls Hot Springs.

Granite Creek to the hot springs, but be cautious of the swift current even at low water levels. It's probably safer in all seasons to drive 0.5 mile farther north on the gravel road to the Granite Hot Springs pool, then take the hiking trail just beyond the pool that leads back to Granite Falls Hot Springs. The trail is fairly level as it follows the east bank of Granite Creek past Granite Creek Falls, then it descends sharply to the hot springs.

The hot springs: The cold waters of Granite Creek cascade directly over one of the largest fault lines in the entire Rocky Mountain region, forming the breathtaking Granite Falls. Stretching for more than 50 miles from east to west, the Cache Creek Fault caused a tremendous upthrust of the surrounding rock layers millions of years ago, forming the entire Gros Ventre mountain range. Shifting of the fault created subterranean fractures in the rock strata that allow surface water to circulate and heat deep in the earth. This heated water returns to the surface along other cracks, creating both Granite Falls Hot Springs and the Granite Hot Springs pool, which lies just upstream from the falls.

Granite Falls Hot Springs consists of a 125-degree-F seep that emerges from a crack in the rock wall about 20 feet above the creekbed. Thermal water flows from the seep into a shallow pool next to the creek, but this pool may be too hot for soaking. A few yards upstream on Granite Creek are two other soaking pools, both rendered a more comfortable 95 to 110 degrees F by the diversion of cold water from Granite Creek to mix with the thermal water. All of the soaking pools are flooded during the high spring runoff from Granite Creek, and in very wet years the pools may be unusable until late summer or fall.

43

Kendall Warm Springs

General description: A series of springs that flows a mere thousand feet before tumbling over a travertine ledge into the Green River. The creek is home to an endangered species of fish found nowhere except in this warm water creek.

Location: Northwest Wyoming, about 31 miles northwest of Pinedale, near the headwaters of the Green River in the Wind River Range.

Primitive/developed: Primitive.

Best time of year: Summer and fall. Snow may close portions of the road during the winter.

Restrictions: The warm springs and creek are closed to bathing and wading to protect the population of endangered fish.

Access: The asphalt and gravel roads leading to the warm springs are accessible to most passenger vehicles. The road beyond Kendall Warm Springs becomes more rutted as it makes its way to Green River Lakes and the Wind River Range but is passable until closed by the winter snows.

Water temperature: 85 degrees F, gradually decreasing in the creek to 81 degrees F where it enters the Green River.

Nearby attractions: Wind River Mountains, Bridger-Teton National Forest, Green River, Green River Lakes.

Services: None. The nearest gas, food, and lodging are available in Pinedale, 31 miles to the southeast.

Camping: Whiskey Grove Campground is located 2 miles south of Kendall Warm Springs. Green River Lakes Campground, located at the headwaters of the Green River in the beautiful Wind River Mountains, is located 14 miles north of Kendall Warm Springs on Forest Service Road 10091.

Map: Wyoming State Highways map.

Finding the springs: From Pinedale, drive 5 miles west on U.S. Highway 191 to Wyoming Highway 352. Go north on WY 352 for 24 miles until the pavement ends. Continue north on the gravel road (Forest Service Road 10091) for 4.3 miles until you cross a bridge over a small creek, the runoff from Kendall Warm Springs. Leave your vehicle in the small parking lot and walk upstream on the north side of the creek to see the springs emerging from the hillside. A couple of interpretive signs explain the story of the fish known as the Kendall

Kendall Warm Springs plunges over a travertine ledge into the Green River.

Kendall Warm Springs

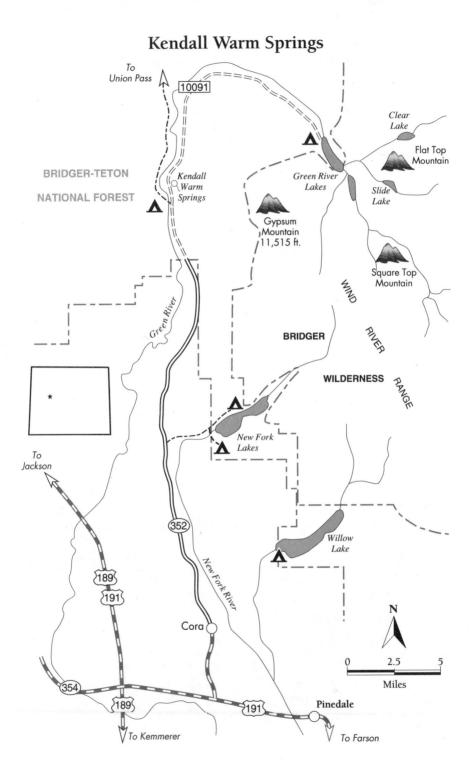

To Union Pass

10091

Clear Lake

Flat Top Mountain

Green River Lakes

Slide Lake

BRIDGER-TETON

NATIONAL FOREST

Kendall Warm Springs

Gypsum Mountain 11,515 ft.

Square Top Mountain

WIND

RIVER

RANGE

BRIDGER

WILDERNESS

Green River

New Fork Lakes

To Jackson

Willow Lake

189
191

352

New Fork River

Cora

N

0   2.5   5
Miles

354

189

191   Pinedale

To Kemmerer

To Farson

Warm Springs dace. Follow the creek downstream, and cross the gravel road to see the limestone ledge and the warm waterfall pouring into the Green River.

The hot springs: Kendall Warm Springs is a unique geological and biological habitat. Several springs emerge from the north face of a limestone hillside. The springs consolidate in two pools and then form a creek that flows 984 feet to the Green River. Just before entering the river the creek passes over a 10-foot-high travertine ledge, formed over thousands of years by the deposition of calcium carbonate from the warm springs.

The temperature of the springs at their source is a constant 85 degrees F, but the water cools to 81 degrees F by the time it enters the Green River. The surrounding air temperature at this 7,840-foot elevation varies significantly, ranging from a record high of 103 degrees F to a bone-numbing record low of minus 54 degrees F.

The springs are the only known habitat of the small fish called the Kendall Warm Springs dace, *Rhinichthys osculus thermalis*. The dace, only 1 to 2 inches long, were confined to the small creek when a travertine ledge slowly rose between the creek and the Green River. The ledge prevented the movement of dace from the Green River into Kendall Warm Springs Creek. Over thousands of years the dace evolved in isolation and are now considered a separate subspecies from the dace found in the nearby Green River (*Rhinichthys osculus yarrowi*). Kendall Warm Springs dace spawn in the warm water year-round, whereas the dace in the colder waters of the Green River spawn only twice a year.

Hungry trout wait in the Green River at the base of the ledge to catch any Kendall Warm Springs dace unlucky enough to be swept over the ledge from their warm water sanctuary.

History: Kendall Warm Springs has a long history of use for bathing, wading, and watering livestock. In 1934, a Forest Service ranger discovered the Kendall Warm Springs dace, but no particular importance was noted about its unique habitat. Three years after the discovery of the dace, members of the Civilian Conservation Corps dug a pool in the creek for use by work crews in the area. In the 1950s and 1960s, bathing and soaking in the creek were popular, and Forest Service rangers reported finding soap bars, shampoo bottles, and beer bottles in the warm waters.

Government officials eventually recognized the fragile nature of the aquatic habitat and moved to protect the stream for the sake of the dace. Cattle grazing was stopped in the 1960s by fencing around the springs. The Kendall Warm Springs dace was listed as an endangered species in the early 1970s, and in 1975 the Forest Service banned bathing and wading in the warm springs and the creek.

44

Chief Washakie Plunge

General description: A warm outdoor pool with hotter indoor private baths, located on the Wind River Indian Reservation.

Location: Northwest Wyoming, 14 miles north of Lander.

Primitive/developed: Developed.

Best time of year: Open year-round.

Restrictions: The Eastern Shoshone and Arapaho tribes of the Wind River Indian Reservation own the plunge. Use of the outdoor pool and private indoor baths requires an admission fee.

Access: Any passenger car can make the trip.

Water temperature: The temperature at the source of the springs is 112 degrees F. The water is 102 degrees F in the private baths and 98 degrees F in the outdoor pool.

Nearby attractions: Gravesites of Sacajawea and Chief Washakie, Shoshone National Forest, Popo Agie Wilderness, Bridger Wilderness, North American Indian Heritage Center.

Services: None at the springs. Gas and food are available at Ethete and Fort Washakie. All services can be found in Lander, 16 miles south.

Camping: Sinks Canyon State Park, 6 miles southwest of Lander on Wyoming Highway 131, offers sites for RV and tent camping.

Map: Wyoming State Highways map.

Finding the springs: From Lander, go 14 miles north on U.S. Highway 287 to the town of Fort Washakie. About 100 yards north of the Sacajawea monument, turn east onto Ethete Road (County Road 335). Go for 2.2 miles on Ethete Road to the hot springs. If you're traveling from Riverton, drive northwest on Wyoming Highway 26 for 18 miles to Kinnear, then south on Wyoming Highway 132 for 11 miles to Ethete. At Ethete, turn west at the stoplight by the Wyoming Indian High School and follow Ethete Road 3.3 miles to the plunge.

The hot springs: Chief Washakie Plunge is located on the Shoshone and Arapaho Recreation Complex. The plunge features a 98-degree-F outdoor pool with a diving board and small water slide, an outdoor Jacuzzi, and a small wading pool. South of the plunge is a large gravel-lined pool that contains the vent of the 112-degree-F hot springs. A headgate controls the amount of water flowing from the pool into the plunge. Inside the bathhouse are nine private plunge rooms. Bathers seated on wooden benches in the 4-foot by 8-foot plunges can lean against whirlpool jets and let the 102-degree-F water soothe aching muscles.

Chief Washakie Plunge

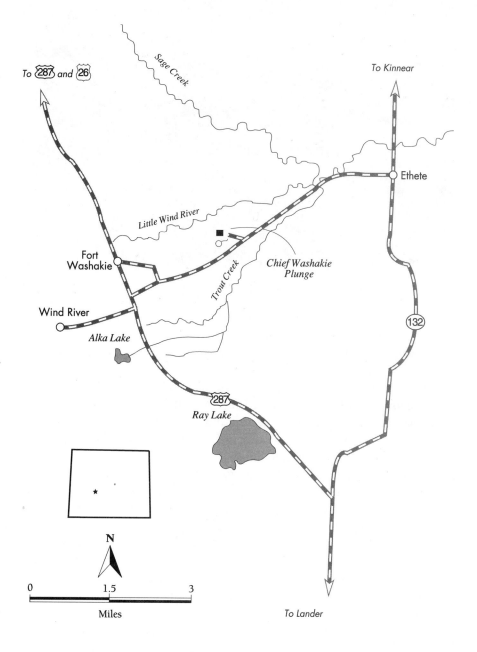

To 287 and 26

To Kinnear

Sage Creek

Ethete

Little Wind River

Chief Washakie
Plunge

Fort
Washakie

Trout Creek

Wind River

132

Alka Lake

287

Ray Lake

N

| 0 | 1.5 | 3 |

Miles

To Lander

Outdoor pool at Chief Washakie Plunge.

Operating hours change with the season. The plunge is open Wednesday through Sunday in the fall, winter, and spring and Tuesday through Sunday in the summertime.

History: Chief Washakie Plunge is named for Chief Washakie, the leader of the Shoshone Tribe from 1840 until 1900. Washakie was a cunning strategist during tribal wars with the Lakota, Arapaho, and Cheyenne but also sought peace with settlers moving into the area. In 1863 Washakie negotiated the treaty that established the Wind River Reservation as a permanent home for the Shoshone tribe, land that included what was to become Chief Washakie Plunge. Chief Washakie's grave is located east of Fort Washakie on North Fork Road.

Also in the vicinity is the gravesite of another famous Shoshone, Sacajawea, the woman who helped the Lewis and Clark Expedition reach the Pacific Ocean. Her grave is located just east of Fort Washakie. Reach it by going west on Trout Creek Road (County Road 294) to Cemetery Lane, then north. (Sacajawea's actual burial place is the subject of controversy, because North Dakota and South Dakota both claim that the courageous young woman is buried in their states, not in Wyoming.)

Little is known about the early uses of the hot water at Chief Washakie Plunge. The first bathhouse was apparently built by U.S. cavalry troops in the 1860s, and at least three other bathhouses have been built on the site since then. The April 1983 *Riverton Ranger* recalled one life-saving benefit of the thermal springs. During a blizzard in the 1930s, a man's car broke down not far from the bathhouse. The man survived the bitterly cold night by submerging himself up to his neck in the hot water and waiting there until the next morning when help arrived.

The current bathhouse was built in 1957 and extensively remodeled in 1996 and 1997.

45

Fountain of Youth RV Park

General description: A huge open-air swimming pool on the banks of the Big Horn River, supplied by a travertine-encrusted hot water well. The adjacent RV park is popular with caravans as well as families.

Location: Two miles north of Thermopolis on U.S. Highway 20.

Primitive/developed: Developed.

Best time of year: The RV park and pool are open from April 1 until at least October 1, sometimes longer if autumn weather stays nice.

Restrictions: The pool is available for use of RV park guests only, although those who don't want to stay overnight can pay a special "day camper" fee.

Access: Any vehicle can make the trip.

Water temperature: The hot well water that supplies the swimming pool emerges from the ground at 128 degrees F. The pool itself is 104 degrees F at the end closest to the well, cooling to 100 degrees F at the far end.

Nearby attractions: Hot Springs State Park, Wind River Canyon, Legend Rock Petroglyphs, Hot Springs Historical Museum, Wyoming Dinosaur Center, Boysen State Park.

Services: A few supplies for campers are available at the RV park. Gas, food, and alternative lodging options are available in Thermopolis, 1.5 miles to the south on US 20.

Camping: The RV park just north of the springs features 60 RV sites with full hookups. Some campers have stayed for up to five months at the resort, using the RV park as a base for exploring Thermopolis and the surrounding area and for relaxing in the shade of the oldest Chinese elm tree in Wyoming.

Map: Wyoming State Highways map.

Fountain of Youth RV Park

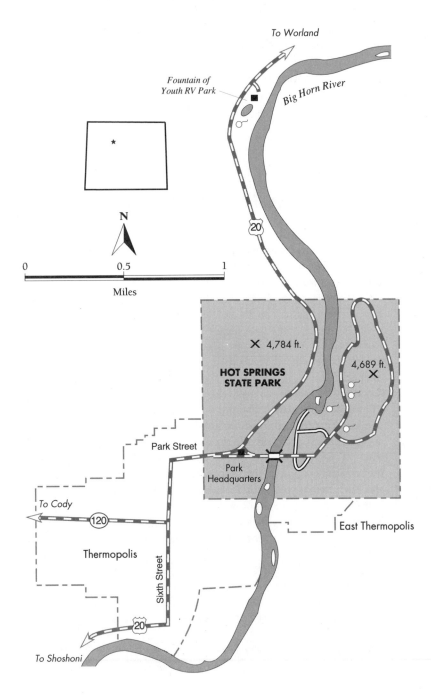

To Worland

Fountain of
Youth RV Park

Big Horn River

N

0   0.5   1
Miles

X 4,784 ft.

4,689 ft.
X

**HOT SPRINGS
STATE PARK**

Park Street

Park
Headquarters

To Cody

East Thermopolis

Thermopolis

Sixth Street

To Shoshoni

Finding the springs: From Thermopolis, drive north on US 20 for 1.5 miles. The RV park is on the east side of the highway near the Big Horn River.

The hot springs: Advertised as the "largest hot mineral pool in Wyoming," the 72-foot by 235-foot swimming pool certainly is immense. The water source for this gargantuan pool is an exploratory oil well drilled in 1918. Instead of oil, the well rig tapped a pressurized reservoir of hot water that erupted with such force that the oil derrick was destroyed. W. B. Garrett, the owner of the well, named it "Sacajawea Well" in honor of the Shoshone guide for Lewis and Clark whose grave is located on the nearby Wind River Indian Reservation. Over the last 70 years the hot water has deposited a colorful travertine cone around the well, which can be seen at the southern edge of the swimming pool.

The 128-degree-F artesian water flows from the well into a small holding pond. No commercial use of the well water was made until 1969, although some locals did use the water for bathing in the years before commercial development. When the current swimming pool was constructed, eight 6-inch pipes were installed in the holding pond to transport water to the new pool. Approximately 1.4 million gallons of water flow into the pool every day, and a complete change of water occurs every 11 hours.

Current owners Tom and Mary Berry, who purchased the RV park in 1978, hold several special events during the April to October season. An interdenominational Easter sunrise service kicks off the spring events, with swimsuit-clad

The immense pool at the Fountain of Youth RV Park.

parishioners soaking in the warm water during the sermon. Other poolside worship services are held on Memorial Day and the Sunday nearest to the Fourth of July. The pool is also used for baptisms, with 75 to 100 baptisms performed annually in the pool by churches from nearby Thermopolis. A Labor Day breakfast signals the approaching end of the soaking season; bathers snack on fruit, donuts, and juices served on floating Styrofoam tables.

Berry notes that accommodating large crowds has never been a problem in the warm water pool at the Fountain of Youth RV Park. He recalls having up to 300 people in the pool at one time, but the pool is so large that "you couldn't even tell it."

46

DeMaris Hot Springs

General description: A sulfurous hot springs pool located deep in the Shoshone River Canyon east of Yellowstone National Park. The hot springs and the surrounding thermal activity in the canyon were named "Colter's Hell" in 1807 by John Colter, a famous explorer from the Lewis and Clark Expedition.

Location: Northwest Wyoming, 2 miles west of Cody.

Primitive/developed: Developed.

Best time of year: The hot springs can be observed anytime.

Restrictions: Though once a popular bathing spot, the springs are now closed to the public.

Access: Any vehicle can make the short trip from Cody to the canyon rim where visitors can view the hot springs in the valley below.

Water temperature: The seven springs nearest to the pool average 81 degrees F, although one spring measures almost 100 degrees F.

Nearby attractions: Yellowstone National Park, Buffalo Bill Reservoir, Buffalo Bill State Park, Buffalo Bill Historical Center, Old Trail Town, Shoshone River.

Services: Gas, food, and lodging are available in Cody, 2 miles east of DeMaris Hot Springs on U.S. Highway 14/16/20. The Irma Hotel, built by Buffalo Bill Cody in 1902, is a great historic place to spend the night.

Camping: Camping is available at Buffalo Bill State Park, 15 miles west of DeMaris Hot Springs. Several Forest Service campgrounds are located along US 14/16/20 between the Buffalo Bill Reservoir and the east entrance to Yellowstone National Park.

Map: Wyoming State Highways map.

DeMaris Hot Springs

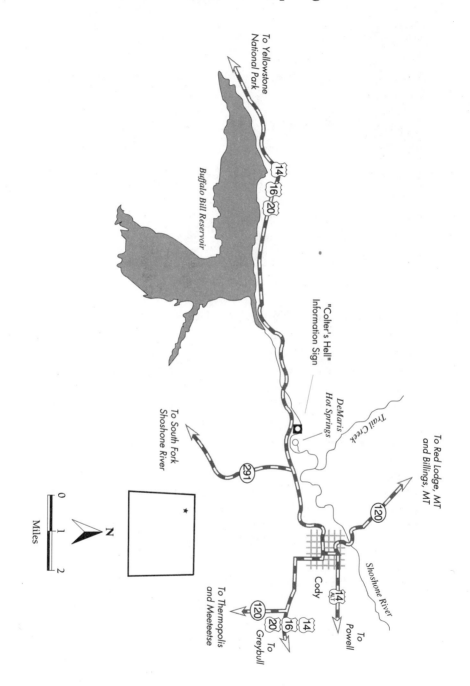

DeMaris Hot Springs at the bottom of the Shoshone River Canyon.

Finding the springs: From Cody, drive 2 miles west on US 14/16/20. About 0.5 mile past the rodeo grounds and Trail Town, look on the north side of the road for a Wyoming Historic Point interpretive sign describing "Colter's Hell." Park at the sign and walk to the canyon rim. Look toward the bottom of the canyon on the far side of the Shoshone River for the open-air swimming pool at DeMaris Hot Springs. Walk east along the canyon rim 100 yards from the interpretive sign to get the best view of the springs. Brightly colored streaks on the canyon wall are indicative of sulfur deposition from past geothermal activity.

The hot springs: DeMaris Hot Springs consists of at least seven distinct hot water vents within a 75-yard span. Water temperatures average 81 degrees F, and flow rates vary from 1 to 500 gallons per minute. The hot springs are very sulfurous, and the "rotten egg" smell is quite strong. The 40-foor by 60-foot pool is privately owned, and no public access is allowed.

History: DeMaris Hot Springs and the other geothermal sites in the Shoshone River Canyon were first described by John Colter in 1807. Colter had been a member of the Lewis and Clark Expedition and was granted permission to leave the expedition upon its return to Fort Mandan in what is now North Dakota. Colter headed back west to lead fur trappers through the newly explored territory. In *The Adventures of Captain Bonneville,* Washington Irving described Colter's sighting of the hot springs along the Shoshone River (formerly known as the

"Stinking River"): "Stinking River, one of the tributaries of the Bighorn, takes its unhappy name from the odor derived from sulphurous springs and streams. This last mentioned place was first discovered by Colter, a hunter belonging to the Lewis and Clarke's [sic] exploring party, who came upon it in the course of his lonely wanderings and gave such account of the gloomy terrors, its hidden fires, smoking pits, noxious streams, and all-pervading 'smell of brimstone' that it received, and has ever since retained among trappers the name of 'Colter's Hell.'" Later the phrase "Colter's Hell" was also applied to Yellowstone National Park, but most historians agree that Colter's" smoking pits and noxious streams" correctly applies to the area around DeMaris Hot Springs.

Members of the Crow Indian tribe frequently visited the springs before settlers arrived, and evidence of tepee rings could be found near the springs until the early 1900s.

In 1886 Charles DeMaris Sr., a Montana cattleman, visited the area in search of new rangeland. DeMaris had operated a large cattle ranch near Billings, but a terrible blizzard the previous winter had reduced his cattle herd to less than 500 head. In poor health from the stress of his business, DeMaris brought his doctor along with him on the trip. One evening the party camped at the hot springs in the bottom of Shoshone Canyon, and DeMaris bathed in the warm water. Feeling much better the next day, he decided to stay at the springs and take more soaks. After a few weeks he sent his doctor back to Montana, and with his health restored DeMaris filed a claim on the springs and settled there permanently. He built a small plunge around one of the spring vents, and for many years settlers and members of the Crow tribe shared the hot, sulfurous water.

In 1902, the same year that Buffalo Bill Cody constructed the Irma Hotel in nearby Cody, DeMaris built a large two-story hotel next to the springs to accommodate guests. Visitation continued to increase at the springs, and DeMaris promoted the health benefits of the water in the local media. A 1907 advertisement in the *Wyoming Stockgrower & Farmer* boasted of the springs' curative properties: "The DeMaris Hot Sulphur Springs radically cure all kinds of skin and blood diseases, all diseases of a scrofulous nature and rheumatism, and are excellent in the nervous diseases, such as St. Vitus's dance, hysteria, etc." DeMaris Springs was also known as "Needle Springs" because of the small, effervescent bubbles in the water. Bursting on contact with bathers, the bubbles created a prickly feeling like thousands of small needles.

Although DeMaris Hot Springs was on the outskirts of Cody, access to the resort at the bottom of the Shoshone River Canyon was difficult. Mail and supplies arrived via a system of pulleys and ropes for lowering items from the canyon rim. Prior to 1924 the main road to Cody and Yellowstone National Park ran on the north side of the canyon, passing just above DeMaris Hot

Crow Indians soaking at DeMaris Hot Springs, circa 1900.
PHOTO COURTESY OF PARK COUNTY HISTORICAL SOCIETY.

Springs. Visitors arrived at the plunge by descending a steep side road that switchbacked along the canyon wall. When the highway moved to its present location on the south side of the canyon, reaching DeMaris Hot Springs required an arduous 16-mile trip that included fording the river. Not surprisingly, business dropped off.

In 1923, the owner of DeMaris Hot Springs erected a large new plunge. A roof enclosed the plunge, but the sulfur gases and odor were so strong that bathers couldn't tolerate being in the building. The owner removed the roof of the plunge, and it remained an open-air pool until 1981, when the flooding Shoshone River destroyed the building.

The public continued to soak in the hot water pools until 1993, when fear of liability and the difficult access to the springs caused the owners to close them to the public.

HOT SPRINGS STATE PARK

The third most visited park in Wyoming after Yellowstone and Grand Teton national parks, Hot Springs State Park is home to one of the largest hot springs in the world. Big Horn Spring produces more than 1.4 million gallons of 135-degree-F water each day. Five separate public and commercial facilities with hot mineral soaking pools, saunas, and steam rooms depend on the ceaseless flow

Hot Springs State Park

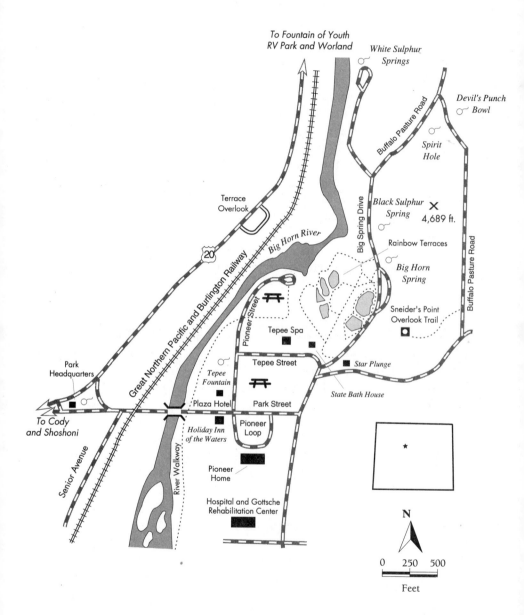

To Fountain of Youth
RV Park and Worland

White Sulphur
Springs

Buffalo Pasture Road

Devil's Punch
Bowl

Spirit
Hole

Terrace
Overlook

Big Horn River

Big Spring Drive

Black Sulphur
Spring

✕
4,689 ft.

Rainbow Terraces

Big Horn
Spring

Buffalo Pasture Road

Great Northern Pacific and Burlington Railway

20

Pioneer Street

Sneider's Point
Overlook Trail

Tepee Spa

Park
Headquarters

Tepee Street

Star Plunge

Tepee
Fountain

To Cody
and Shoshoni

Plaza Hotel

Park Street

State Bath House

Holiday Inn
of the Waters

Pioneer
Loop

Senior Avenue

River Walkway

Pioneer
Home

Hospital and Gottsche
Rehabilitation Center

★

N

0   250   500

Feet

from Big Horn Spring for their hot water. Big Horn Spring is also responsible for the colorful Rainbow Terraces, a series of colorful travertine ledges built up over thousands of years by the deposition of minerals from the thermal water. Several other hot springs can be seen on the loop road through the buffalo pasture to the north, including Black Sulphur Spring, White Sulphur Springs, and the Devil's Punch Bowl. You may also catch a glimpse of the two dozen buffalo that roam the pastures along the loop road to the north and east of Big Horn Spring.

One of the first explorers to describe Big Horn Spring was Captain Bonneville, whose exploration of the springs in 1832 was recorded by Washington Irving in *The Adventures of Captain Bonneville.*

Having forded Wind River a little above its mouth, Captain Bonneville and his three companions proceeded across a gravely plain until they fell upon Popo Agie, up on the left bank of which they held their course nearly in a southerly direction . . . and then "turned in" for the night and slept soundly like weary and well-fed hunters.

At daylight they were in the saddle again, and skirted along the river, passing through fresh grassy meadows, and a succession of beautiful groves of willows and cottonwood.

Toward evening Captain Bonneville observed smoke at a distance rising from some hills directly in the route he was pursuing. Apprehensive of some hostile band, he concealed the horses in a thicket, and accompanied by one of his men, crawled cautiously up a height, from which he could overlook the scene of danger. Here with a spyglass he reconnoitered the surrounding country, but not a lodge nor fire, not a man, horse, nor dog, was to be discovered; in short, the smoke which had caused such alarm proved to be the vapor from several warm, or rather hot springs of considerable magnitude, pouring forth streams in every direction over a bottom of white clay. One of the springs was about twenty-five yards in diameter, and so deep that the water was of a bright green color.

The hot springs with the "bright green color" described by Bonneville is most certainly Big Horn Spring, which still retains its verdant hue more than 150 years after Bonneville's visit.

Big Horn Spring and the surrounding area were most likely visited by members of the Crow, Shoshone, and Arapaho tribes for thousands of years. Native Americans ascribed sacred powers to the springs, which were considered neutral territory by the warring tribes.

Big Horn Spring, advertised as "The Largest Hot Springs in the World."

The hot springs and surrounding area were included in the Shoshone Indian Reservation Treaty of 1868. Pressure to settle the area increased over the next three decades, and in April 1896 Chief Washakie of the Shoshone tribe sold 10 square miles of the land around the springs to the U.S. government for $60,000. The anniversary of this treaty is remembered every year during the first week of August, when the "Gift of the Waters" pageant is held near the springs. A reenactment of the signing ceremony highlights the celebration.

Testimonials abound as to the curative power of the water from Big Horn Spring. A 1925 promotional brochure produced by the Thermopolis Chamber of Commerce made this remarkable claim: "There are hundreds of cases of skin, blood, kidney, nervous and kindred diseases that come to Thermopolis every month for treatment. NO FAILURE HAS EVER BEEN KNOWN." Another claim reported in an article of unknown date from the *Thermopolis Independent Record* was the following: "These waters restore vitality to elderly folks and actually prolong life that has flickered faint and dim."

According to the *Thermopolis Independent Record* of April 25, 1946, a fellow named Bill Pickering stated that the hot water not only made him "feel twenty years younger" but also had convinced him to "quit telling lies and stealing." But perhaps the most amazing cure attributed to the thermal water from Big Horn Spring was reported in the November 27, 1952, edition of the *Thermopolis Independent Record,* concerning the physical condition of 79-year-old Jesse Smith. According to the article, Smith had arrived at Thermopolis

The "Pageant of the Waters" celebrates the transfer of the hot springs from the Shoshone and Arapaho Tribes to the United States. PHOTO COURTESY OF HOT SPRINGS COUNTY MUSEUM.

with "snow-white hair and no teeth." After Smith spent three months drinking water from Big Horn Spring, the newspaper reported that "his hair was turning black and he was even sporting seventeen new teeth!"

So prevalent were the stories of miracle cures from the springs that some visitors sought to use the water not only for the ills of man but also those of machines. The December 11, 1941, edition of the *Thermopolis Independent Record* tells the story of two ladies from Nebraska traveling through the area during a bitter cold spell. The ladies asked one of the Thermopolis locals if the water from Big Horn Spring ever froze and were reassured that it did not. The next morning the ladies drove their car to a service station in Thermopolis, with the radiator steaming and the engine damaged. "We can't understand it," the women complained, "he said that it never freezes!" Apparently the ladies had drained the antifreeze from their radiator the night before and then refilled it with the mineral water from Big Horn Spring, thinking that the "water that never freezes" would do a better job than the chemical antifreeze in the frigid Wyoming weather.

Hot Springs State Park is located on the northeast edge of the town of Thermopolis. The park headquarters is located at the intersection of U.S. Highway 20 and Park Street, just east of the high school and Hot Springs County Fairgrounds. Stop at the park headquarters for more information and a detailed map of the park.

Thousands visit Hot Springs State Park every year to see the thermal springs and beautiful travertine deposits. Within the boundaries of the park are a myriad of soaking options, including hot pools at two motels, two commercial recreational facilities, and a free public soaking facility. Detailed descriptions of these five soaking options are provided in the following sections.

Big Horn Hot Spring
Thermopolis, Wyoming

Here I am at last in the good old town,
Thermopolis! The city of renown.
Famed for its wonderful Hot Water Springs,
Of its healing merits the poets sing.

If you are ill and cannot sleep at night,
Then come and bathe and you will feel all right.
If you are weary and tired of life,
Of its tribulations and ceaseless strife,
If you are old and worn and feeling blue,
Then drink Hot Springs water, it will renew.

If your brain feels numb from overapplication,
Of Bookkeeping Fractions, and Multiplication,
The Hot Springs Water will restore your brain,
To its normal condition and relieve the strain.

Have your deepest affections been misplaced?
Is your heart broken and sadly defaced?
Do you look in the future with hopeless despair?
No hope of love, no pleasure awaits you there?

If these afflictions are you, my friend,
Then cheer up! for these troubles will end.
If you will come to the Hot Springs and soak
As long as you can without going broke,
And dive and swim from morning till night,
Till your grief is submerged and your heart is bright,
And drink 5 gallons of water a day,
Then you'll be happy, and then you'll be gay.

—Poem from a 1916 Thermopolis postcard (author unknown)

47

Holiday Inn of the Waters

(See map on page 185)

General description: A modern hostelry that features an exotic wildlife theme, a gourmet restaurant, and hot mineral water soaks. The Holiday Inn is also a great base of operations for exploring Hot Springs State Park.
Location: Northwest Wyoming, inside Hot Springs State Park in Thermopolis.
Primitive/developed: Developed.
Best time of year: The hotel and hot mineral pools are open year-round.
Restrictions: Holiday Inn is privately owned. Hotel guests have free use of the outdoor mineral and swimming pools. Private indoor Jacuzzis and steam rooms are available to anyone for an hourly fee.
Access: Any vehicle can make the trip.
Water temperature: Like all swimming and soaking facilities in Hot Springs State Park, the mineral pools and steam rooms at the Holiday Inn of the Waters are supplied with hot water from nearby Big Horn Spring. The seasonal outdoor freshwater pool is kept between 75 and 85 degrees F. The outdoor mineral pool averages 103 degrees F, as does the indoor private Jacuzzi. The temperature of the individual indoor soaking tubs can be adjusted.
Nearby attractions: Wind River Canyon, Legend Rock Petroglyphs, Hot Springs Historical Museum, Wyoming Dinosaur Center, Boysen State Park.
Services: Food and lodging are available at the Holiday Inn. Other lodging and dining services, as well as gasoline and other supplies, are available in Thermopolis.
Camping: Camping is not allowed at Hot Springs State Park. Lower and Upper Wind River campgrounds are located 14 and 15 miles south of Thermopolis on U.S. Highway 20. Several other campgrounds are located in Boysen State Park, 20 miles south of Thermopolis on US 20.
Maps: Wyoming State Highways map, Hot Springs State Park visitor map.

Finding the springs: From the entrance to Hot Springs State Park, head east on Park Street. The Holiday Inn is on the south side of the road immediately after you cross the bridge over the Big Horn River.

The hot springs: Although the standard Holiday Inn sign outside this motel might lead you to believe there's nothing special inside, you will be pleasantly mistaken. The combination of the exotic game theme, several mineral water

Outdoor mineral pool at Holiday Inn of the Waters.

soaking options, and a gourmet restaurant make the Holiday Inn of the Waters worthy headquarters for your visit to the Thermopolis area.

Upon entering the Holiday Inn you'll see hundreds of photos of safari trips and outdoor adventures decorating the hallway and lobby walls, attesting to the globe-trotting adventures of general manager Jim Mills and his family. The Safari Club Restaurant and Lounge add to the exotic wildlife theme of the hotel, featuring more than 100 big-game trophies. (Note to trivia buffs: If you can name all of the trophy mounts on the walls of the Safari Club Lounge, the bartender will give you a free drink. Of course your friends will think it a bit weird that your own trophy head is filled with such information, but a free drink is a free drink.)

After you've built up your appetite trying to name all the water buffaloes, leopards, and other exotic animals, try a gourmet meal in the Safari Club Restaurant. In recognition of its great cuisine, the restaurant has received the coveted Epicurean Plate Award from the Culinary Guild of America. Breakfast, lunch, and dinner are served.

One of the many unique features of the Holiday Inn of the Waters is the outdoor hot mineral Jacuzzi, located within sight of the Bighorn River. Naturally heated 110-degree-F water enters a holding reservoir at one end of the soaking pool but cools to 103 degrees F by the time it flows into the main pool used by bathers. The 6-foot by 24-foot soaking pool is open year-round from

7:00 A.M. to 10:00 P.M., making it a great place to start or end your day's exploration of Hot Springs State Park or the Wyoming Dinosaur Center. The adjacent 20-foot by 50-foot outdoor fresh water pool is open Memorial Day to Labor Day.

The motel's full-service athletic club features separate men's and women's exercise rooms outfitted with free weights, treadmills, cross-country ski machines, and Universal exercise machines. Two racquetball courts are also available. After a workout (or in lieu of a workout) head to the health spa, which features private soaking tubs, steam rooms, a sauna, and a private two-person Jacuzzi room. A masseuse and a tanning bed are also available.

48

Quality Inn Plaza Hotel

(See map on page 185)

General description: An historic hotel and apartment complex that has been newly renovated into a modern lodging facility. A natural outdoor mineral pool can offer a relaxing conclusion to a day of sightseeing in Hot Springs State Park.

Location: Northwest Wyoming, inside Hot Springs State Park in the town of Thermopolis.

Primitive/developed: Developed.

Best time of year: The hotel and hot mineral pool are open year-round.

Restrictions: The Quality Inn Plaza Hotel is privately owned. Hotel guests have free use of the outdoor mineral pool.

Access: Any vehicle can make the trip.

Water temperature: Like all swimming and soaking facilities in Hot Springs State Park, the mineral pools and steam rooms at the Quality Inn Plaza Hotel are supplied with hot water from nearby Big Horn Spring. The hotel features an outdoor mineral pool. At this writing, the hotel was still under renovation, and water temperatures were not available.

Nearby attractions: Wind River Canyon, Legend Rock Petroglyphs, Hot Springs Historical Museum, Wyoming Dinosaur Center, Boysen State Park.

Services: Food and lodging are available at the Quality Inn. Other lodging and dining services, as well as gasoline and other supplies, are available in Thermopolis.

Camping: Camping is not allowed at Hot Springs State Park. Lower and Upper Wind River campgrounds are located 14 and 15 miles south of

The Quality Inn Plaza Hotel, scheduled to open in April 1999.

Thermopolis on U.S. Highway 20. Several other campgrounds are in Boysen
State Park, 20 miles south of Thermopolis on US 20.
Maps: Wyoming State Highways map, Hot Springs State Park visitor map.

Finding the springs: From the entrance to Hot Springs State Park, head east
on Park Street. The Quality Inn Plaza Hotel is on the north side of the road
immediately after you cross the bridge over the Big Horn River.

The hot springs: Closed for several years, the Plaza Hotel has been recently
renovated and is scheduled to reopen to the public in the spring of 1999. The
35-room hotel will feature an outdoor hot mineral pool. Other soaking facilities are unknown at this writing—call the Quality Inn reservations number for
current information.

49

State Bath House

(See map on page 185)

General description: A free thermal soaking facility managed by the state of Wyoming, featuring indoor and outdoor soaking pools and private individual soaking tubs.

Location: Northwestern Wyoming, on the grounds of Hot Springs State Park in Thermopolis.

Primitive/developed: Developed.

Best time of year: Open year-round.

Restrictions: Swimsuits are required in the indoor and outdoor soaking pools but are optional in the private soaking tubs. Soaking time is limited to 20 minutes in the pools and 15 minutes in the private tubs, but guests can return after a two-hour interval for additional soaks.

Access: Any vehicle can make the trip.

Water temperature: 104 degrees F in the indoor and outdoor pools; adjustable in the private tubs.

The first State Bath House, built in 1902.
PHOTO COURTESY OF WYOMING DIVISION OF CULTURAL RESOURCES.

The second State Bath House, built in 1921. PHOTO COURTESY OF HOT SPRINGS COUNTY MUSEUM.

Nearby attractions: Wind River Canyon, Hot Springs Historical Museum, Wyoming Dinosaur Center, Boysen State Park, and Legend Rock State Petroglyph Site.

Services: Lodging and meals are available at the Holiday Inn of the Waters and the Quality Inn Plaza Hotel, both within the boundaries of Hot Springs State Park. Other lodging and dining services, as well as gasoline and other supplies, are available in Thermopolis.

Camping: Camping is not allowed at Hot Springs State Park. Lower and Upper Wind River campgrounds are located 14 and 15 miles south of Thermopolis on U.S. Highway 20. Several other campgrounds are located in Boysen State Park, 20 miles south of Thermopolis on US 20.

Maps: Wyoming State Highways map, Hot Springs State Park visitor map.

Finding the springs: From the entrance to Hot Springs State Park, head east on Park Street to its intersection with Buffalo Street. Go north for one block on Buffalo Street, then turn west onto Tepee Street. The State Bath House is located on the north side of Tepee Street about 100 feet past the Buffalo Street turnoff.

The hot springs: State Bath House is a fine introduction to the variety of thermal soaking facilities at Hot Springs State Park and is the only facility in the area that doesn't charge an admission fee. The facilities are maintained by the

The outdoor pool at State Bath House, dedicated in 1967.

state of Wyoming and have trained attendants on hand who ensure that bathers don't exceed the 15 or 20 minutes allotted for each soak. Suits and towels are available for rent.

The glass-enclosed central soaking pool is maintained at 104 degrees F. It is flanked by separate men's and women's private soaking areas, each containing four individual tubs as well as lockers that can be rented from the attendants. The outdoor soaking pool is shaded by a canopy and has a view of the travertine deposits of Rainbow Terrace to the north.

The State Bath House is open from 8:00 A.M. to 5:30 P.M. Monday through Saturday and from noon to 5:30 P.M. on Sundays and summer holidays. The facility is closed during winter holidays.

History: Prior to signing the treaty in 1896 that granted ownership of the area around Big Horn Spring to the U.S. government, Chief Washakie of the Shoshone tribe specified that one-quarter of the hot water from the spring was to be available free for public soaking. This foresighted action by Chief Washakie resulted in the development of the State Bath House, which has provided free soaks for generations of people who are indebted to Chief Washakie's vision.

In the years after the treaty was signed, several crude structures were used to shelter the free baths until the first officially sanctioned state bathhouse was built in 1902. The 32-foot by 44-foot stone structure contained seven private rooms furnished with tubs and benches. A larger bathhouse was built in 1921, and the current facility was constructed in 1967.

For many years the State Bath House was open to anyone, but in 1927 the decision was made that only the indigent or the medically needy would be allowed to soak in the thermal water. This ruling enraged many people, according to Dorothy Milek's 1975 history of the area, *The Gift of Bah Guewana—A History of Wyoming's Hot Springs State Park*. One incensed local was Thermopolis saloon owner Tom Skinner, who shot down the posted notice of the new rules with his revolver. The sign was reposted, and Skinner shot it down again. After a third attempt to post the sign resulted in another spray of bullets, the sign was permanently removed, although the policy remained in place.

After two years of restrictive bathing rules, the Wyoming State Board ruled that the general public could soak at the State Bath House whenever it wasn't being used by the sick or indigent. But additional restrictions were in the works. In 1932 a rule was passed that only residents of Wyoming could partake of the free baths—visitors from out of state were forbidden to use the hot water.

Eventually the "Wyoming only" rule was also eliminated, and today the pools and tubs at the State Bath House are available to anyone, regardless of race, creed, medical condition, or Wyoming citizenship.

50

Star Plunge

(See map on page 185)

General description: Offering soaking, swimming, and sunning options to suit most any desire, Star Plunge is the granddaddy of commercial resorts in Hot Springs State Park.

Location: Northwest Wyoming, inside Hot Springs State Park in Thermopolis.

Primitive/developed: Developed.

Best time of year: Open year-round.

Restrictions: Star Plunge is privately owned. An admission fee is charged to use the facilities. The resort is open from 9:00 A.M. to 9:00 P.M.

Access: Any vehicle can make the trip.

Water temperature: Like all swimming and soaking facilities in Hot Springs State Park, the pools and steam room at Star Plunge are supplied with hot water from nearby Big Horn Spring. The large indoor and outdoor pools are kept between 90 and 98 degrees F. The outdoor Jacuzzi averages 104 degrees F, while the steamy "Lobster Pot" indoors tops 115 degrees F.

Nearby attractions: Wind River Canyon, Legend Rock Petroglyphs, Hot Springs Historical Museum, Wyoming Dinosaur Center, Boysen State Park.

Services: A snack bar is available at the plunge. Lodging and meals are available at the Holiday Inn of the Waters and the Quality Inn Plaza Hotel, both within the boundaries of Hot Springs State Park. Other lodging and dining services, as well as gasoline and other supplies, are available in Thermopolis.

Camping: Camping is not allowed at Hot Springs State Park. Lower and Upper Wind River campgrounds are located 14 and 15 miles south of Thermopolis on U.S. Highway 20. Several other campgrounds are located in Boysen State Park, 20 miles south of Thermopolis on US 20.

Maps: Wyoming State Highways map, Hot Springs State Park visitor map.

Finding the springs: From the entrance to Hot Springs State Park, head east on Park Street to its intersection with Buffalo Street. Go north for one block on Buffalo Street, then turn east into the Star Plunge parking area.

The hot springs: Billing itself as a "full recreational facility," Star Plunge overflows with swimming and soaking opportunities for both indoor and outdoor hot water enthusiasts.

Interior shot of Star Plunge in the early 1900s.
PHOTO COURTESY OF WYOMING DIVISION OF CULTURAL RESOURCES.

Outdoor pool at Star Plunge.

The roof over the 40-foot by 120-foot indoor pool consists of exposed wood beams alternating with skylights. The pool's southern end contains a 2-foot wading pool (called the "baby pool") and an 8-foot by 15-foot Jacuzzi with plenty of bubblers to soothe aching back muscles. The indoor pool temperature ranges from 94 to 98 degrees F, and the sides and bottom of the pool are lined with a porcelain-smooth layer of pale pink mineral deposit, the result of decades of contact with the thermal water.

Located on the west deck of the indoor pool is the 8-foot by 30-foot "Lobster Pot." At 115 degrees F, it is the hottest soak at Star Plunge. Signs advise users to limit themselves to no more than ten minutes in the Lobster Pot, lest they end up mimicking the shell color of the pool's namesake.

North of the pool at the end of a short tunnel is an 8-foot by 20-foot steam cave hewn out of the rock hillside. Guests sit on wooden benches in a semicircle facing a travertine-encrusted hot water fountain that fills the cave with 115-degree-F vapor. Skylights in the ceiling illuminate the occupants of the cave, many of whom sit motionless in a satisfying, heat-induced stupor.

Outdoor facilities at Star Plunge are as varied as those indoors. The 50-foot by 120-foot outdoor pool varies from 3 to 11 feet deep, with a 15-foot jumping platform located above the deep end. Water temperature averages 90 to 94 degrees F. An 8-foot by 15-foot Jacuzzi bubbles with 104-degree-F water on the deck near the north end of the outdoor pool. Twenty yards northwest of the Jacuzzi is a 10-foot by 10-foot wading pool that features a 4-foot vertical center pipe cascading 100-degree-F water onto cavorting children. Ten sundecks are scattered on the hillside north of the pool.

Star Plunge also features three water slides. A 60-foot slide north of the outdoor pool is great for smaller kids during the summer months. Next up in size is the 338-foot enclosed tube called "Blue Thunder," which empties into the indoor pool. It's open all season. Last but certainly not least is the granddaddy of the Star Plunge slides, the "Super Star 500," which snakes down the adjacent hillside for 500 feet before emptying into its own exit pool. The Super Star 500, advertised as "one of the world's largest water slides," is open only in the summertime.

History: Built in 1900, Star Plunge is the oldest commercial resort in Hot Springs State Park. The plunge has attracted many famous visitors including Buffalo Bill Cody, Butch Cassidy, Marlon Brando, and Robert Redford.

Decades before water slides began appearing at swimming pools, Star Plunge had installed its own rustic prototype, named "The Screaming Mimi." Adventurous youngsters would climb a staircase on the steep hillside above the outdoor pool, then sit on a small wooden toboggan fitted with steel wheels instead of sled runners. The toboggan would whoosh down a grooved wooden ramp into the warm pool below, where it would skid across the water's surface for several yards before it sank. The Screaming Mimi was torn down in 1980, but one of the old wooden toboggans is on display in the main lobby.

Wolfgang Luehne is the current owner of Star Plunge.

51

Tepee Spa

(See map on page 185)

General description: A family-oriented resort offering a number of indoor and outdoor swimming and soaking options.
Location: Northwest Wyoming, within Hot Springs State Park in Thermopolis.
Primitive/developed: Developed.
Best time of year: Open year-round.
Restrictions: The resort is privately owned. An admission fee is charged to use the pools. The resort is open daily from 9:00 A.M. to 9:00 P.M.
Access: Any vehicle can make the trip.

Water temperature: Like all swimming and soaking facilities in Hot Springs State Park, the pools at Tepee Spa are supplied with hot water from nearby Big Horn Spring. The large indoor and outdoor pools are kept at 90 degrees F. The smaller soaking pools range from 100 to 105 degrees F.

Nearby attractions: Wind River Canyon, Legend Rock Petroglyphs, Hot Springs Historical Museum, Wyoming Dinosaur Center, Boysen State Park.

Services: Lodging and meals are available at the Holiday Inn of the Waters and the Quality Inn Plaza Hotel, both within the boundaries of Hot Springs State Park. Other lodging and dining services, as well as gasoline and other supplies, are available in Thermopolis.

Camping: Camping is not allowed at Hot Springs State Park. Lower and Upper Wind River campgrounds are located 14 and 15 miles south of Thermopolis on U.S. Highway 20. Several other campgrounds are located in Boysen State Park, 20 miles south of Thermopolis on US 20.

Maps: Wyoming State Highways map, Hot Springs State Park visitor map.

Finding the springs: From the entrance to Hot Springs State Park, head east on Park Street to its intersection with Buffalo Street. Go north for one block on Buffalo Street, then turn west onto Tepee Street. Drive about 200 feet past the State Bath House. You'll see the golden-domed Tepee Spa on the north side of the street.

The hot springs: Tepee Spa is referred to by several different names (and a couple of different spellings), but staff and visitors don't seem to mind. Many long-time visitors still call the resort by its old name of "Hot Springs Water Park," and t-shirts in the gift shop misspell the resort's name "teepee" instead of "tepee." But no matter what it's called, Tepee Spa offers something to satisfy most any thermal bather.

The dark interior of the large domed structure, punctuated by shafts of sunlight entering through the high wooden ceiling, provides bathers with a feeling of being inside an old Indian lodge. The large indoor pool is divided into three sections. The biggest section is a lap pool between 3.5 and 5 feet deep, maintained at 90 degrees F. A smaller section of the large pool consists of a shallow wading pool, which is kept at about 100 degrees F. A third section consists of a 104-degree-F soaking pool about 3.5 feet deep, with a small Jacuzzi at one end. Tepee Spa also features an indoor steam room at 115 degrees F and a sauna. A 162-foot indoor water slide empties into the big pool.

The outdoor hot water offerings are as diverse as those inside. A 45-foot by 90-foot outdoor pool is kept at a constant 90 degrees F and is filled by hot water cascading from a pipe suspended 5 feet above the pool. Lounge chairs on the surrounding deck and a small tree-shaded picnic area offer bathers a place

Outdoor pools at Tepee Spa.

to relax between soaks. Other outdoor facilities include three soaking pools, each about 10 feet square and 3 feet deep, with temperatures between 100 and 104 degrees F. A 272-foot-long blue water slide to the north of the main pool resounds with screams of delight from the younger set during the summer months.

History: Tepee Spa was built by Darrell Hunt, the former administrator for the Gottsche Rehabilitation Center, which is also located at Hot Springs State Park. Hunt had been a physical therapist with the Mayo Clinic prior to moving to Thermopolis in 1959. The first project built in Hot Springs State Park in 50 years with private capital, the $250,000 building was completed in June 1968. The original wooden tepee-shaped roof burned in 1975, but it was soon rebuilt with the dome-shaped roof seen today.

Tepee Spa was probably named for nearby Tepee Fountain, a travertine mound with mineral water bubbling from its apex. Although it's now one of the most visited attractions at Hot Springs State Park, Tepee Fountain began in 1903 as a vertical vent pipe installed in the park's plumbing system to relieve pressure and prevent mineral deposition in the pipes. The plan worked well, and mineral deposits built up around the vertical pipe instead of in the underground pipes. Over the years the mineral deposits increased in height and width, and today Tepee Fountain is about 30 feet tall and 25 feet wide.

SOUTHEAST WYOMING

Southeast Wyoming is rich with the history of pioneer families headed West. More than 350,000 individuals traveled along the Oregon Trail through this part of the state in the mid-1800s. Southeast Wyoming contains the largest cities in the state, including Casper, Laramie, and Cheyenne. The Medicine Bow National Forest, which includes the beautiful Snowy Mountain Range and several wilderness areas, is also located here.

Even though the hot springs in southeast Wyoming are separated from each other by more than 50 miles, they all lie within 1 or 2 miles of the banks of the North Platte River. The hot springs of Saratoga, the plunge near Douglas, and the warm springs along the Oregon Trail near Guernsey are all linked to the earliest history of discovery and settlement in the area.

52

Saratoga Hot Springs

General description: A picturesque hot springs within Saratoga City Park. Soaking options include a warm water municipal swimming pool, the always open and always free Hobo Pool, and several thermal seeps on the banks of the North Platte River.

Location: Southeast Wyoming in the town of Saratoga.

Primitive/developed: Developed.

Best time of year: Hobo Pool (named for the transients who used to soak there) is open year-round, but its high temperature makes it best for soaking on crisp fall and winter days. The temporary pools on the banks of the North Platte River are flooded during spring runoff, so late summer and winter are probably best for soaking there. The municipal swimming pool is open from May to October.

Restrictions: Hobo Pool is owned by the city of Saratoga and is free to the public 24 hours a day, 365 days a year. The chlorinated municipal pool is open May to October and charges an admission fee. Swimsuits are required in both pools.

Access: Any vehicle can make the trip.

Water temperature: The Lobster Pot at one end of Hobo Pool is a steamy 120 degrees F. The main soaking pool surrounding the Lobster Pot averages 110 degrees F. Primitive rock pools filled with the runoff from the Hobo Pool average 102 to 104 degrees F, depending on the amount of cold water mixed in from the North Platte River.

Nearby attractions: Saratoga Museum, North Platte River, Snowy Range Scenic Byway, Medicine Bow National Forest, Snowy Range Ski Area.

Services: Gas, food, and lodging are available in the town of Saratoga. The posh Saratoga Inn Resort and Hot Springs offers luxurious lodging with guest-only outdoor hot plunges. The historic Wolf Hotel, located on Bridge Street, is another great lodging choice.

Camping: Tent and RV camping is available at Saratoga Lake Campground 1 mile north of Saratoga. The Foote Fishing Access, located on the North Platte River 5 miles north of Saratoga, also has a campground. There are also at least six Forest Service campgrounds scattered along the Snowy Range Scenic Byway east of Saratoga.

Map: Wyoming State Highways map.

Finding the springs: From Walcott and Interstate 80, take Wyoming Highway 130 south for 20 miles to downtown Saratoga. Continue through town on WY 130 (now called First Street) past the Wolf Hotel at the corner of First and Bridge streets. Go south on First Street for four more blocks to Walnut Street. Turn south on Walnut Avenue for two blocks. Walnut Avenue curves along the North Platte River, terminating in a parking lot in front of the Saratoga Municipal Pool. Park your car, grab your towel and suit, and walk about 50 yards on the paved sidewalk around to the back of the municipal pool. The Hobo Pool is located just behind the municipal pool, just above the banks of the North Platte River.

The hot springs: The quiet Wyoming town of Saratoga was named after the famous resort of Saratoga Springs, New York. Located in the beautiful North Platte River Valley, this Western community of under 2,000 people is famous not only for its hot springs but also for the world-class trout fishing in the North Platte River that bisects the town. The fishing is so well-known that Saratoga adopted the slogan "Saratoga—Where the Trout Leap on Main Street."

The most popular hot spring in Saratoga is the city-owned Hobo Pool. This hot plunge is about 50 feet by 50 feet square and is surrounded by cement block walls built by the Civilian Conservation Corps in the 1930s to keep the North Platte River from flooding the springs. Two benches in the 3-foot-deep pool allow seated bathers to submerge themselves up to their necks. The rock-lined 10-foot by 10-foot Lobster Pot at one end of Hobo Pool stays between 120 to 128 degrees F, and the surrounding pool is usually around 110 to 117

Saratoga Hot Springs

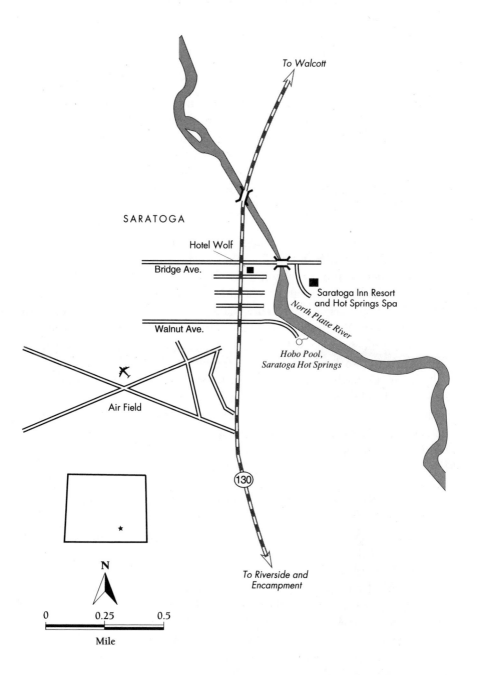

To Walcott

SARATOGA

Hotel Wolf

Bridge Ave.

Saratoga Inn Resort
and Hot Springs Spa

North Platte River

Walnut Ave.

Hobo Pool,
Saratoga Hot Springs

Air Field

130

To Riverside and
Encampment

★

N

0   0.25   0.5

Mile

degrees F. There are no restrictions on soaking in the Lobster Pot, but be warned that it is quite hot and you don't want to stay in there very long. Free dressing rooms, toilets, and showers stand adjacent to Hobo Pool.

Hot water flows continuously from the Lobster Pot into Hobo Pool, and then drains into the North Platte River. Hot springs aficionados have constructed several rock-lined pools to capture the hot water runoff, and these riverside soaking spots are almost as popular as Hobo Pool itself. There is also a seep on the banks of an island 20 yards across the river from Hobo Pool that provides a warm, muddy soak for bathers willing to ford the North Platte River. Use caution when deciding whether to wade the river to reach the island pool—it's easy enough in the late summer and fall, but when the river level is high it's probably safer simply to soak in Hobo Pool. Springtime high water can wash out all of the volunteer pools, although their patrons always return to rebuild them when the runoff subsides.

History: The hot springs at Saratoga were well-known to Native American tribes long before settlers moved into the North Platte River Valley. The thermal waters figured prominently in a tragic smallpox epidemic in 1874. Both the Sioux and Cheyenne tribes were suffering terrible losses from the deadly disease and desperately sought a cure. Native Americans had long used the hot springs along the North Platte River for healing a variety of ailments, and they hoped the springs would also be effective against smallpox. Infected tribal members were placed in a swing attached to the end of a long pole. They were carefully lowered into the hot springs to soak for several minutes, then lifted out and immediately plunged into the cold water of the North Platte River. The treatment was used many times, but to no avail. Traces of hundreds of burial sites on the banks of the river surrounding the hot springs are mute testimony to this futile attempt to cure the deadly disease.

Two years after the smallpox epidemic, William Cadwell built a small hotel and bathhouse at the hot springs. Fenimore Chatterton, surveyor for the town site of Saratoga, mentioned Cadwell's bathhouse in his 1879 memoirs quoted in a date-unknown newspaper story titled "Warm Springs Takes Root:" "Bill Cadwell owned a three-room cabin and a bath house with two wooden tubs, which he operated as a hotel with medicinal baths where cowboys came to boil out their afflictions after a winter in Cheyenne."

Before electric pumps were available, Cadwell used an ingenious system to bring hot water into his hotel for baths. He hitched an old horse to a turnstile attached to a manual pump near the springs. Whenever a customer wanted a bath, Cadwell would yell out of the hotel window at the horse. The animal would then trudge around the turnstile, pumping hot water through a pipe to the hotel until the bathtub was full.

The stone-lined "Lobster Pot" at one end of Hobo Pool.

A 1913 brochure promoting the benefits of the hot water claimed that Saratoga Hot Springs:

> . . . . closely resemble in their different properties the famous springs at Carlsbad, Ems, Teplitz and Aix la-Chapelle. Their properties may be summed up as stimulating, absorptive, alterative and reconstructive. It is difficult to say what diseases are most benefited by a course of baths in these thermal waters. Among those on the list of maladies which have been most relieved at the hot springs are the following: All acute and chronic diseases of the mucous membrane, such as catarrh of the nasal passages and bronchial tubes; the stomach and the whole alimentary canal; dyspepsia; gastric ulcers; congestion of the liver and catarrh of the bile ducts; cirrhosis; acute and chronic catarrh of the whole genito-urinary tract. The water acts not only by its chemical ingredients, but also mechanically as a sluice upon the system. It is well, therefore, for patients to drink the water very freely.

Others claimed the crisp mountain air and the hot springs joined forces to cure all manners of ailments. According to A. B. Bartlett's 1926 book *Mineral Springs of Wyoming,* "The tonic air from the mountains and the freedom from alkali [in the hot springs] produce unusually good conditions for recuperation from overwork, nerve and brain fatigue, tubercular troubles, etc.

Catarrh and hay fever are relieved and cured by the water and pure air. Helpless rheumatics have been cured in from two to six weeks. Victims of the liquor and tobacco habits have been entirely cured. Sufferers from stomach and intestinal diseases have been sent away happy at the first freedom from pain, completely cured."

In 1917 the state of Wyoming purchased the hot springs and a few hundred surrounding acres, and created a state park. The state relinquished its ownership of the springs to the town of Saratoga in 1982, which incorporated the hot pools into its city park system. Hobo Pool was extensively renovated in 1997 and 1998, and further improvements are planned.

53

Saratoga Inn Resort and Hot Springs Spa

(See map on page 205)

General description: A luxurious Western-style resort featuring five hot soaking pools, a swimming pool, a gourmet restaurant, an on-site microbrewery, and a variety of outdoor activities.

Location: Southeast Wyoming in the town of Saratoga.

Primitive/developed: Developed.

Best time of year: Previously open only during the summer months, the resort began year-round operations in 1998.

Restrictions: Private resort. The hot springs pools and other resort facilities are for the use of registered guests only. Swimsuits required.

Access: Any passenger car can make the trip.

Water temperature: The swimming pool is kept at 90 degrees F; the five hot soaking pools vary from 104 to 114 degrees F.

Nearby attractions: Saratoga Hot Springs, Saratoga Museum, historic Wolf Hotel, North Platte River, Snowy Range Scenic Byway, Medicine Bow National Forest, Snowy Range Ski Area.

Services: Saratoga Inn Resort offers more than 50 guest rooms and suites and a restaurant with an extensive gourmet menu. All other services are available in the town of Saratoga.

Camping: Guests of the resort won't be camping, but if you're planning on staying in the area before or after your visit, there are several camping options. Sites for RV and tent camping can be found at Saratoga Lake Campground, 1 mile north of Saratoga. A campground fee is usually charged, but true to the town's pride in piscatorial pursuits, campers who catch a ten-

pound or bigger fish from Saratoga Lake get one night of free camping. The Foote Fishing Access located on the North Platte River 5 miles north of Saratoga also has a campground. At least six Forest Service campgrounds are scattered along the Snowy Range Scenic Byway east of Saratoga.
Map: Wyoming State Highways map

Finding the springs: From Walcott and Interstate 80, take Wyoming Highway 130 south 20 miles to the town of Saratoga. Continue on WY 130 (which becomes First Street) to the corner of First Street and Bridge Street in downtown Saratoga (look for the historic Wolf Hotel on the corner). Turn west on Bridge Street, go two blocks, cross the bridge over the North Platte River, then immediately turn south on East River Street. Follow East River Street south for two blocks to the resort.

The hot springs: Located just across the North Platte River from Saratoga Hot Springs, the original Saratoga Inn and swimming pool were built in the summer of 1951 after a private developer obtained a 99-year lease on the property from the state of Wyoming. In the mid-1990s, a multimillion-dollar renovation of the inn resulted in the present gorgeous resort.

The refurbished and renamed Saratoga Inn and Hot Springs Spa is certainly one of the most elegant hot springs experiences available in Wyoming or

Saratoga Inn Resort and Hot Springs Spa.

Montana. Many of the guest rooms face the interior open-air courtyard, site of the hot water mineral pools. The 35-foot by 70-foot swimming pool, varying from 3 to 8 feet in depth, is maintained at 90 degrees F. Next to the swimming pool is a 108-degree-F soaking pool large enough to hold ten people. It is flanked by two smaller five-person pools, one approximately 104 degrees F, the other 110 degrees F. Just south of these are the two hottest and smallest pools, each comfortably holding two or three people in steamy water kept between 112 and 114 degrees F. None of the mineral water at the resort is high in sulfur, and there's no detectable odor. All of the natural-rock pools have rock-slab benches and steps and natural river-rock walls. The pools are available to resort guests 24 hours a day. Strategically placed lighting keeps nighttime soakers from stumbling while still allowing them to enjoy the starry Wyoming sky. For the truly decadent, the inn offers professional massage and aromatherapy for post-soak bliss. The inn also has a nine-hole golf course (three of the holes have tee shots over the North Platte River) and opportunities for mountain biking, tennis, and guided fly-fishing trips.

From the rawhide lampshades to the Pendleton woolen blankets and goose-down feather quilts on the handcrafted lodgepole pine beds, the Western resort motif is evident in each of the 45 guest rooms and seven suites. Large rock fireplaces in the reading room and bar provide cozy gathering places for guests, and an outdoor fireplace facing the courtyard and hot pools beckons on crisp fall evenings. The inn has its own on-site microbrewery specializing in ales, wheat beer, and root beer. Restaurant entrées include pecan-crusted catfish, sautéed trout, and homemade bread containing grain mash from the microbrewery. To top off the culinary delights, freshly baked chocolate chip cookies are delivered every evening to the guest rooms.

The Saratoga Inn Resort and Hot Springs Spa is advertised heavily in nearby Colorado (the reservations office is located in Denver), and advance reservations are strongly encouraged.

54

Emigrants' Laundry Tub

General description: Wyoming's most famous thermal spring in the mid-nineteenth century, located on the Oregon Trail, a day's wagon journey from Fort Laramie. The warm water pool and nearby gurgling springs are of mainly historical interest, frequented more by thirsty cattle than by thermal bathers.

Location: Southeast Wyoming, 2.5 miles southwest of Guernsey.

Primitive/developed: Primitive.

Best time of year: The springs can be visited year-round, although winter snows and spring rains may render the dirt road impassable. The relatively low temperature of the springs makes them best suited for summertime soaks, at least for those bathers who don't mind sharing the muddy water with a herd of cattle.

Restrictions: The springs are on the property of the Wyoming Army National Guard. Obtain permission to visit by calling the National Guard headquarters in Guernsey. This isn't as formidable as it sounds, and permission is usually granted without a hassle. Because the springs are near the National Guard rifle range, visitors may not be allowed to enter the property during firing practice.

Access: The dirt road leading to the springs is rough, and high-clearance vehicles are recommended for the last mile. If you don't mind a longer walk, any passenger vehicle can park at the green steel gate accessing the military property and you can walk the 2 miles to the springs.

Water temperature: 70 degrees F.

Nearby attractions: Guernsey State Park, Register Cliff National Historic Site, Fort Laramie National Historic Site, Oregon Trail Ruts National Historic Site.

Services: None at the springs. Gas, food, and lodging are available in Guernsey, 2.5 miles northeast.

Camping: Guernsey State Park, 3 miles northwest of Guernsey, has RV and tent sites at seven campgrounds surrounding the Guernsey Reservoir. The park was constructed by the Civilian Conservation Corps in 1933. The beautiful bridges, hiking trails, and museum are considered to be "the finest examples of CCC work in the Rocky Mountain Area," according to promotional information from the Wyoming Division of State Parks and Historic Sites. Larsen Park Campground, privately owned, is on the southern edge of Guernsey.

Maps: Wyoming State Highways map, USGS Wheatland NE WY.

Emigrants' Laundry Tub

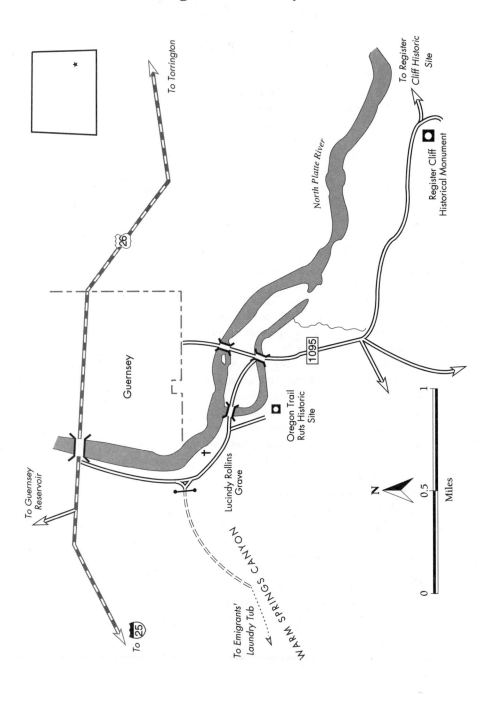

Finding the springs: Before going to the springs, obtain permission to visit by calling the Wyoming Army National Guard at (307) 836-2823. After you've gotten the green light, drive west from Guernsey on U.S. Highway 26. Immediately after crossing the North Platte River, turn south on a gravel road that parallels the river. Drive south for 0.5 mile until you see a green steel gate on the west side of the road. A "no trespassing without permission" sign on the gate identifies the property as belonging to the Wyoming National Guard. Presuming you've obtained permission to enter the military area, open the gate, close it behind you, and proceed 0.6 mile on a dirt road until you reach a second gate that says "no military vehicles." Leave your car, walk through the gate, and continue west on a dirt trail for about 250 yards. You'll enter a wide, shallow wash containing a small creek, the runoff from the warm springs. Walk west on a dirt path toward a large cedar tree on the north bank of the creek. Just past the tree is a gurgling warm spring that issues from a vertical limestone crack. The larger but more quiescent upper pool is located 200 feet west of the springs.

The hot springs: In spite of having to contend with military bureaucracy, obstinate cattle, and occasional low-flying National Guard helicopters, it's still worth a trip to visit the warm springs seen by tens of thousands of emigrants on the Oregon Trail.

The larger pool, once used for laundering pioneer clothing, is about 15 feet in diameter and a foot deep. The 70-degree-F springs bubble up through a sandy bottom in the center of the pool. There's lots of mud and cow manure on the pool's heavily trampled edge.

The lower springs issue from a crack in a 3-foot ledge of snow-white limestone and enter an oblong pool 1 foot deep and 10 feet across. The spring water is crystal clear when it gushes from the limestone but becomes murky as it passes over a muddy area trampled by thirsty cattle. Ten yards from its source, the lower springs joins the outflow from the upper springs, forming a creek that meanders toward the North Platte River. Interpretive signs provided by the Oregon-California Trails Association detail the springs' importance to pioneers.

History: Emigrants' Laundry Tub is located 11 miles from Fort Laramie. The fort stood at the convergence of the Mormon, Oregon, and Texas cattle trails. As the last outpost of civilization before pioneers headed farther west, Fort Laramie was one of the most important stops on the Oregon Trail. Westbound travelers leaving the fort often spent their first night 10 miles away at Emigrants' Laundry Tub.

The explorer John C. Fremont, one of the first to blaze the trail from Missouri to Oregon, described the springs in a diary entry on July 21, 1842: "At the distance of 10 miles from the fort [Fort Laramie], we entered the sandy bed

A thirsty cow drinking from Emigrants' Laundry Tub.

of a creek, a kind of defile shaded by precipitous rocks, down which we wound our way for several hundred yards to a place where on the left bank, a very large spring gushes with considerable noise and force out of the limestone rock. It is called 'the Warm Spring' and furnishes to the hitherto dry bed of the creek a considerable rivulet."

The Warm Spring became more commonly known as the Emigrants' Laundry Tub or, by some accounts, the Immigrants' Washtub. An 1850 entry in pioneer Pusey Graves' diary described the activity that led to the popular name for the springs: "After I finished my letter to send back to the Fort, I proceeded to the spring a distance of 1 miles with my bucket of dirty clothes."

Not all sojourns to the springs were as tranquil as Pusey Graves' laundry-day visit. A February 14, 1930, editorial in the *Guernsey Gazette* recalled the following: "At a location on a knoll about a half mile beyond the Springs was mute evidence of a wagon train disaster. Here a train of eight or ten wagons had drawn into its circle for the night, or for defense. Here they witnessed an attack upon the train. It was burned to the ground by the Indians. For many years there lay the stark evidence of this tragedy—old wagon irons of each wagon and its contents were in place, with only here and there a piece of the charred spoke of a wheel or like fragment of charred wood, as evidence of what took place."

Starting with one small group of travelers in 1841, the westward migration along the Oregon Trail peaked at over 50,000 emigrants a year in the early 1850s. By the early 1860s, when the Union Pacific Railroad to the West Coast was built 100 miles to the south, the migration had slowed to a trickle. Emigrants' Laundry Tub diminished in importance as a landmark, and today the water that once refreshed travelers on the Oregon Trail is used by cattle instead.

Historic reminders of the Oregon Trail abound within a few miles of the springs and are well worth visiting. Backtrack from the springs to the green steel gate that marked the entrance to the military land, and drive south on the gravel road another 0.2 mile. On a ridge to your left near the North Platte River you'll see a monument to Lucindy Rollins, a pioneer who died near there in 1849. Continue another 0.3 mile down the road to the Oregon Trail Ruts National Historic Site. Here the pioneers turned away from the North Platte River, crossing a bed of soft sandstone as they headed uphill. The pressure of thousands of heavy wagons carved a small canyon in the rock.

After you've visited the wagon ruts, return to the gravel road and drive another 0.5 mile east along the North Platte River to the intersection with paved County Road 109S south of Guernsey. Turn south and drive 1.8 miles to the Register Cliff National Historic Site. Register Cliff, a sandstone island near the Oregon Trail, is covered with the signatures of thousands of emigrants who carved their names and dates of travel into the soft rock. It's a poignant reminder of the hardy spirit of those early pioneers moving west toward uncertain futures.

Fort Laramie is another historic site well worth visiting. With the waning threat of Native American attacks and the declining need for an outpost on the Oregon Trail, the stronghold was abandoned in 1890. The National Park Service took charge of the decaying fort in 1936 and has restored the original barracks and several other buildings. To reach the fort from Emigrants' Laundry Tub, drive from Guernsey 11 miles southeast on US 26 to the town of Fort Laramie, then southwest 3 miles on Wyoming Highway 160.

55

Jackalope Plunge

General description: An Olympic-sized warm water swimming pool and picnic area located along the banks of the North Platte River, just south of Douglas. The pool has been closed since the early 1990s.
Location: Southeast Wyoming, 7 miles south of Douglas.
Primitive/developed: Developed.
Best time of year: The pool and picnic area are currently closed to the public.
Restrictions: The pool and picnic grounds are currently closed, although you may ask permission to look at the old resort.
Access: Any vehicle can make the trip.
Water temperature: 84 degrees F.
Nearby attractions: Thunder Basin National Grassland, Medicine Bow National Forest, Wyoming Pioneer Memorial Museum, Ayers Natural Bridge, Douglas Railroad Interpretive Center, Oregon Trail Historic Marker, Fort Fetterman State Historic Site, Wyoming State Fair, and what is probably the biggest jackalope statue in the world (the town of Douglas claims to be the home of the mythical hybrid between an antelope and a jackrabbit).
Services: None available at the hot springs. Gas, food, and lodging can be found in Douglas, 7 miles to the north. The historic Hotel La Bonte is a good choice for overnight accommodations.
Camping: Esterbrook Forest Service Campground is south of Jackalope Plunge. Reach it by driving 23 miles south on Esterbrook Road, then 3 miles east on a Forest Service road to the campground. Another nearby campground is at Ayers Natural Bridge, 12 miles west of Douglas. A KOA and an RV park are located in the town of Douglas.
Map: Wyoming State Highways map.

Finding the springs: From Douglas, take Exit 140 on Interstate 25. Head south at the exit for about 0.5 mile to Wyoming Highway 94 (Esterbrook Road). Continue on Esterbrook Road for 7 miles to Converse County Road 3 (at milepost 7). Stay on Esterbrook Road for another 200 yards, then turn east (toward the North Platte River) onto a gravel road. Drive 0.2 mile to a brown brick house where the owners of Jackalope Plunge live and ask them about the current status of the pool. The plunge itself is located about 0.2 mile north of the house in a lush grove of cottonwood trees.

The hot springs: Also known as Douglas Warm Spring, the 84-degree-F water at Jackalope Plunge flows at 400 gallons per minute into a 10-foot-diameter

Jackalope Plunge

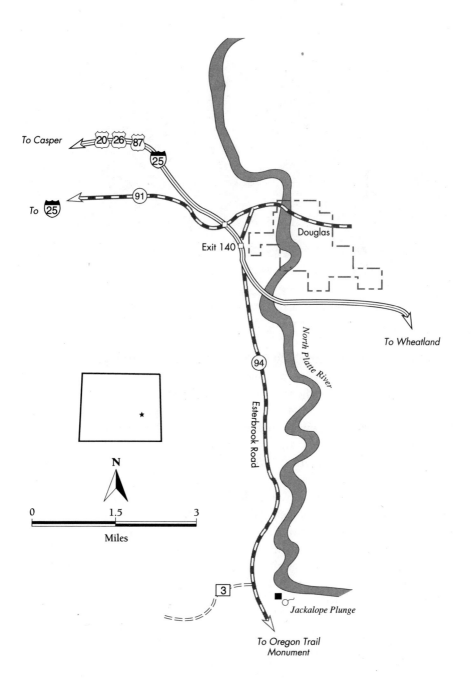

Jackalope Plunge in the 1960s. POSTCARD COURTESY OF JACKIE WEISS.

steel tank located 100 yards from the North Platte River. At one time the water was pumped 0.2 mile from the tank to a swimming pool.

History: Little is recorded about the early history of the warm springs, although its proximity to the Oregon Trail suggests it may have been used by travelers in the 1800s. (You can see the ruts of the Oregon Trail and an Oregon Trail historic marker if you drive 2.4 miles south of Jackalope Plunge on Esterbrook Road.) The warm springs were used for irrigation and bathing during the 1920s.

Jackalope Plunge was opened in the summer of 1961, and the current owners purchased the resort in 1981. The swimming pool was open Memorial Day to Labor Day and was the only swimming pool available in the Douglas area until a municipal pool was built. During the Wyoming State Fair (held every autumn in Douglas), Jackalope Plunge was filled with bathers. A former lifeguard at the plunge (now a librarian in Douglas) recalled that during the state fair the pool would become so crowded that "you could walk across the heads in the pool without getting your feet wet." Many visitors came just to enjoy the beautiful picnic grounds set among tall cottonwood trees on the banks of the North Platte River. With the opening of the municipal swimming pool in Douglas, the number of summer bathers at Jackalope Plunge declined and the pool closed in 1993. Current owners George and Jackie Weiss have no immediate plans to reopen the pool, although they have considered leasing it to be managed by others.

BIBLIOGRAPHY

Bartlett, A.B. *The Mineral Hot Springs of Wyoming.* Bulletin 16, Wyoming Geologist's Office. Laramie, Wyo.: Wyoming Geological Survey, 1926.

Berry, George. "Thermal Springs List for the United States." *NOAA Key to Geophysical Records Documentation,* no. 12. Boulder, Colo.: National Geophysical and Solar-Terrestrial Data Center, 1980.

Binns, Niles Allen. *Habitat Structure of Kendall Warm Springs, With Reference to the Endangered Kendall Warm Springs Dace, Rhinichthys Osculus Thermalis.* Fisheries Technical Bulletin No. 4. Cheyenne, Wyo.: Wyoming Game and Fish Department 1978.

Birkby, Jeff. "Montana's Geothermal Resources: An Overview." *Geo-Heat Center Quarterly Bulletin* (Fall/Winter 1982): 3–9.

Breckenridge, Roy M., and Bern S. Hinckley. *Thermal Springs of Wyoming.* Bulletin 60. Laramie, Wyo.: Wyoming Geological Survey, March 1978.

Brown, Keith E. *Geothermal Energy in Montana: Site Data Base and Development Status.* Klamath Falls, Oreg.: OIT Geo-Heat Utilization Center, 1978.

Bryan, T. Scott. *The Geysers of Yellowstone.* Boulder, Colo.: Colorado Associated University Press, 1986.

Chittenden, Hiram Martin. *The Yellowstone National Park.* Cincinnati, Ohio: The Robert Clarke Company, 1895.

DeVoto, Bernard, ed. *The Journals of Lewis and Clark.* Boston: Houghton Mifflin Co., 1953.

Fanestil, Richard E. "History of Warm Springs State Hospital and the Division of Mental Hygiene 1875–1973." Hospital Operating Policies and Procedures (internal memo). Warm Springs, Mont., 1973.

Federal Writers' Project. *The WPA Guide to 1930s Montana.* Tucson, Ariz.: The University of Arizona Press, 1994.

Fitch, William. *Mineral Waters of the United States.* Philadelphia and New York: Lea & Febiger, 1927.

Franzwa, Gregory. *The Oregon Trail Revisited.* Tucson, Ariz.: The Patrice Press, 1997.

Heasler, Henry. *Geothermal Resources of Wyoming.* Laramie, Wyo.: Wyoming Geological Survey, 1983.

Hunger, Bill. *Hiking Wyoming.* Helena, Mont.: Falcon Publishing, 1992.

Irving, Washington. *The Adventures of Captain Bonneville: or, Scenes beyond the Rocky Mountains of the Far West.* Paris: A. and W. Galignani, 1837.

Leeson, Michael A. *History of Montana.* Boston, Mass.: Warner, Beers & Co., 1885.

Long, Philip S. *Early History of Sleeping Buffalo Resort.* Billings, Mont.: Cypress Books, 1976.

McMillan, Marilyn Johnson. "Taking the Waters—Montana's Early Hot Springs Resorts." Master's thesis, Montana State University, 1982.

Milek, Dorothy G. *The Gift of Bah Guewana—A History of Wyoming's Hot Springs State Park.* Thermopolis, Wyo.: Pronghorn Press, 1975.

Miller, Joaquin. *An Illustrated History of the State of Montana.* Chicago: The Lewis Publishing Co., 1894.

Parent, Laurence. *Scenic Driving Wyoming.* Helena, Mont.: Falcon Publishing, 1997.

Schneider, Bill. *Hiking Yellowstone National Park.* Helena, Mont.: Falcon Publishing, 1997.

Smith, R. B., and R. L. Christiansen. "Yellowstone Park as a Window on the Earth's Interior." *Scientific American* (February 1980): 104–17.

Snyder, S. A. *Scenic Driving Montana.* Helena, Mont.: Falcon Publishing, 1995.

Sonderegger, John L., and R. N. Bergantino. *Geothermal Resources of Montana—Hydrogeologic Map HM4.* Butte, Mont: Montana Bureau of Mines and Geology, 1981.

Whithorn, Bill, and Doris Whithorn. *Photo History of Chico Lodge.* Livingston, Mont.: Self-published, 1981.

Whittlesey, Lee H. *Death in Yellowstone—Accidents and Foolhardiness in the First National Park.* Boulder, Colo.: Roberts Rinehart Publishers, 1995.

—————. *Yellowstone Place Names.* Helena, Mont.: Montana Historical Society Press, 1988.

FOR MORE INFORMATION

Northwest Montana

Quinn's Hot Springs Resort
P.O. Box 1280
Plains, MT 59859
(406) 826-3150

Sun River Hot Springs
Rocky Mountain District Ranger Office
USDA Forest Service
1102 Main Avenue NW
Choteau, MT 59422
(406) 466-5341
or
Klick's K Bar L Ranch
Box 287
Augusta, MT 59410
(406) 562-3551 (summer)
(406) 562-3589 (winter)

Symes Hot Springs Hotel and Mineral Baths
209 Wall Street
P.O. Box 651
Hot Springs, MT 59845
(406) 741-2361
Website: www.ronan.net/~hscofc/symes.htm

Wild Horse Hot Springs
P.O. Box 629
Hot Springs, MT 59845
(406) 741-3777

Southwest Montana

Alhambra Hot Springs
Evergreen Clancy Health and Rehabilitation Center
474 Highway 282
Clancy, MT 59634
(406) 933-8311

Boulder Hot Springs
P.O. Box 930
Boulder, MT 59632-0930
(406) 225-4339
E-mail: hotsprng@initco.net
Website: www.boulderhotsprings.com

Bozeman Hot Springs
81123 Gallatin Road
Bozeman, MT 59715
(406) 586-6492

Broadwater Athletic Club & Hot Springs
4920 Highway 12 West
Helena, MT 59601
(406) 443-5777
E-mail: bac@thebroadwater.com
Website: www.thebroadwater.com

Chico Hot Springs Lodge
#1 Chico Road
Pray, MT 59065
(406) 333-4933, 1-800-HOT-WADA
E-mail: chico@chicohotsprings.com
Website: www.chicohotsprings.com

Corwin/La Duke Hot Springs
USDA Forest Service
Gardiner Ranger District
P.O. Box 5
Gardiner, MT 59030
(406) 848-7375

Elkhorn Hot Springs Resort
P.O. Box 514
Polaris, MT 59746
(406) 834-3434, 1-800-722-8978
E-mail: info@elkhornhotsprings.com
Website: www.elkhornhotsprings.com

Fairmont Hot Springs Resort
1500 Fairmont Road
Anaconda, MT 59711
(406) 797-3241, 1-800-332-3272
E-mail: fairmontmt@aol.com
Website: www.fairmontmontana.com

Jackson Hot Springs Lodge
P.O. Box 808
Jackson, MT 59736
(406) 834-3151

Jerry Johnson Hot Springs (Idaho)
Lochsa Ranger Station
Clearwater National Forest
P.O. Box 398
Kooskia, ID 83539
(208) 926-4275

The Lodge at Potosi Hot Springs
P.O. Box 688
Pony, MT 59747-0688
(406) 685-3594, 1-800-770-0088
Website: www.ranchexit.com/potosi

Lolo Hot Springs
38500 West Highway 12
Lolo, MT 59847
(406) 273-2290, 1-800-273-2290
E-mail: stoen@bigsky.net

Lost Trail Hot Springs Resort
8321 Highway 93 South
Sula, MT 59871
(406) 821-3547, 1-800-825-3574
E-mail: lths@bigsky.net
Website: www.losttrailhotsprings.com

Norris Hot Springs
P.O. Box 2916
Norris, MT 59745
(406) 685-3333

Spa Hot Springs Motel
202 West Main Street
Box 370
White Sulphur Springs, MT 59645
(406) 547-3366

Upper Potosi Hot Springs
Deerlodge-Beaverhead National Forest
Sheridan Ranger District
P.O. Box 428
Sheridan, MT 59749
(406) 842-5432

Warm Springs
Director of Public Relations
Warm Springs State Hospital
Warm Springs, MT 59756
(406) 693-7000

Weir Creek Hot Springs (Idaho)
Lochsa Ranger Station
Clearwater National Forest
P.O. Box 398
Kooskia, ID 83539
(208) 926-4275

Northeast Montana

Gigantic Warm Springs
David Vaneck
Route 3, Box 3108
Lewistown, MT 59457
(406) 583-9825

Sleeping Buffalo Resort
HC 75
Box 13
Saco, MT 59261
(406) 527-3370
E-mail: ereaux64@msn.com
Website: www.ereaux.org/sleeping.htm

Southeast Montana

Angela Well
Charles and Linda Moore
Angela, MT 59312
(406) 354-6471

Yellowstone National Park

Yellowstone National Park
National Park Service
Park Headquarters
P.O. Box 168
Yellowstone National Park, WY 82190
(307) 344-7381

Yellowstone National Park
Backcountry Office
P.O. Box 168
Yellowstone National Park, WY 82190
(307) 344-2160, (307) 344-2163

Northwest Wyoming (Outside Yellowstone)

Astoria Hot Springs
Box 18
Star Route
Jackson, WY 83001
(307) 733-2659

Chief Washakie Plunge
Shoshone Tribal Cultural Center
Box 1008
Fort Washakie, WY 82514
(307) 332-9106, (307) 332-4530

Fountain of Youth RV Park
P.O. Box 711
250 North Highway 20
Thermopolis, WY 82443
(307) 864-3265

Granite Hot Springs
Star Route, Box 44A
Jackson, WY 83001
(307) 733-6318

Holiday Inn of the Waters
115 East Park
P.O. Box 1323
Thermopolis, WY 82443
(307) 864/3131, 1-800-HOLIDAY

Hot Springs State Park
220 Park Street
Thermopolis, WY 82443
(307) 864-2176
Website: www.commerce.state.wy.us/sphs/textual/hot.htm
or
Thermopolis-Hot Springs Chamber of Commerce
700 Broadway
P.O. Box 768
Thermopolis, WY 82443
(307) 864-3192, 1-800-SUN-N-SPA
E-mail: hotspot@wyoming.com
Website: www.wyoming.com/~hotspot/

Huckleberry/Polecat Hot Springs
Grand Teton National Park
P.O. Drawer 170
Moose, WY 83012
(307) 739-3300

Quality Inn Plaza Hotel
Hot Springs State Park
Thermopolis, WY 82443
(307) 864-2939, 1-800-228-5151

Star Plunge
P.O. Box 627
Thermopolis, WY 82443
(307) 864-3771

Tepee Spa
P.O. Box 750
Thermopolis, WY 82443
(307) 864-9250

Southeast Wyoming

Emigrants' Laundry Tub
c/o Wyoming Army National Guard
Camp Guernsey
P.O. Box 399
Guernsey, WY 82214
(307) 836-2823

Jackalope Plunge
George and Jackie Weiss
684 Esterbrook Road
Douglas, WY 82633
(307) 358-2820

Saratoga Inn Resort and Hot Springs Spa
601 East Pic Pike Road
P.O. Box 869
Saratoga, WY 82331
Phone: (307) 326-5261
Reservations: (303) 825-2779

Saratoga Hot Springs
Saratoga Chamber of Commerce
P.O. Box 1095
Saratoga, WY 82331
(307) 326-8855

INDEX

Page numbers in *italic* type refer to maps.
Page numbers in **bold** type refer to photos.

ABOUT THE AUTHOR

Jeff Birkby soaked in his first hot springs in 1976, after leaving the cornfields of Iowa to attend graduate school at Montana State University in Bozeman where he earned his master's degree in plant ecology in 1979. Shortly after earning his degree, Jeff was hired as a geothermal energy specialist for the Montana Department of Natural Resources and Conservation. Over the next five years Jeff traveled throughout Montana, assessing geothermal energy use at both public and private hot springs. During these trips Jeff developed a passion for the history of the region's thermal areas.

For the last 20 years Jeff has shared his knowledge of hot springs through Elderhostel sessions, evening lectures, workshops for kids, and in several technical publications.

When not soaking in thermal springs, Jeff manages sustainable development and renewable energy programs for the National Center for Appropriate Technology in Butte, Montana.

If you have comments, corrections, or fresh information about any Montana or Wyoming hot springs, send your insights to Jeff Birkby c/o Falcon Publishing, or e-mail Jeff at jbirkby@hotmail.com. He'll check out your information for future editions of this guide.

Author Jeff Birkby warms his heels at Camas Hot Springs.

SCENIC DRIVING GUIDES

Scenic Driving Alaska and the Yukon
Scenic Driving Arizona
Scenic Driving the Beartooth Highway
Scenic Driving California
Scenic Driving Colorado
Scenic Driving Florida
Scenic Driving Georgia
Scenic Driving Hawaii
Scenic Driving Idaho
Scenic Driving Michigan
Scenic Driving Minnesota
Scenic Driving Montana
Scenic Driving New England
Scenic Driving New Mexico
Scenic Driving North Carolina
Scenic Driving Oregon
Scenic Driving the Ozarks
Scenic Driving Pennsylvania
Scenic Driving Texas
Scenic Driving Utah
Scenic Driving Washington
Scenic Driving Wisconsin
Scenic Driving Wyoming
Scenic Driving Yellowstone and
    the Grand Teton National Parks
Scenic Byways East
Scenic Byways Far West
Scenic Byways Rocky Mountains
Back Country Byways

HISTORIC TRAIL GUIDES

Traveling California's Gold Rush Country
Traveling the Lewis & Clark Trail
Traveling the Oregon Trail
Traveler's Guide to the Pony Express Trail

WILDLIFE VIEWING GUIDES

Alaska Wildlife Viewing Guide
Arizona Wildlife Viewing Guide
California Wildlife Viewing Guide
Colorado Wildlife Viewing Guide
Florida Wildlife Viewing Guide
Indiana Wildlife Vewing Guide
Iowa Wildlife Viewing Guide
Kentucky Wildlife Viewing Guide
Massachusetts Wildlife Viewing Guide
Montana Wildlife Viewing Guide
Nebraska Wildlife Viewing Guide
Nevada Wildlife Viewing Guide
New Hampshire Wildlife Viewing Guide
New Jersey Wildlife Viewing Guide
New Mexico Wildlife Viewing Guide
New York Wildlife Viewing Guide
North Carolina Wildlife Viewing Guide
North Dakota Wildlife Viewing Guide
Ohio Wildlife Viewing Guide
Oregon Wildlife Viewing Guide
Puerto Rico & the Virgin Islands
    Wildlife Viewing Guide
Tennessee Wildlife Viewing Guide
Texas Wildlife Viewing Guide
Utah Wildlife Viewing Guide
Vermont Wildlife Viewing Guide
Virginia Wildlife Viewing Guide
Washington Wildlife Viewing Guide
West Virginia Wildlife Viewing Guide
Wisconsin Wildlife Viewing Guide